MUSIC ON THE FRONTLINE

For Mary and Ronald Wellens

Music on the Frontline

Nicolas Nabokov's Struggle against
Communism and Middlebrow Culture

IAN WELLENS

Ashgate

Published by
Ashgate Publishing Limited
Wey Court East
Union Road
Farnham
Surrey, GU9 7PT
England

Ashgate Publishing Company
110 Cherry Street
Suite 3-1
Burlington
VT 05401-3818
USA

Ashgate website: http://www.ashgate.com

British Library Cataloguing in Publication Data

Wellens, Ian
    Music on the frontline : Nicolas Nabokov's struggle against Communism and middlebrow culture
    1. Nabokov, Nicolas 2. Congress for Cultural Freedom 3. Communism and culture 4. Composers – Soviet Union – Biography 5. Music – Political aspects
    I. Title
    780.9'2

Library of Congress Cataloging-in-Publication Data

Wellens, Ian
    Music on the frontline : Nicolas Nabokov's struggle against communism and middlebrow culture / Ian Wellens
        p. cm.
    Includes bibliographical references (p.).
    1. Music and state – Soviet Union. 2. Nabokov, Nicolas, 1903 – Contributions in cultural policy. 3. Congress for Cultural Freedom. 4. Soviet Union – Cultural policy – History. 5. United States – Cultural policy – History – 20th century. 6. United States. Central Intelligence Agency – Influence. 7. Music – Social aspects – History – 20th century. I. Title.

ML3917.S65 W45 2002
780'.947–dc21   2001048708

Transferred to Digital Printing in 2011

ISBN 978-0-7546-0635-2

MIX
Paper from
responsible sources
FSC
www.fsc.org   FSC® C004959

Printed and bound in Great Britain
by Printondemand-worldwide.com

Contents

Preface

The roots of this book can be traced back to 1993 when, as a mature student at Dartington College of the Arts, I found myself needing a subject for a final-year dissertation. The idea of 'Music and the Cold War' was intriguing, irresistible. Part of the attraction was down to timing: the Cold War – always in the background as I grew up, dominating the political landscape – had just ended. I had even had a small part in it, as a foot soldier of the anti-nuclear movement – organising, demonstrating and cutting the wire at St Mawgan airbase – in the years leading up to the deployment of cruise missiles in 1983. Then, suddenly, it was over. Only ten years after the missiles arrived at Greenham Common, it was scarcely credible that monolithic communism, the log-jam of the Cold War, the spiralling arms race – that all of this could have come, so abruptly, to an end. Looking back at all this, I felt there must have been places where the worlds of art, music and Cold War politics crossed, and so set out to look for them, producing a study which considered dissident musicians in the East and West, institutional controls over composers and the changing Western reception of Shostakovich and his music. In the final section I suggested that perhaps the issue of contemporary musical language might have been pulled into the Cold War in some way – was it possible that the Western avant-garde's contest with traditional musical language might have formed a parallel, yet connected, struggle with the Cold War? All of this was tentative, limited by the time and space available for an undergraduate project. At that time, I had no idea I would spend the next few years pursuing this idea, and I had never heard of the Congress for Cultural Freedom (CCF) or Nicolas Nabokov.

Having decided, encouraged by my tutor Max Paddison, to take this area of research on to doctoral level, I spent some time looking for a focus. Somewhere – I don't recall where exactly – there was a brief reference to an émigré Russian composer, CIA money and music festivals in the Cold-War 1950s. Strange but true. Looking into the matter further, it seemed that no-one had bothered to study either Nabokov or his festivals. The decision was made for me: I had found my focus. However, the subsequent research process had some surprises in store. It is not unknown for researchers to set off with a hunch that they secretly hope to prove, and I had, by that time, discovered Eva Cockcroft and Max Kozloff's articles linking Abstract Expressionism to the CIA. It was only a short hop sideways to suppose that the CIA could have had a hand in the Darmstadt-driven lurch towards the musical 'difficulty' of the early 1950s. In fact, given that this was happening when the temperature of the Cold War was somewhere near absolute zero, given Kozloff and Cockcroft's work, given that there clearly was a Nabokov–CCF musical *something* linked to the CIA, it seemed highly probable. It was an appealing, exciting idea – I am not the only person to have pursued it, and am unlikely to be the last. In time, however, as I dug into archives in Austin and Chicago, I was forced to conclude that the evidence pointed another way. Through Nabokov, the CIA *was* indeed promoting musical modernism, but in a loose, broad way. There is no evidence that they discriminated between serialism and neoclassicism, no evidence that they sought to push the most 'advanced' postwar trends. And if music had, at times, a high profile in the CCF's events, this cannot be taken to suggest that the Agency accorded it special importance. This was merely the consequence of having a composer sitting at the top of the CCF's structure. Why had that man been chosen? For a range of reasons: his qualities as communicator, showman, impresario, for his range of contacts, his knowledge of the arts and his language skills, because he was a friend of the main CIA agent involved, perhaps even for his status as a practising artist – but *not* as a composer *per se*.

The thesis that eventually emerged, in 1999, looked at Nabokov and the festivals he organised for the CCF, his writings on music and politics, and considered the whole undertaking in context. I had not, however, been the only person working in this area. In *Journey to the Centre of the Earth*, Jules Verne's hero follows the trail left by an earlier explorer, Arne Sackneusen, who has left the initials 'AS' scrawled on the cavern walls. Ploughing through the Nabokov papers in Austin, Texas, I came across my own trail – a paper trail of 'SS' bookmarks. This was Frances Stonor Saunders, who I had already met in London. Her book *Who Paid the Piper? The CIA and the Cultural Cold War* appeared the same year. I had expected it to be a major study, and so it is: with her intellect, dogged perseverance and substantial detective skill, there is no doubt that Stonor Saunders is now *the* authority in this area, having given us not only the 'big picture' of US cultural intervention, but also tremendous detail, especially in the area of the key personalities and their relationships, and the underlying CIA connection. All this in spite of the total non-availability of relevant official documents.

Reading her book, I realised with some relief that this substantial work still left a space for my own. It would be misleading to say now – as I did in the Introduction to this work in its doctoral incarnation – that there are 'no existing studies of Nabokov himself or the musical activities of the CCF', because both feature in Stonor Saunders' story (and, where necessary, I have revised my story to take account of her discoveries). In some respects, however, I believe that my work, whilst admittedly on a less ambitious scale than hers, stands alone. I have been less interested in creating an inventory of all that was done – every composer featured, every work performed, every conference paper delivered – than in looking closely at the terms in which this work was justified by Nabokov. The further I went on, the *less* it seemed to be an anomaly, a peculiar footnote to music history, a mildly diverting cul-de-sac, and the *more* it seemed utterly connected to important processes driving postwar art music. So, here you will find, examined for the first time, the ideas on music and politics which Nabokov spread across a large number of texts – ideas which, together, formed the rationale for his CCF festivals. On this foundation, I then look for links with other important currents in mid-twentieth-century cultural life, reaching the conclusion that this anti-communist struggle was closely linked to fears for a high culture which many felt to be threatened by the increasing cultural influence of the middle classes. Nabokov, I believe, was fighting both communism *and* 'middlebrow' culture.

This book is fundamentally interdisciplinary in nature, having stubbornly refused to remain within subject boundaries. I have attempted to accommodate the varied backgrounds of my potential readership, by giving potted histories and background as necessary: where this seems to be over- or underdone, I can only apologise (if anything, I have leaned towards the assumption that readers, whilst familiar with the basic contours of twentieth-century music, may welcome assistance in other areas – the New York Intellectuals, 'mass' and 'middlebrow' culture, Adorno and so on). I must recognise that, for some, there may be a disappointing lack of musical detail and even, perhaps, a specific frustration that Nabokov's own output as a composer is not examined. Whilst, as a musician myself, I sympathise, my defence would be that I have been led by the material, and by a desire to make sense of it. This book is the result, and it is what it is: a story of the *politics* of culture, of how culture – in this case, music – was used for political ends. It is also a story of the *sociology* of culture: about the interest groups that form around culture, about their ideology and how they function. It is not about culture – about music – itself, simply because there seemed to be nothing of value along that route. And as for Nabokov: it is Nabokov the Secretary-General of the Congress for Cultural Freedom, Nabokov the impresario that interests us here. His life as a composer was a quite separate thing (and very much put on hold during the Congress period). To be sure, it would have been possible to locate a few dusty, neglected scores, but I make no apology for not having done so: I am convinced that what we need to know we can learn from the writings.

The book divides into two halves, the first half being broadly chronological, starting with relevant aspects of Nabokov's life and career in the 1940s, then moving on to consider the writings, most of which appeared in the 1940s and very early 1950s. All of this forms the foundation for Chapter 4, on the CCF's Paris festival of 1952 ('Masterpieces of the XXth Century'). From this point on we move to context, with a chapter each on the idea of the CCF as an American 'Ministry of Culture', and on the split Nabokov's policy produced between the CCF in Paris and its New York-based American affiliate. Finally, Chapters 7 and 8 – very much the core of the book – draw out connections between this project and the growing concerns of many intellectuals for the health – even the survival – of high culture in general and art music in particular.

Acknowledgements

Over the six years it has taken to reach this point, many people have been generous with their time and advice. Chief among these were my doctoral supervisors at Dartington College, Bob Gilmore and Kevin Thompson, whose faith, support and criticism – contributed in equal measure – were invaluable throughout. Richard Taylor and Rosemary Burn tolerated my endless requests for books with surprising good humour. I would also like to thank the following College staff – tutors and, later, colleagues – for their encouragement and general help over the years: Trevor Wiggins, Nick Virgo, Julian Marshall and Ruth Herbert. I was lucky to have David Fanning and Frank Denyer read a late draft of the thesis: the final result benefited greatly from their comments and corrections. Along the way, discussions with Martin Brody have been much appreciated, likewise, Anne-Marie Schuffels, a fellow toiler in the vast IACF archive at the Regenstein. Frances Stonor Saunders generously pointed me towards some source material which might otherwise have been overlooked. Also, I could never have undertaken the project without the College's financial support which came in the form of a studentship and a research grant for travel to the USA: thanks are due to Edward Cowie and the College's administrative staff, particularly Margaret Eggleton and Jane Bishop. In the USA, the staff of the Harry Ransom Humanities Research Center of the University of Texas at Austin (especially Pat Fox), and the Special Collection of the Joseph Regenstein Library at the University of Chicago were all extremely helpful.

Finally, I must thank three people slightly more detached from the research, but crucial nonetheless. The pre-history of this work involved an undergraduate dissertation, and I owe a tremendous debt to Max Paddison not only academically but also for his belief in both the subject and in my capacity to do it justice. Max saw the further potential in that work before I did, suggesting that there might be a thesis in it; later, I again drew on his advice when seeking publication. Dartington's loss is Durham's gain. Further back still, John Railton's inspirational piano lessons proved to be a turning point for a thirty-something furniture-maker seeking a new direction, beginning a process which has, with this book, borne an unlikely fruit! Finally, thanks are due to my wife, Susie Honnor, for providing the solid foundation which made the work possible.

List of Abbreviations

ACCF	American Congress for Cultural Freedom
AIF	Americans for Intellectual Freedom
CCF	Congress for Cultural Freedom
CIA	Central Intelligence Agency
DP	displaced person
EAG	Europe–America Groups
HICOG	High Command in Germany (US)
IACF	International Association for Cultural Freedom In Bibliography denotes the archives of the IACF, held in the Special Collection of the Joseph Regenstein Library, University of Chicago
ILGWU	International Ladies Garment Workers Union
IOD	International Operations Division
IRCAM	Institut de Recherche et Coordination Acoustique/Musique
MJ	In Bibliography denotes the Michael Josselson papers held at the Harry Ransom Humanities Research Center, University of Texas at Austin
NCL	'Non-communist Left'
NMC	National Music Council
NN	In Bibliography denotes the Nicolas Nabokov papers held at the Harry Ransom Humanities Research Center, University of Texas at Austin
OMGUS	Occupation Military Government of the United States
PCF	Parti Communiste de la France
PR	*Partisan Review*
PSB	Psychological Strategy Board
SW	In Bibliography denotes the Secker and Warburg papers held at the University of Reading
USIE	United States Information and Education

Chapter 1

Great Books and Wise Men: Nabokov's Road to the 1950 Berlin Congress

Nicolas Nabokov was born at Lubcza, Belorussia (now Belarus) on 4 April 1903 into a wealthy family with liberal inclinations. His early years – comfortable and unremarkable – included musical studies with Rebikov in St Petersburg and Yalta. All of this ended in 1919 with the family's decision to flee the advancing Red Army. Making his way via Greece to Germany, where he arrived the following year, he studied at the Stuttgart Conservatory (1920–22) and then at the Hochschule für Musik in Berlin with Juon and Busoni (1922–23). Whilst in Berlin he also worked as a music critic for the Russian émigré daily *Rul*, edited by his uncle Vladimir Nabokov (whose son – also Vladimir – would go on to become the author of *Lolita*). Moving to Paris, he studied at the Sorbonne in 1926 and became friends with many of the leading composers, including Prokofiev and Stravinsky; having received a commission from Diaghilev his ballet-oratorio, *Ode*, was presented in Paris (and subsequently in London and Berlin) by the Ballets Russes in 1928. A *Symphonie Lyrique* followed in 1930, and two more ballets, *La Vie de Polichinelle* and *Union Pacific*, were produced in 1934 in Philadelphia and Paris respectively. After lecturing in the United States on European music, at the invitation of Alfred C. Barnes, Nabokov took a teaching post at Wells College, Aurora, where he stayed from 1936 to 1941, opting for American citizenship in 1939.

In 1941 he moved to St John's College in Annapolis, Maryland, later to the Peabody Conservatory in Baltimore, where he taught intermittently until 1951. The war years also found him translating for the Department of Justice in Washington, before enlisting in 1945 and leaving for occupied Germany, where he became engaged in the re-establishment of Berlin's cultural life as part of the American Sector's Information Control Division. Returning to the USA, the years 1947–49 saw the completion of his *Second Symphony* ('Biblical'), two commissions for Koussevitsky and the Boston Symphony Orchestra (a cantata, *The Return of Pushkin*, and a 'vocal concerto', *La Vita Nuovo*) and one for the Philadelphia under Ormandy (*Studies in Solitude*). At this time he also worked on Voice of America's Russian Broadcast Service, becoming its first chief.

In 1951, when he became secretary-general of the Paris-based Congress for Cultural Freedom (CCF), Nabokov became involved with the work which will form the central focus of this study. In this role he produced four music festivals (alongside many non-musical events): 'L'Oeuvre du XXème Siècle' (Paris, 1952); 'Music in the XXth Century' (Rome, 1954); 'Tradition and Change in Music' (Venice, 1958) and

1

the 'East–West Music Encounter' (Tokyo, 1961). This led on to the Directorship of the Berlin Festival (1963–66), during which period his involvement with the CCF became rather more distant (ending completely in 1967). He continued to compose – although with some difficulty as a result of the demands of the heavy workload in both Paris and Berlin – producing two operas: *Rasputin's End*, written with the poet Stephen Spender, came first, in 1959, with a Köln premiere followed by performances in Paris and Catania. In 1973 *Love's Labour's Lost*, with a libretto by W.H. Auden and Chester Kallman, was produced by the Deutsche Oper in Brussels. In the late 1960s he taught at the City University of New York, then from 1970–73 was composer-in-residence at the Aspen Institute for Humanistic Studies in Colorado. Married five times, he was survived by his wife, the photographer Dominique Cibiel, when he died in New York on 6 April, 1978.[1]

In the following pages there will be little more to say of Nabokov the composer – a neglect which only mirrors the indifference of the musical world at large. Our interests lie elsewhere, for Nicolas Nabokov was that rare thing, a composer actively engaged in politics. In the 1940s he began to seek ways of working politically within the world of music or, more specifically, marrying his musical interests to his anti-communism. This led in 1951 to his CCF post.[2] The CCF, which lasted until 1967, was a body of anti-communist intellectuals owing its existence to a perception – in the early Cold War years – that the Soviets were winning the battle of ideas. In his broadly sympathetic account of the organisation, Peter Coleman summarised it as follows:

It lasted for seventeen years and at its height had offices or representatives in thirty-five countries ... it thought of itself as 'a movement' leading a liberal offensive against the Communists and their fellow-travelers ... . It sponsored a network of magazines ... . It conducted large and small international seminars ... . It orchestrated international protests against oppression of intellectuals. ... It organized festivals and helped refugee writers. ... Above all, the Congress helped to shatter the illusions of the Stalinist fellow-travelers ... . (Coleman, 1989, p. 9).

The appearance of independence was crucial in pursuit of the CCF's primary purpose – winning the allegiance of intellectuals. It presented itself as a body of autonomous individuals partisan only in their unswerving support for freedom; beholden to no-one. Predictably then, the revelation, in a celebrated scandal of 1966, that it had been secretly funded by the CIA proved terminal.[3] Although reconstituted

---

    1   All biographical details have been taken from Nabokov (1975) and Glanville-Hicks and Carr (1980).
    2   Hereafter described as 'Congress', 'the Congress', or the 'CCF'.
    3   In April 1966 the *New York Times* ran a major five-part series on the CIA, attributed jointly to 'Tom Wicker, John W. Finney, Max Frankel, E.W. Kenworthy and other Times staff members'. In the third part, a brief but – as it turned out – devastating passage runs:

Through similar channels [bogus foundations] the CIA has supported ... liberal organisations of intellectuals such as the Congress for Cultural Freedom, and some of their newspapers and magazines. *Encounter* magazine, a well-known anti-Communist intellectual monthly ... was for a long time ... one of the indirect beneficiaries of CIA funds. (Wicker *et al.*, 1966, p. 28)

as the International Association for Cultural Freedom (IACF) with new sources of funding, it essentially never recovered, closing down in 1977.[4]

Nabokov had launched the CCF in 1952 with a large, and mainly musical, festival in Paris – 'L'Oeuvre du XXème Siècle'. This event, which seemed to signal an intention to make the arts prominent in the Congress's activities, proved controversial within the organisation and – perhaps partly as a result – Nabokov never again attempted anything on quite the same scale. Nonetheless there were, as we have already mentioned, three more music festivals. In addition, Nabokov and the CCF assisted the composer Andrzej Panufnik on his defection to the West in 1954, and also helped in the creation of the Philharmonia Hungarica out of musicians who had fled Hungary in 1956.

What sort of man was Nabokov? Among his most valued and long-term friends were Isaiah Berlin and Igor Stravinsky: their impressions may help give a sense of the person at the centre of this study. The philosopher offered me this character sketch in a 1997 interview. Nabokov, he said, had been charming – good company and a great raconteur, but also extremely well-read and multilingual. He had had a great deal of respect for Nabokov, adding that he had been the best organiser of music festivals in his day. Pressed for possible weaknesses, he said that Nabokov could be an exhausting talker, and that he had a restless quality – an inability to be at ease anywhere. Furthermore, he was perhaps not always entirely truthful: Berlin gave as an example Nabokov's claim that he had once been smuggled into Moscow 'in the baggage of an American General'. Berlin was convinced this had never happened, but thought that Nabokov himself may have believed it. Asked if there may have been something of the fantasist about Nabokov, Berlin replied: 'Just that'.[5]

In his *Selected Correspondence*, Robert Craft explains the value of Nabokov's friendship to Stravinsky in terms of both social and intellectual qualities. In relation to Nabokov's work in cultural administration in occupied Berlin and, later, for the CCF, Craft describes him as:

> ... uniquely qualified for this, speaking German and French as fluently as Russian and English, and possessing a knowledge of European culture ranging far beyond music ... Moreover, as a member of a prominent family in the Russian liberal movement, Nabokov was at least as informed about East–West politics as were the leaders of the Allied governments. (Craft, 1984, p. 365)

And, like Berlin, he stresses that Nabokov was good company, and that his 'warmth, his sense of the ridiculous, his parodies of accents and speech' were all much valued by Stravinsky. This humour did not, according to Craft, translate well into print, but in person Nabokov was 'unrivalled' as a raconteur and mimic (ibid., p. 367). For example, in 1959 Nabokov, Craft and the Stravinskys met up in Kyoto:

---

4   The archives of the IACF – which cover the full period of the Congress for Cultural Freedom – have since been acquired by the Special Collections of the Joseph Regenstein Library at the University of Chicago (hereafter: 'IACF').

5   Sir Isaiah Berlin, interviewed by the author, 11 June 1997.

N.N.'s impersonations ... are even more brilliant, and once he has been heard in such set pieces as 'The American Fulbright Student in Florence' and 'Stephen Spender and the Sanskrit Poet Reciting Their Verses to Each Other', to say nothing of improvisations like the hilarious 'Noh' play he puts on for us tonight, the butt of the mimicry can never again be seen in the same, pre-N.N. way. (Craft, 1972, p. 85)

The combination of intellectual, administrative and social skills was the foundation on which the 'culture generalissimo' as Stravinsky called him, would build his postwar career. This, however, would owe as much – and perhaps more – to contingency, to alliances formed by chance and circumstance, as to any personal qualities. To understand how the cash-strapped emigré composer of the 1930s became, in less than two decades, a globe-trotting musical-political impresario, a high-profile *bon viveur* impeccably connected to the 'Great and the Good' and playing a key role in the vast constellation of individuals and groups that formed the CIA's cultural Cold War effort, we must first consider a few key episodes in Nabokov's pre-Congress life.

Early years in America: politicisation

In the early war years, whilst teaching the 'Great Books' course at St John's College in Annapolis, Maryland, Nabokov made two friendships that were to prove highly influential. One was with the career diplomat Charles 'Chip' Bohlen who had, in 1942, taken up a post as Assistant Chief of the Russian Section of the Division of European Affairs in Washington. A Russian specialist since the 1920s, Bohlen had spent two periods in the American embassy in Moscow – 1934–35 and from 1938–42. Bohlen's friend Isaiah Berlin, the British diplomat and philosopher, spent the period 1942–46 at the British embassy in Washington, after a spell working for the Ministry of Information in New York.[6] Bohlen's Dumbarton Avenue house formed the centre for what Nabokov called the Washington 'Russian Circle'.[7] It was, for a mere college lecturer, a high-powered group, but Nabokov later came to think that he had had a distinct role within it – a special value to Bohlen and Berlin. As he describes it, the relationship between these two was a symbiotic one, to which each – one a 'kremlinologist', the other an expert on Russian culture – brought complementary skills. And yet there was something missing, namely:

> ... neither ... was in the remotest sense Russian by instinct. How could they be? One of them was English, the other American. As Chip once said, 'The only one of us who is gut-wise Russian is you.' In other words their words, their reflexes, their intuition, their instinctive reactions were of necessity non-Russian, whereas mine could be gauged as such. (Nabokov, 1975, p. 215–16)[8]

---

6   Nabokov's (1975) memoir has him meeting Bohlen in Washington either in 1940 (p.211) *or* 1941 (p.205). If either one of these is correct, presumably Bohlen must have been home on leave. He met Berlin in 1943 (p.208). For Bohlen's career, see Bohlen (1973, pp.123–5).

7   Nicolas Nabokov to Mike Bessie, 3 November 1958, p. 3.

8   In an interview with the author, Isaiah Berlin agreed that this was probably true.

The Dumbarton Avenue group found itself very much at odds with public opinion. This was a time when only the Soviet Union seemed to be actually *fighting* Hitler, and sympathy for the struggle of the Russian people tended to exclude all criticism of the Soviet state, a situation which the Russian Circle found both misguided and dangerous. As Nabokov describes it:

> These new friends had few if any illusions about 'Uncle Joe', about Russian Communism and the future shape of the Socialist Motherland. In more ways than one, they were an anachronistic group in the Washington of those years, perhaps even in all of America. America was in a state of Sovietophilic euphoria, which none in the house on Dumbarton Avenue shared. (Nabokov, 1975, p. 212)

Bohlen's views had been shaped decisively by his experiences in Moscow: during his second posting, in 1938, he had witnessed the final round of the notorious show trials of 1936–38. Ambassador Joseph E. Davies, however, did not share his subordinate's disgust at the process. For, according to Bohlen:

> [Davies] had gone to Russia sublimely ignorant of even the most elementary realities of the Soviet system and of its ideology. He was determined ... to maintain a Polyanna attitude ... He took the Soviet line on everything except issues between the two governments. (Bohlen, 1973, p. 44)

Bohlen adds that Davies accepted 'as gospel truth' the evidence presented at the trials. Similarly, the senior military figure in the Embassy, Colonel Phillip R. Faymonville was 'inclined to favour the Soviet regime in almost all its actions ... he would stoutly defend the purges, insisting that they were uprooting traitors and enemies of the people ...'. Back in Washington Bohlen and a few likeminded colleagues fought for what they considered a 'realistic', rather than an 'emotional' attitude to the USSR. Although it was to be some years before their prescriptions were taken up, they nonetheless provided a seed-bed for the ideas which would later constitute America's Cold War foreign policy.

Undoubtedly this was an extremely influential group. Walter Isaacson and Evan Thomas include Bohlen and another of the Dumbarton Avenue circle, George Kennan, among the six 'Wise Men' who were the 'Architects of the American Century':

> By breeding and training, this handful of men and a few of their close colleagues knew that America would have to assume the burden of a global role ... [They] shaped a new world order ... authored a doctrine of containment and forged an array of alliances that has been the foundation of American policy ever since. ... Their world view was shaped by a fascination with the emergence of the Soviet Union as a world power and an unabashed belief in America's sacred destiny (and their own) to take the lead in protecting freedom

---

Bohlen, incidentally, does seem to have been interested in Russian culture; in his auto-biography we learn that, on his first visit to Moscow, he made many friends in the worlds of ballet and theatre, including writer Mikhail Bulgakov (*The Master and Margarita*). See Bohlen (1973, pp.20–21). However, according to Nabokov, his immersion in Russian politics in reality left little time for the study of Russian culture.

around the world and create ... 'the American Century'. (Isaacson and Thomas, 1986, pp.19 and 26).

We are not, fortunately, required to believe in sacred destinies, 'American Centuries' or, indeed, to share Isaacson's and Thomas's heroic view of the Wise Men's legacy; the point is to note the sense in which this group foreshadowed a postwar American policy of *internationalism* (for which read leadership – or domination) and *containment*, and the significance of Nabokov having come under their influence – an influence he was happy to admit to, describing the period as a watershed which led to 20 years of political involvement in the world of music.[9]

At the beginning of the 1940s Nabokov had been a little-known émigré composer. By pure chance he made close personal friendships with men who would later become central figures in the American establishment during the Cold War. When, 10 years after that first meeting, Nabokov emerged from relative obscurity to become the highly visible figurehead of the Congress for Cultural Freedom, this would be directly traceable to the soirées at Dumbarton Avenue.

Joining the Bohlen set prompted a political reorientation, creating a Nabokov ready for some sort of engagement. Before the war's end, another meeting would prove crucial in terms of determining what form that engagement would take. In 1945, after a spell teaching at Peabody Conservatory, Nabokov joined up, following his friend W.H. Auden into the Morale Division of the US Strategic Bombing Survey. Once in Germany he became deeply affected by the return of the 'DPs' (displaced persons) to Russia. To one newly politicised by the 'Russian Circle', this – the DP's return 'to slavery and certain destruction' (Nabokov, 1975, p. 224) – was a monstrous crime, and he would later describe this as the moment when 'my old nostalgia, my deep-rooted illness ... left me. I knew then that my Russia, the Russia of an exile's wish-dream, had been wiped out' (Nabokov, 1951d, p. 182). He resolved to stay within the Allied apparatus *specifically* as an anti-Stalinist working from within to change official policy on the DPs, and in August moved to Berlin and the Information Control Division of OMGUS,[10] his job there being to work towards the

---

9   He adds 'No wonder! At that time it [politics] was in the air. It was the concern of intelligent people all over the world. Men and women of goodwill and integrity readily abandoned their professional occupations, their private lives and interests in order to help win the war against what seemed to be obvious evil' (Nabokov, 1975, p. 214). One is tempted to note that, whilst he is happy to associate himself with the fight against fascism, in practice Nabokov was *not* moved to abandon his Washington friends and the vital war work of teaching music in order to join it. Not, at least, until that fight was practically ended.

10   Occupation Military Government of the United States. See Nabokov (1975, pp. 218–19 and 1951d, p. 182). He gives most detail, however, in the 1951 article 'Music under the Generals', itself extracted from the latter book:

Officially we were supposed to be concerned only with the following:
1. To eject the Nazis from German musical life and license those German musicians whom we believed to be 'clean' Germans.
2. To control the programs of German concerts and see to it that they would not turn into nationalist manifestations.

re-establishment of German musical life. It was here that he met Michael Josselson, the man who would go on to become the cornerstone of the Congress for Cultural Freedom, serving, from 1950 to 1967, as its executive director, for most of that time alongside Nicolas Nabokov.

Born in Estonia in 1908, Josselson, like his new friend, had found himself in Berlin after the Revolution where he worked for the American Gimbel-Saks chain of stores. Following his emigration to the USA he joined up in 1943 and served as an interrogator in the Psychological Warfare Division, staying on after the war to work on the de-Nazification programme. It had always been supposed that he was a CIA agent by the time the Congress was born in 1950, and this was established beyond doubt by Frances Stonor Saunders in *Who Paid the Piper? The CIA and the Cultural Cold War* (1999). In Berlin, Nabokov and Josselson formed an effective and congenial partnership, sharing both the experience of exile and an attachment to America, and taking a pragmatic approach to the business of de-Nazification (Stonor Saunders, 1999, pp. 11–16).

Whilst Josselson stayed on (while still in Berlin, he was recruited to the CIA in 1948), Nabokov returned to the USA for a six-month stint working with Chip Bohlen's brother-in-law Charles Thayer, helping to establish the Voice of America's Russian Service, before an unfortunate conclusion to his government service. According to one source, before issuing a security clearance, the FBI 'grilled him over his bohemian private life', leading to the composer's resignation (Coleman, 1987, pp. 43–4).[11] Stonor Saunders has a different account: for her, the evidence suggests that Nabokov applied to join the CIA, but was refused security clearance – quite possibly on similar, character-related, grounds (Stonor Saunders, 1999, pp. 42–4).

Around this time he seems to have become involved with a group who would find a prominent place in the CCF a few years later. It is commonplace now to identify a particular world of writers, academics and polemicists as the 'New York Intellectuals'. Coalescing in the late 1930s, the group owed its character to a combination of literary modernism with anti-Stalinism (see Chapter 6), the chief vehicles for its ideas being a range of 'little magazines' – *New Leader, Politics, Commentary* and, most importantly, *Partisan Review.* The Intellectuals were united by a shared flight from orthodox communism in the late 1930s. With revolutionary idealism rapidly dissolving, the early postwar years were to see them taking on a new role, moving, on the one hand, to cultural concerns, whilst also supplying, as Richard Pells has described it, 'the philosophical ammunition for the cold war' (Pells, 1985, p. 76).

---

3. To guard and protect the 'monuments' and 'treasures' of Germany's culture which had by virtue of conquest fallen into our hands.

He goes on to list the numerous practical problems that this entailed – repairing, heating and lighting buildings, acquisition of paper, ink, parts and scores, costumes etc. See Nabokov (1951a, pp.50–51). Incidentally the Nicolas Nabokov papers held by the University of Texas at Austin contain various de-Nazification documents including those relating to Herbert von Karajan and Wilhelm Furtwängler, along with the proceedings of a committee considering the case of the former.

11   There is no mention of this in *Bagázh*; but there *is* enough to suggest that Nabokov's private life was probably not a model of restraint and propriety.

In 1948 the editor of *Politics,* Dwight Macdonald, embarked on a short-lived venture known as the 'Europe–America Groups' (EAG), together with Mary McCarthy, Albert Camus and the Italian anarcho-pacifist Nicola Chiaromonte. Hugh Wilford has described EAG as an attempt to create 'a practical non-Marxist radical politics,' and the project clearly had Atlanticism at its core (Wilford, 1995, p. 163). Its manifesto speaks of the isolation – in a bipolar world – of those European leftists 'outside the mass parties', and the need to combat their 'distress and desperation' via what Camus called a 'community of dialogue', creating a counterbalance on the democratic Left. It appears that this programme appealed to Nabokov since he took part, in the spring of 1948, in two EAG benefits – a lecture ('The Soviet Attack on Culture') at the Rand School, and a fund-raising auction, to which he donated some music (ibid., p. 132).[12] Within a year the EAG had folded, after an attempted takeover by a particularly hard-line anti-Stalinist group closely associated with *Partisan Review.* However, this short-lived organisation arguably formed the starting point for a process which would lead to the creation of the Congress for Cultural Freedom, and the following year was to see Nabokov and elements of both factions (Macdonald's EAG and the *PR* 'boys') engaged in a high-profile exercise which would drive that process powerfully forward.[13]

Into the cultural Cold War

By the late 1940s the Soviet strategy of holding 'peace conferences' held under the auspices of apparently independent front organisations was well established. The 1947 German Writer's Congress in East Berlin was followed the next year by the Cultural Conference for Peace in Wroclaw, Poland, establishing a pattern in which the supposed independence of the proceedings was exposed by the fact of rigid control in all its aspects (in each case, however, there were some small pro-Western protests, for example by Melvin Lasky in Berlin, and A.J.P. Taylor in Wroclaw). This policy was stepped up dramatically in March and April of 1949, when peace conferences were arranged for New York and Paris, the first being the Cultural and Scientific Conference for World Peace, held at the Waldorf-Astoria Hotel. Sponsored by Albert Einstein, Charlie Chaplin, Paul Robeson and Leonard Bernstein, among others, conference participants included Dmitri Shostakovich and Aleksandr Fadeyev from the Soviet Union with American speakers including Clifford Odets, Lillian Hellman, Norman Mailer and Aaron Copland (Coleman, 1989, pp. 4–7).[14]

Highly visible, and aimed squarely at influencing American intellectuals, it was

---

12   The lecture was chaired by Mary McCarthy, and followed by a panel discussion including Macdonald, Meyer Schapiro and Lionel Trilling. It raised $300. The auction was accompanied by a short play acted by Kevin McCarthy and Montgomery Clift.

13   Wilford has underlined both the significance of the EAG and the irony implicit in the situation: 'When Macdonald, McCarthy and Chiaromonte undertook the creation of an organisation designed to rejuvenate the international left they could not have suspected that, within the space of one and a half years, it would mutate into a propaganda front for the US government' (Wilford, 1995, p. 200).

14   The Paris conference of April was the World Peace Congress.

inevitable that this conference would generate opposition. Under the leadership of New York University philosophy professor Sidney Hook, and including Nabokov, Dwight Macdonald and Mary McCarthy, a group calling itself Americans for Intellectual Freedom (AIF) was established. Working alongside this group in the Waldorf's bridal suite, and appearing to foot the bill, was one David Dubinsky of the International Ladies Garment Workers Union. In fact, Dubinsky merely acted as a CIA conduit, setting a pattern by which the Agency would secretly subsidise groups whose aims and policies meshed with those of government (Stonor Saunders, 1999, pp. 54–5). Thus funded, AIF set out to counter the conference in every possible way: they exposed the communist connections of its organisers, asked loaded questions of the speakers, and held a counter-rally.

Without any doubt, the star of the conference was Dmitri Shostakovich.[15] After his speech, in which he 'condemned most Western music as decadent and bourgeois, painted the glories of the rising Soviet music culture … [attacking] the demon Stravinsky as the corrupter of Western art', it fell naturally to Nabokov to mount a counter-attack (Nabokov, 1951d, pp. 204–5). It is conventional today to view Shostakovich as a man deeply opposed to communism, and even to find that opposition coded into the music. There was little or no suggestion of this in the 1940s, however, and Nabokov's attitude to the Russian composer was straightforward: Shostakovich *must* be considered a thoroughgoing communist, and 'any doubt as to the sincerity of this devotion, any suspicion as to the honesty of his intentions, should definitely be put aside' (ibid., p. 198). Granted, Shostakovich appeared 'uncomfortable and awkward', indeed 'a spectacle of human misery and degradation'. Nabokov put this down partly to a personal sensitivity unsuited to the heat of public attention, partly to his being a man who had *voluntarily* renounced his free will in favour of the superior wisdom of the Party. Having been attacked in the pages of *Pravda* only a year before, it was clear that:

> … this speech of his, this whole peace-making mission was part of a punishment, part of a ritual of redemption he had to go through before he could be pardoned again. He was to tell, in person, to all the dupes at the Waldorf conference and to the whole decadent bourgeois world that loved him so much that he, Shostakovich, is *not* a free man, but an obedient tool of his government. He told in effect, that every time the Party found flaws in his art, the Party was right, and every time the Party put him on ice, he was grateful to the Party, because it helped him to recognise his flaws and mistakes. (Nabokov, 1951d, p. 205)

In both his published accounts of this engagement, Nabokov professes sympathy for Shostakovich and a certain reluctance to 'embarrass a wretched human being'. However, as the situation demanded a confrontation, following the speech, Nabokov asked whether Shostakovich – as an individual, not as a delegate of the Soviet government – agreed with the characterisation of Stravinsky, Hindemith and Schoenberg in *Pravda* as ' "obscurantists", "decadent bourgeois formalists" and "lackeys of imperialism" '. The reply was brief and in the affirmative (Nabokov, 1975, p. 238).

---

15   Irving Howe wrote of the audience as ' … breathless middlebrows, half grasping and half fearful in their culture-hunger (*did you* SEE *Shostakovich?*) …' (Howe, 1949, p. 505).

At the counter-rally Nabokov gave a speech entitled 'Music and Peace' which sought to expose the true position of artists in the Soviet Union, listing some of Stalin's victims,[16] and detailing the attacks on Western music and the restrictions on composers. As for Shostakovich, in this public speech the idea of the composer's self-abasement before the Party is replaced by the less ambiguous, politically clearer image of a man coerced. Perhaps an acknowledgement of his widespread popularity, this removes any element of *personal* criticism, and indeed allows Nabokov to position himself *on Shostakovich's side*:

> Like dirty laundry, Shostakovich was thrown in a clothes hamper; then suddenly, picked up, washed, ironed out, and sent to America with five other colleagues in blue serge suits (with overly long sleeves *à la Stalin*) to meet Dr Harlow Shapley and a motley crew of Iron Curtain parrots, each with an olive branch in his mouth, gathered for a press conference in the Parrot Room of the Waldorf Astoria. No one who saw him ... his pale, sensitive face twitching, his fingers nervously crushing the butt of a Russian cigaret [*sic*], could help but feel compassion for the young and timid artist, and feel an overpowering wish to take him by the arm and lead him out of the clatter, the parody of that noisy conference, into a quiet place, far and safe from the realities of the political world, far and safe from Stalin and his henchmen. (Nabokov, 1949b, unpublished, pp. 1–2)

After giving his speech, Nabokov reports that he saw at the back of the hall:

> ... a familiar face ... an acquaintance ... from Berlin who, like me, had worked for OMGUS. He congratulated me warmly. 'This is a splendid affair you and your friends have organised,' he said. 'We should have something like this in Berlin.' (Nabokov, 1975, pp. 238–9)

The 'acquaintance' was Michael Josselson, monitoring the proceedings on behalf of his new employers at the CIA, and so the stage was set for the first 'Congress for Cultural Freedom', held in Berlin in 1950. This was set up as an explicit response to Soviet 'cultural conferences' such as the Waldorf affair. The Berlin Philharmonic played Beethoven (*Egmont* overture[17]) and the anti-Stalinists had scored a powerful propaganda coup in the blockaded German capital. Among Nabokov's contributions was a fighting speech in the session devoted to 'Freedom and the Artist':

> Out of this Congress we must build an organisation for war. We must have a standing committee. We must see to it that it calls on all figures, all fighting organisations and all methods of fighting, with a view to action. If we do not, we will sooner or not all be hanged. The hour has long struck 12. (Coleman, 1989, p. 29)

He had made his mark. When, in November of that year, the Executive Committee of a permanent, Paris-based, Congress was set up, Nicolas Nabokov was appointed

---

16   He cites Dimitry Mirsky, Isaac Babel, Boris Pilnyak, Mikhail Bulgakov, Ivan Katayev, Professor Platonov, Vsevolod Meyerhold, Anna Ahkmatova and Boris Pasternak. See Nabokov (1949b) undated typescript 'Music and Peace', p. 3.

17   Apparently, '[Arthur] Koestler had wanted Benjamin Britten and Louis MacNeice to compose a "Free Europe Anthem", but nothing came of it' (Coleman, 1989, p. 27).

secretary-general. Working out his notice at the Peabody Conservatory, he left for Europe in May 1951, to become the chief organiser and 'public face' of the CCF, a task which would occupy him until he left in 1962 to become director of the Berlin Festival.

Until 1999, and the publication of *Who Paid the Piper?*, much regarding the relationship of the CIA to the CCF remained unknown, and it remains the case that *all* the relevant papers are classified 'operational' and, as such, exempted from the provisions of the Freedom of Information Act.[18] Against this background, Stonor Saunders' achievement is substantial, and any reader seeking to understand this area – the funding mechanisms, the personnel, the power struggles and policy shifts, not just in the CCF but in the wider operation of which it formed a part – will naturally turn to her work, both now and in the foreseeable future. The facts in outline, however, have been clear for over 30 years. Following the 1966 *New York Times* article, which revealed CIA funding of the CCF, and the placement of agents within it and *Encounter* magazine, an extraordinary justification of the CIA's covert funding of front organisations appeared in the *Saturday Evening Post*, setting out the context in which the CCF was born, and some of the forces operating behind the scenes. Its author was Tom Braden, who had been the begetter and first head of the CIA's International Operations Division (IOD). Braden explained how the formation of the IOD reflected the fear that the West was losing the Cold War, and losing it crucially because of the Soviets' success in their use of apparently benign and independent front organisations. The aim of the new Division was, quite simply, to play the Soviets at their own game. Braden's article set out the ground rules for working through front organisations which, along with the CCF, included the International Committee of Women, the World Assembly of Youth, and Force Ouvrière, an anti-communist French trades union:

> 'Limit the money to amounts private organisations can credibly spend.' The other rules were equally obvious: 'Use legitimate, existing organisations; disguise the extent of American interest; protect the integrity of the organisation by not requiring it to support every aspect of official American policy.' (Braden, 1967, p. 14)

Charitable foundations were set up to act as conduits for CIA monies, and agents placed within the fronts: Braden cites the CCF and its journal, *Encounter*, as examples of organisations in which this was done. These agents could then suggest that certain generous American foundations might be approached for funds – exactly what happened with the Congress, where the bulk of the funds were supplied by the Farfield Foundation, created expressly for the purpose (Stonor Saunders, 1999,

---

18   In response to a letter to the CIA dated 21 November 1996, the author received a reply dated 25 June 1997 from Lee S. Strickland, 'Information and Privacy Coordinator'. He wrote that '... records on this subject, if any exist, would be found in operational files. You should be aware of the provisions of the CIA Information Act, 50 USC 431, under which operational files of the CIA have been exempted from the Freedom of Information Act, 5 USC 552. The pertinent section of the CIA Information Act defines "operational files" as: "(1) files of the Directorate of Operations which document the conduct of foreign intelligence or counterintelligence operations or intelligence ..."'

pp. 125–7). Braden also underlines another aspect of CIA thinking which must be understood if its support of Congress is to make any sense: its belief, in the late 1940s and early 1950s, in the Cold War utility of the 'non-Communist left'. He reminds his readers:

> The fact, of course, is that in much of Europe in the 1950s, socialists, people who called themselves 'left' – the very people whom many Americans thought no better than Communists – were the only people who gave a damn about fighting Communism. (Braden, 1967, p. 10)

In an atmosphere – as the CIA perceived it – of widespread European support for the Soviets, a corresponding mistrust of America, and a general desire for some sort of 'third way', the 'non-Communist left' were potentially a vital asset. What was needed was somehow to enlist – unknowingly, if necessary – intellectuals who could combine left-wing credibility with anti-communism and an Atlanticist outlook (Pells, 1997, pp. 66–70). Arthur Schlesinger Jr, the historian, author of the influential *The Vital Center* (1949), referred to the 'quiet revolution' that overtook the State Department in the late 1940s, through which this non-communist Left became so central to its Cold War strategy that it came to be referred to simply by the abbreviation 'NCL'. As Peter Coleman has put it:

> Now, at a unique historic moment, there developed a convergence, almost to the point of identity, between the assessments and agenda of the 'NCL' intellectuals and that combination of Ivy League, anglophile, liberal, can-do gentlemen, academics, and idealists who constituted the new CIA. (Coleman, 1989, p. 46)

Schlesinger also credited the revolution to the influence of 'Chip' Bohlen, George Kennan and Isaiah Berlin: Nabokov's Dumbarton Avenue friends were no longer voices crying out in the wilderness, and it is unlikely to be an accident that *their* victory in the battle of ideas coincides with *his* emergence as a public figure.[19]

And the degree of control exercised by the CIA is beyond doubt. An unclassified internal Agency account of the origins of Congress confirms their close involvement, and reveals the pivotal role of Josselson.[20] It shows that the CIA were impressed by the AIF's Waldorf-Astoria action, and took a close interest in the group that had

---

19   Whether they used their influence in support of Nabokov is not known. Bohlen, however, did advise him to attend the 1950 Congress in Berlin: 'You should go,' said Bohlen, 'if only to tell your Kulturnye colleagues that it is a mistake not to invite artists. They've been *the most persistent whipping boys of both the Soviets and the Nazis* [my italics]' (Nabokov, 1975, p. 241). This is an incredible statement, but one which tended to be echoed by Nabokov's speeches painting artists as prime victims of totalitarianism. Jews, socialists, homosexuals, democrats and gypsies, among others, might want to take issue with this view.

20   The unattributed, undated document is titled *Origins of the Congress for Cultural Freedom, 1949–51*. Marked *Unclassified*, a footnote adds: 'This article is an excerpt from a larger classified draft study of CIA involvement with anti-Communist groups in the Cold War. The author retains a footnoted copy of the article in the CIA History Staff. This version of the article has been redacted for security considerations (phrases in brackets denote some of the redactions)' (p. 11). The document was enclosed with the letter cited in note 18.

coalesced around it; they went on to pay the expenses of German, Italian and American delegates to another counter-conference, in April 1949 in Paris, looking all the while for some way of creating an ongoing organisation. The Berlin Congress was organised chiefly by Josselson, who kept the CIA informed of developments and, as the momentum generated by Berlin carried the group on towards the formation of the CCF proper, he contrived to have at least one individual, Melvin Lasky – whom the Agency found unacceptable – removed from its leadership.

This last point is important in terms of the focus of this study. We are concerned with the musical activities of Nicolas Nabokov as CCF secretary-general; his attempt, effectively, to enlist the arts for the anti-communist cause. This project was undertaken alongside the agent Josselson, and yet he always maintained that the whole business of CIA funding was unknown to him.[21] We may think this incredible, and indeed Stonor Saunders, in her exhaustive study, is highly sceptical, without being able to prove conclusively that Nabokov knew (Stonor Saunders, 1999, pp. 395–6). For our present purposes, however, the important point is that the CIA, through Josselson, controlled appointments in the CCF, as the example of Lasky's removal shows. Top positions in the organisation were *only* filled with the blessings of the Agency. The fact of Nabokov's appointment, and his close collaboration with Josselson for more than 15 years, can only suggest that his policies met with their approval.

21　In *Bagázh* he presents himself as having been both surprised and amused to discover the source of the CCF's funding (see pp. 243–6). Some others involved in the enterprise, however, have cast doubt on this innocence. Isaiah Berlin told the present writer he suspected Nabokov *did* know the true state of affairs, commenting on how closely he had worked with Josselson (Sir Isaiah Berlin, interviewed by the author, 11 June 1997). The sociologist Edward Shils, a prominent member of the CCF's American affiliate, recalls asking Nabokov in October 1955 about a rumour that the Congress was receiving Agency support: in return, he was sent an accountant's report on the Farfield Foundation, later revealed as a front. He comments that Nabokov 'did not accompany that boring, uninformative and, as it turned out later, false, document with any denial of the report which I had transmitted ... That was a cynical thing to do ...' (Shils, 1990, p. 85).

Chapter 2

Waking the Twilight Sleepers I: On Soviet Music and Shostakovich

> … from 1943 onward my life changed. First imperceptibly, then radically. For nearly twenty years I became involved in politics and in political action. Not that I abandoned my basic profession; I became politically involved within that profession. (Nabokov, 1975, p. 214)

In his 1975 autobiography Nabokov describes the far-reaching personal consequences which can be traced back to his meeting 'Chip' Bohlen and Isaiah Berlin in the early 1940s. The first consequence of this was that he began to write on music and politics, and an article titled 'Music under Dictatorship' duly appeared in *Atlantic Monthly* in 1942, followed by one on Prokofiev and another on Shostakovich for *Harper's Magazine* the following year. Silenced by the demands of teaching at Baltimore's Peabody Conservatory (1943–45) and two years' military service in Europe, his return to the USA in 1947 marked the beginning of a whole series of articles and a book, *Old Friends and New Music*, produced between 1948 and 1953. After that, the output is sparse, notable mainly for the autobiography, *Bagázh: Memoirs of a Russian Cosmopolitan*, which appeared in 1975, two years before his death.[1]

Almost all this writing is concerned with the situation of music in the Soviet Union and Eastern Europe, and clearly shows the marks left by the Chip Bohlen–Isaiah Berlin 'Russian Circle'. The newly politically aware Nabokov, seeking a means of engagement, finds it within his own, musical, world. As we have observed, the Dumbarton Avenue group, which also included the US diplomat George Kennan (who would later become famous as the author of the 1947 'X article'[2]), found itself at odds with the mood of widespread public sympathy towards the Soviet Union which followed the German invasion of June 1941. They considered such attitudes naive, ill-informed and dangerous: the USSR was seen as internally brutal (Bohlen had been decisively influenced by witnessing the purges and show trials of 1934–38 whilst stationed in the Moscow embassy), innately at odds with the West – whatever the contingencies of wartime alliance – and, above all, expansionist. In their work,

---

1   Along with the two books and the journal articles, I have also drawn on the texts of various unpublished (and sometimes undated) speeches, talks and press releases.

2   Kennan published an article, 'The Sources of Soviet Conduct' in the July 1947 issue of *Foreign Affairs*, under the name 'X'. This is generally viewed as decisive in the formation of Truman's policy of 'containment'.

Bohlen, Berlin and Kennan strove to promote these views in both Washington and London.

In this atmosphere Nabokov was becoming politicised. As he describes it:

> ... political perspectives, which until then had been 'simplistic', gradually acquired a degree of sophistication. I began to perceive the basic nature of the twentieth century's political scene: that the evil spirit of this century was double-headed. Hitler and Stalin were two parts of the same phenomenon. Stalinism was the opposite side of the same coin as Herr Hitler. (Nabokov, 1975, p. 213)

Sophisticated? Perhaps not, but for Nabokov this was clearly a watershed, and it does seem to have been a political *shift*, not just a hardening of existing attitudes. Isaiah Berlin recalled that early in their friendship Nabokov had made a comment to the effect that anti-Soviet feeling was got up 'for the benefit of General Electric', and American big business generally, but that under the influence of Bohlen and himself 'that never happened again' – that he lost any pro-Soviet leanings he may previously have entertained.[3] Another suggestion that Nabokov's politics may have been less clear-cut in the 1930s comes when, in the book *Old Friends and New Music*, he seeks to account for the return of his friend Sergei Prokofiev to the Soviet Union in 1934. There are, he argues, two important points to bear in mind:

> First, the Soviet Union of that period was not quite the same thing as the Soviet Union of today [1951]. Second, the feelings of a forward-looking and revolutionary-minded Russian intellectual towards his fatherland and its government were quite different then from what they are now and were on the whole rather mixed. (Nabokov, 1951d, p. 127)

Perhaps we may read this as an apology for the author's *own* former views (it would certainly not be the only place in the writings where there seems to be an identification with Prokofiev, as the next chapter will show). However, the question for the new Nabokov of the 1940s, who was no politician after all, was how to act on this new-found awareness. It was to be some time before the ideal vehicle arrived, although later in the war he would begin to undertake cultural–political work, first in the Information Control Division of OMGUS, the American authorities in Berlin, then in the Voice of America's Russian Service, where he worked with Bohlen's brother-in-law, Charles Thayer. He began, in effect, to move in a world of information and administration, and this path would lead, ultimately, to the secretary-generalship of the Congress for Cultural Freedom. In the meantime, he shared the view of his new political friends that a well-meaning but disinformed public had to be alerted to the Soviet danger.

In his memoir, *Witness to History*, Bohlen recalls this period, and a conversation with Isaiah Berlin in which the two worked out a metaphor for public attitudes to the Soviet Union. It is, as he says, an 'involved figure of speech', the finer details of which need not concern us, but, broadly, communism is compared to a train whose engineer and firemen, knowing the destination and how to get there, are the card-carrying Party members, and whose passengers, happily to be moving rapidly

---

3   Sir Isaiah Berlin, interviewed by the author, 11 June 1997.

in a direction they generally approve of, are the 'fellow travelers'. Conductors and brakemen have their place in the metaphor too: they know the destination but are relatively powerless – unable to affect the speed of the train.

> The final group were the twilight sleepers, who did not know what was going on. They stood on the edge of the tracks waving handkerchiefs and hats, pleased at seeing the train moving. They didn't know where the train was going but they enjoyed the sight. (Bohlen, 1973, p. 126)

These 'twilight sleepers' encompassed the large mass of people who, as Bohlen and his friends saw it, in their appreciation for the efforts of the Red Army and sympathy for the plight of the Russian people, failed to appreciate the true nature of the Soviet state.

We know that Nabokov shared this general view; there is, moreover, evidence suggesting that he knew of the Bohlen/Berlin metaphor which expressed it so succinctly. Years later, in 1958, he was trying to interest the publishers Secker and Warburg in an autobiography. In a 'tentative outline' of the book, provisionally entitled *Ages of Lives*, he sketched a chapter on his postwar return to the USA. This was to be concerned with 'New York in the postwar years. Fellow-travelers, twilight sleepers, Communists, anti-Communists. The Waldorf-Astoria meeting.'[4] It seems reasonable to assume that the phrase has the same meaning as in the Bohlen account.

In the view of Nabokov and his friends, the 'twilight sleepers' were politically uncommitted, only supporting the Soviet Union by virtue of their ignorance and passivity.[5] The task ahead must be to enlighten them. As a composer, Nabokov could make his contribution by increasing awareness of the true state of music in the USSR, and the true situation of its composers: his writings were therefore part of an attempt to awaken the twilight sleepers.

Nabokov's writings: an overview

The major task of this and the following chapter will be to demonstrate Nabokov's preoccupations by reference to this body of written work. What are the key characteristics of the texts? First, and most obviously, they form a coherent body of work by virtue of the fact that all except one are concerned, in whole or in part, with music and politics in relation to the Soviet Union.[6] Frequently the aim is to inform the

---

4   The outline of the proposed book *Ages of Lives* is attached to a letter from Nicolas Nabokov to Mike Bessie dated 3 November 1958, Secker and Warburg papers, University of Reading.

5   It might also be said that the image displays the same elitist disdain towards the public embodied in the fears of a mass culture which many of the CCF's most prominent American supporters would voice in the 1950s. See Chapter 6.

6   Strictly speaking, this should be qualified, since *Old Friends and New Music* contains elements of pure reminiscence such as 'Christmas with Stravinsky', along with chapters on Prokofiev and Shostakovich that are more directly relevant to our current purposes.

reader of current developments – such as the 'music purge' of 1948 – which illustrate the controls exercised over composers and its effects; Nabokov exposes the Soviet 'line' on music, both domestic and foreign, and its consequences. Sometimes he moves beyond reportage to offer a historical and cultural context for what he sees as the corrosion of Russian musical life by Soviet aesthetics – this usually involves some characterisation of the latter as 'middle-class' or 'petit-bourgeois'.

Inevitably, the two principal Soviet composers make regular appearances: Shostakovich – as archetypal new Soviet artist, sometime target of Zhdanov, and as celebrity in the West – and the rather different case of Prokofiev, who Nabokov frequently linked to Diaghilev, both of whom he had known in Paris of the 1920s. A juxtaposition of the cosmopolitan with the provincial is woven into the pieces as a sort of motif, although the author never feels the need to define these terms: on the contrary, there appears to be an assumption that author and readers will share an understanding of their meaning, validity and evaluative content. A small amount of the writing ventures into two other areas, the first being personal reminiscence, which within our period is concentrated in the book *Old Friends and New Music*. This leaves two articles on issues in contemporary music – 'Festivals and the Twelve Tone Row' (1951b) and 'The Atonal Trail' (1948b). Although the former piece does not have the adversarial character its title may suggest, in the latter, Nabokov enters the fray, somewhat uncharacteristically, as a protagonist in the resumed postwar debate over the Schoenberg system.

Reading through these texts, the author's character emerges. For an anti-communist, he is not particularly 'hawkish', and, in the wartime articles at least, is careful not to assume a bellicose tone. Even in the later, Cold War, period his writing on Shostakovich, for example, shows an apparently genuine sympathy for the difficult position of the Russian composer, whilst entertaining no doubts about the sincerity of the latter's communist beliefs.[7] The moderate anti-communist was an equally moderate modernist. From what we can tell of Nabokov's musical values (he preferred to write on cultural politics and personalities than musical ideas) he was no sectarian. Unable to understand the magnetic pull of Schoenbergian or post-Weberian systems, impatient with their more aggressive and dogmatic proponents, he was, however, generally unwilling to enter the lists wearing the favours of tonality. In fact, he seems to have taken a 'broad church' approach to programming his festivals, which was perhaps appropriate, given his linking of music and freedom. His article 'The Atonal Trail: A Communication' – a public blast at the certainties of postwar twelve-toners – is something of an exception: stung into a defence of Stravinsky by a René Leibowitz piece in *Partisan Review*, the response nonetheless espouses a catholic approach to contemporary musical language.

A distinct style emerges in these pieces. Their author enjoys introducing humour, often at the expense of his opponents, and the language and terms of Soviet art

---

This, after all, is not a biography. It remains true, however, that *all* the other texts bar one – 'The Atonal Trail' (1948b) – are Cold War interventions.

    7   'Any doubts as to the sincerity of this devotion [to communism], any suspicion as to the honesty of his intentions, should be definitively put aside' (Nabokov, 1951d, p. 198). See Chapter 1 on Nabokov's confrontation with Shostakovich at the Waldorf-Astoria 'peace conference' of 1949.

controls are often ridiculed. At least one of his editors questioned the good taste and appropriateness of these elements, requiring them to be toned down for publication. In 1951 Nabokov was preparing a piece to be broadcast on the Third Programme, and had sent a draft to the BBC. By way of response, the Corporation's Anna Kallin asked that he should:

> ... keep in mind the fact that – forgive the pompousness – we are dealing with ideas, and that we can stand a lot of them, but that we cannot stand facetiousness or propaganda ... all you say is so funny apart from being tragic that it is not necessary to emphasise and over-elaborate the joke.[8]

The IACF papers held at the University of Chicago contain a typescript of this talk: comparing this with the version published in *The Listener* (which we may assume to be the text of the broadcast) reveals a number of excisions which Kallin may have required or encouraged. Take, for example, the opening of the draft version:

> Everyone knows that the romance of Soviet authorities with the art of music has been a bumpy affair. *The indigenous Melpomene of the Socialist motherland has apparently been quite an erratic lady for in these last 20 years she has undergone treatment varying from the tender and lavish caresses due a beloved concubine, to something resembling police action against a dissolute trollop* [my italics]. Soviet composers have seen themselves elevated .... (Nabokov, nd 4, unpublished, p. 1)

The second, italicised, sentence is entirely missing from the published version. One more instance will suffice; again, the text in italics was edited out:

> Yet suddenly in the midst of this *heroic* idyll *of cajolment and caress, the wrath of the fierce Soviet gods descended upon the unsuspecting honorary firemen and chess champions. They* [Soviet composers] were suddenly told they were not heroes at all, but a sorry lot of inveterate formalists, *of caterers to decadent bourgeois tastes, resembling the most dangerous enemies of Soviet society, namely deviationists and diversionists.* Parallel to the excommunication of Russian composers came the wholesale condemnation of Western music. *Composers of the Western world were called such curious names, such as 'insatiable sadistic erotomaniacs' or 'degenerate blackguards'* [my italics] ... .

Kallin's editing leaves the body of Nabokov's argument intact, but reduces considerably the first two pages of his draft – just where the author is enjoying himself most at the expense of Soviet officialdom. The result is sparer, and certainly drier; it is more to the point and less 'facetious'. Nabokov loved to mock the Soviet system and it is quite possible to question, like Anna Kallin, whether this tendency really helped further his arguments.

---

8   Letter from Anna Kallin to Nicolas Nabokov, dated 7 August 1951. An annotated copy of Nabokov's draft was enclosed with the letter: this was not found in the Nabokov archive. The draft, which is here assumed to be an original version or at least an early version of *The Listener* piece, was found in the IACF papers at the University of Chicago. To avoid confusion, note that *The Listener* piece (1951c) is 'Changing Styles in Soviet Music', whilst the Chicago typescript is headed 'The Changing Styles of Soviet Music'.

Nabokov also takes pleasure in the use of anecdotes to illustrate a point, and this is linked to a quality of display in the writing – display of his own connections and travels, of his own learning (according to Isaiah Berlin he may indeed have been as well-read as he liked to imply) and his aristocratic, high-cultural background (typically Brahmin, Nabokov takes the value and superiority of Western music and high culture very much for granted[9]). The language itself can be extravagant or showy, and contains examples of English usage that are, to say the least, novel (this was not, of course, his first language).[10] Overall, the style may be described as inelegant but lively; the arguments perhaps less than profound, yet transparent and sincere. We should now consider the content of this work in detail.

Reporting on Soviet music

Reading Nabokov's articles the central preoccupations are clear and consistent, and indeed there is little apparent development in the period under consideration. This very consistency – the sense in which the writings are almost wholly about the relationship between music and (Soviet) totalitarianism, with only slight shifts of focus – makes the production of a clear summary a little difficult. The reader should bear in mind that a significant degree of overlap will exist between any themes that might be identified: here is a body of work which, by virtue of its single-mindedness, stubbornly resists separation into discrete components. For example, whilst it may be asserted that Nabokov is interested in both Shostakovich *and* Soviet music controls, he does, however, use the career of the former to illustrate the character of the latter; likewise, Prokofiev is considered sometimes because of his intrinsic interest to the author, and sometimes because the Soviet authorities attitude to him allows the introduction of another favourite theme – the exposure of what he sees as their 'provincial' tastes. Nonetheless, some untangling of strands *is* necessary if this chapter is to amount to more than a mere chronicle or précis. This said, we may turn to the sense in which these pieces function as reports on Soviet musical life.

Most of these pieces have some element of reportage, of the author detailing current or recent events in the world of Soviet music. This information is never wholly separable from his own analyses and conclusions; indeed, frequently the former acts as a springboard for the latter, so that, although the texts have this aspect, they are always more than mere reports. However, where there are particular recent events to relay, the 'news' aspect of a text sometimes carries more emphasis. So it is with 'The Music Purge' (1948a) which, appearing in the spring of 1948, was largely

---

9   As a qualification it should be added that his later activities show a real and developing interest in non-European musics and the developing area of ethnomusicology. See below on the East–West Music Encounter of 1961. It would also appear, however, that he continued to view music in strictly hierarchical terms.

10   Here, to give the flavour, is one example: 'To lead a rational, ice-cold, determinedly intellectual war against Stalinism without falling into the easy Manichean trap of phony righteousness seemed essential to me, especially at a time when in America that ideological war was getting *histrionically hysterical and crusaderishly paranoiac*' (Nabokov, 1975, pp. 242–3, my italics).

concerned with Zhdanov's attack, in February of that year, on 'anti-Soviet' musical trends (prompted by Muradeli's opera, *The Great Friendship*). The host magazine on this occasion was *Politics*, edited by Dwight Macdonald, the maverick leftist critic and founder of the Europe–America Groups.

Nabokov's opening paragraph ensures that the reader will understand the political context in which Russian composers must operate, and his own attitude to it:

> Soviet Russia is an autocratic oligarchy in which 200 million people are governed by an 'apparatus' as they say in the Soviet Union, of two million elected, or, better, selected people, who, in turn are controlled by a group of about two hundred persons – the Central Committee of the CP. (Nabokov, 1948a, p. 102)

Further up the pyramid of 'democratic centralism' are the 15 members of the Politburo, with Stalin himself at its apex. As a preface to describing the regime's recent intervention in the world of music, Nabokov offers some historical context. We have seen similar things before, he argues, at various times in the years since 1929 (and most notably in 1937), albeit with a more relaxed attitude prevailing 'for opportunistic reasons' during the war years. Then, in 1946, under the auspices of Zhdanov, restrictions on cultural life began to intensify, starting with literature and the theatre, before moving on to the fields of science and philosophy. The guiding principle throughout, we are told, has been opposition to 'formalism' in art – a Western trend that can apparently lead only to decay and regression – and its pernicious influence on Soviet artists. On 11 February 1948 the Central Committee issued a decree, published in *Izvestia*, concerning Muradeli's opera and conclusions drawn from it. As an appendix to the Nabokov article, *Politics* gives the full text, mischievously thanking the New York *Daily Worker* for the translation.[11] Here, Nabokov argues, the cultural position of the Soviet leadership is made clear, for 'it classifies under "formalism" all those Soviet composers who were in any way part of the general European evolution of modern music ...'.

This decree has, Nabokov continues, been followed by a series of articles in the Soviet press which amplify and elaborate its themes, and he singles out a piece by Tikhon Khrennikov (1948) in *Soviet Art*. As the new, post-purge, leader of the Union of Soviet Composers (replacing one of its 'victims', Khachaturyan), Khrennikov's views can, he suggests, be regarded as authoritative: coming from a composer, they also provide a more musically detailed version of the official position. The piece in *Soviet Art* apparently makes much of the link between 'anti-popular' Soviet composers and Western influence, which must inevitably be negative, since, according to Khrennikov:

> ... it is impossible to name a single composer in the Western world who is not afflicted with formalist vices, with subjectivism, mysticism, and with an utter lack of principles ... This music ... openly harks back to the primitive, barbaric cultures of prehistoric society,

---

11   In an Editor's Note, Macdonald writes: ' "The Worker" printed the text "as a service to musicians, composers, and the general public which has shown such great interest in this notable cultural event." We agree that a service has indeed been rendered, though perhaps not precisely the one the editors had in mind' (Nabokov, 1948a, p. 104).

and extols the eroticism, psychopathic mentality, sexual perversion, amorality and shamelessness of the bourgeois hero of the 20th Century. (Nabokov, 1948a, p. 103)

In the following year Nabokov prepared a longer and updated version of this article for the larger-circulation *Partisan Review* under the title 'Russian Music after the Purge' (hereafter referred to as 'After the Purge'). This new piece retains the opening section (which sketches Zhdanov's reactivation of the campaign against decadent bourgeois culture from 1946) and the conclusion linking music to freedom. Now, however, Nabokov is able to examine the impact of the previous year's decree on the prominent Soviet composers it named: Prokofiev, Shostakovich, Khachaturyan, Shebalin, Popov and Miaskovsky. The opening statement is interesting. 'To our knowledge', he writes, 'none of these six has "bodily" disappeared from Soviet musical life. No direct punitive action has been taken' (Nabokov, 1949a, p. 843). In light of this, it is worth reflecting on Nabokov's persistent description of the 1948 events as a 'purge'. The following pages go on to detail criticism, loss of conservatory professorships and a severe reduction in the number of pieces programmed, but do not suggest that any of the six have lost their status and salaries as composers, still less their life or liberty. A purge, then? It is a strange purge that leaves its targets alive, pursuing their chosen vocations and still in the employ of the purging state itself. Perhaps the Russian understanding of the word 'purge' is broader than our own: certainly if a purge can be understood to mean a purge of *ideas* – in the sense of purifying, removing impurities – then Nabokov's usage has, perhaps, some validity. In 1948, however, the term 'purge' as applied to the USSR would not have been understood in this way. In 1948, only 10 years on from the Moscow show trials, a Soviet 'purge' meant a removal of people, and, as such, this 'music purge' would have to be judged spectacularly unsuccessful! We should, then, consider Nabokov's use of this term as a polemical device, calculated to promote outrage by associating the control of music with the Soviet Union's rather more seriously repressive acts – rather than description.

In this piece, as in the *Politics* article, a post-decree text is used to clarify the meaning and consequences of the decree itself. The author, this time, is Marian Koval, 'editor of Sovietskaya Muzyka and a party-line whip' (Nabokov, 1949a, p. 845). According to Nabokov, Koval's analysis of Shostakovich's music gives us 'a fairly clear picture of what kind of music Stalin expects his composers to write', which he summarises, adding a second list to set out that which is musically proscribed. Attention is also drawn to the potentially serious consequences, in the totalitarian environment, of personal jealousies, given that the bureaucratic machine has such control over the careers of individuals, and Nabokov cites Boris Asafiev's 'bitter grudge' against Prokofiev, which resulted – or so he claims – in the composer's inclusion in the 1948 list.

Again, like its predecessor, 'After the Purge' illustrates Soviet attacks on Western music, although here in more detail, and this time Nabokov instances various mistakes and contradictions in the official statements. These, he argues, show how little they know of it. For example, Asafiev brackets Hindemith with 'Schoenberg, Berg, Krenek and Webern, as an "antiharmonic atonalist", which, of course, he has never been'; Walter Piston's work is described in *Sovietskaya Muzyka* as 'brilliant', despite what Nabokov describes as the close links between his style and that of

Hindemith; Poulenc, meanwhile, is sometimes bracketed with Milhaud and Auric as 'servile teasers of the snobbish, bourgeois tastes of a capitalist city', and at other times highly commended.

The aim in these articles is never merely that of disseminating information, and even where the element of reportage is relatively large (as it is in the two pieces discussed above) Nabokov will customarily use it as a vehicle for the introduction of larger issues, such as the relationship between music and freedom, or the cultural influence of the middle classes – favourite themes that we will examine below. The drama of 1948, of course, offered opportunities for reporting not afforded by other years where developments were less sensational and less visible. As a result, later articles tend to recap the general situation, usually with references to the events of 1937 and 1948, by way of introduction: there is, in these cases, little *news*. The year 1953, however, brought the death of Stalin and a consequent opportunity to consider any possible repercussions in the world of music. That year also saw the launch of the CCF's English-language journal *Encounter*, based in London and edited by Stephen Spender and Melvin Lasky. Nabokov (by then secretary-general of the CCF) wrote 'No Cantatas for Stalin?' for the first issue. The opening tone is sarcastic:

> Where are the funeral cantatas for Stalin? Why has the task of lamenting his death been left, so far, almost exclusively to the solemn marches of Beethoven and Chopin? Why have the composers of the USSR – the Great and Small Russians, the White Russians, the Uzbeks, the Ugro-Finns, the Armenians, the Georgians – failed to render homage to Him who is no longer with us? (Nabokov, 1953, p. 49)

After all, he continues, composers had previously written numerous works in praise of their leader: 'It was neither Marx nor Engels nor Lenin, but always Stalin and only Stalin who was thus hymned in the inevitable major key of Soviet self-glorification.' Contrasting this seven-month silence with the speed with which composers produced 'works of penance and rehabilitation' in 1948, Nabokov considers possible explanations. Observing that Stalin is suddenly – and surprisingly – absent from the pages of *Pravda*, he leaves the reader to consider whether there may have been some official decision not to overcommemorate him. Or could there be an explanation rooted in the history of Soviet music itself?

> ... is it that Soviet composers have become so used to the musical language of joy, with its abundant major 'intonations' – to use a term dear to Soviet musical theorists – that they experience some difficulty or disinclination in venturing upon the *stilisticheskaya pereustanovka* ('stylistic re-orientation') required for the composition of lamentations in minor keys? (Nabokov, 1953, p. 49).

A following paragraph sketches the harmonic constraints which have been in force in the Soviet Union, leading to a reiterated suggestion that its composers have perhaps shied away from the task simply because they lack the experience and skills necessary to accomplish it. Are we to take this claim seriously? It is surely difficult to believe that Soviet composers found themselves actually bereft of the imagination and technical resources the occasion required, and just as hard to imagine that Nabokov really believed this. Nonetheless, the elaboration of this idea – backed up with historical context – suggests that the author wants the reader to accept this as a serious explanation. It is, however, scarcely credible, and certainly not in light of the picture of Soviet music painted by Nabokov's own writings. After all, if Soviet composers were bound to follow the dictates of their political masters, as he repeatedly asserted, a lack of cantatas could only mean that no cantatas were demanded. If Nabokov's written output represented any implied claim to authoritative analysis of his subject, it was undermined here by an instinctive drive to ridicule Soviet music.

Looking at the broader field of Soviet music since Stalin's death, however, there are apparently some encouraging signs, however small. Nabokov sees a gradually widening repertory, including more early music – Bach and Monteverdi – as well as a loosening of the strictures against twentieth-century music: 'Debussy, Ravel, da Falla and Richard Strauss have ... recently penetrated the iron curtain which marks the limit of the Soviet musical repertoire.' Furthermore, closer contacts with the satellite states of Eastern Europe, where controls, he says, were less effective, bode well, along with 'a new atmosphere of thought' in the music and arts journals. Replacing pieces merely expounding the post-1948 party line one now finds genuine historical studies (albeit ones often based on 'a questionable and tendentious theory of music') and serious accounts of new works. The article ends on what, in light of the anti-communist project of both *Encounter* and its parent organisation, we may consider a generous note:

> Admittedly, these are only very faint indications. One would have to have much stronger signs before one could confidently say that a new spirit is alive in Russia. But in the immense refrigerator in which Stalin had confined the life of the Russian people, these barely perceptible signs of life are significant. ... So long as the door of the refrigerator remains even slightly ajar, there will be an opportunity for some of the outer atmosphere to reach the frozen regions of the interior. (Nabokov, 1953, p. 52)

In Soviet music of the 1940s and 1950s one name naturally looms larger than any other: Shostakovich. Already the Soviet Union's most celebrated composer, equalled only by Prokofiev, and held up as the model of a new type of socialist artist, his sudden popularity abroad owed much to wartime sympathy for the USSR after the German invasion of 1941. The newly politicised Nabokov of the early 1940s was faced with a composer whose music evidently had remarkable appeal for Western concertgoers, and whose example could be interpreted in a manner favourable to communism. Here was a composer who had turned his back on doctrines of 'art-for-arts sake'; here was a composer who had placed his skills and inspiration at the service of the people; and here, at last, was a composer whose work was both new *and* accessible. It could surely be no coincidence that such an artist should rise from the Soviet Union, audiences might reason. For its part, Moscow was unlikely to waste the propaganda opportunities that this development afforded. Frustrated anti-communists found Shostakovich's reputation inflated and the conclusions drawn from it erroneous; it only remained for someone with appropriate musical expertise – and an appetite for polemics – to set about bursting the bubble.[12] He set out to do this in an

---

12   Nabokov was not alone on the anti-Stalinist Left in wishing to do so. A critical article in *The New Leader* by Kurt List – 'Seven Reasons for Shostakovich' – provoked a

article, 'The Case of Dmitri Shostakovich', written in 1943 for *Harper's Magazine*. Later, a revised version of this piece was included in the 1951 collection of essays, *Old Friends and New Music*.

Writing in 1949 about Zhdanov's campaign of the previous year, the journalist Alexander Werth commented: 'The decree ... made a deplorable impression abroad ... *Time* and *Life* and *Newsweek* had all become terrific Shostakovich fans' (Werth, 1949, p. 91). Nicolas Nabokov, however, had never joined the throng. Taken overall, the immediate impression gained from his many references to Shostakovich is a concern to downgrade the value of the composer and his work. There are, as we shall see, shades of grey – and perhaps contradictions – in Nabokov's view, yet it remains true that he could find in the works of Shostakovich technical quality at best, but little artistic merit.[13] Consider just some of the adjectives deployed in the *Harper's Magazine* piece of 1943: the music is retrospective, orthodox and well-behaved; synthetic, impersonal and conservative; *Lady Macbeth of Mtsensk* is old-fashioned, provincial and unimaginative. A single paragraph identifies the use of 'naive and dated formulae ... the most emphatic and banal musical language', 'wooden rhythm ... [and] commonplace metrical patterns', the whole amounting to 'a verbose and brassy style which soon becomes dreary and monotonous' (Nabokov, 1943, p. 430). The previous year he had found the *Fifth Symphony* to be banal, trite and 'always reminiscent of late nineteenth-century music' (Nabokov, 1942a, p. 95). If we consider this criticism as a whole, two substantial objections to Shostakovich's work emerge. They are encapsulated in his description of the *First Symphony* as 'synthetic' and 'retrospective' (Nabokov, 1943, p. 423).

In 'The Case of Dmitri Shostakovich',[14] Nabokov recalls his first encounter with the Russian composer's music: after a trip to Russia his friend Prokofiev had brought back some piano pieces to Paris in 1927 or 1928. He felt immediately that this was old-fashioned music: 'so reminiscent of older Russian piano music that it was odd to

---

defence from Olin Downes of the *New York Times* (1944). Downes would later appear on the platform beside Shostakovich at the Waldorf-Astoria 'peace conference' of 1949 (see Chapter 1).

In another article, List wrote in terms that suggest Nabokov's own views: 'Russian music is being used abroad for political purposes. Whether our music will succumb to the shallowness and the easy success of the present Russian style will largely depend on the future political influence of the Soviet Union' (List, 1944, p. 108). The threat presented by 'shallow' and 'easy' Russian music was shared by Nabokov, as we shall see in Chapter 7. Nabokov wrote for the same journal, *Politics*, being, in the late 1940s, an associate of its editor Dwight Macdonald and his EAG group – see Chapter 1.

13   There is the odd exception: in the first article of this 'series', written in 1942, he describes the *Piano Quintet* of 1940 as 'an attractive piece, every bar of which rings true' (Nabokov, 1942a, p. 95). Nabokov would never be so complimentary again.

14   This piece, especially as revised for inclusion in the 1951 book, *Old Friends and New Music*, represents the fullest account of Nabokov's position and much of what follows will draw upon it. The revisions are largely concerned with bringing the piece up-to-date, with the exception of a few significant omissions, to which this study will return. Fundamentally, however, Nabokov did not see fit to alter his basic assessment of either man or music, which appeared to be unchanged, and, for the sake of consistency, where the pieces are identical this study will refer to the earlier version.

realize that they had emanated from the most revolutionary land in the world'. This becomes a recurrent motif in the criticism, and indeed, as we have seen in comments on the *Fifth Symphony*, the source of this allegedly dated style is often located specifically in the late nineteenth century. Again, it is difficult to decide what view to adopt – was Nabokov serious, or was this line merely calculated to be especially wounding? After all the 'discoveries' and 'progress' of modernism, what could be more damning than to describe music as 'late nineteenth-century', especially when that music issued from the loudly 'progressive' USSR? Yet, however we are to take these comments, they are consistent. *Lady Macbeth of Mtsensk*, for example, is 'neither daring nor particularly new. It sounds very much like many naturalistic Russian operas written in the eighties and now happily forgotten' (Nabokov, 1943, p. 428).[15]

This theme also emerges again in two pieces written after 1948 although in both cases what Nabokov now saw as nineteenth-century characteristics were ascribed to that year's 'purge' (perhaps forgetting that he has already described *Lady Macbeth*, composed in 1934, in the same terms). So, for example, considering the scores for the two Shostakovich films, *The Young Guard* and *Michurin*, through which 'his comeback has been accomplished', he writes: 'These two frightened little fragments sound more like a *devoir d'écolier* from a Prussian conservatory of approximately 1880 than anything else' (Nabokov, 1948a, p. 844). Four years later, again describing the Zhdanov legacy, this would-be withering image appears in an extended form:

> ... if one looks over the latest production of Soviet composers, one finds that their musical language is composed of the most outworn clichés of the 19th Century's musical language. In fact when you hear such works as the latest cantata 'Song of the Forests' by Shostakovich and the Seventh Symphony by Prokofiev, you may think that these works are written by a half-educated conservative student of the second year harmony class in a provincial conservatory in Germany at the end of the 19th Century. (Nabokov, nd 3, unpublished, p. 8)[16]

Nabokov's apparent lack of discrimination in making the charge, however, hardly adds weight to the argument. We have seen, after all, both the work which raised Stalin's ire, *Lady Macbeth* of 1934, *and* the work of rehabilitation, the *Fifth Symphony* of 1937, both described as essentially nineteenth-century in style. This same characteristic is later judged to be a consequence of the Central Committee's

---

15   In light of Nabokov's comments, consider this passage from the autobiography – it is 1927, and Nabokov has just played his *Ode* to Stravinsky, Diaghilev, George Balanchine and Serge Lifar in his Paris flat. Afterwards, Stravinsky comments: ' "You know what it's like? It's as if it were written by a predecessor of Glinka, someone like Gurilyov or Alyabiev ... from where do you know all this Russian salon music of the 1830s? It is unmistakably and naïvely Russian". I did not know what to answer ...' (Nabokov, 1975, p. 162).

16   Although no date is given, the references to Stalin's death suggest sometime after 1953. There is no indication that this piece was published. Parts of it are heavily corrected, in what appears to be Nabokov's own hand, to improve the writing, add points and correct what appears – on the basis of numerous spelling errors – to have been very badly-taken dictation. In drawing on this text, the present writer has used the corrected version.

1948 decree. Perhaps Nabokov was identifying different *degrees* of nineteenth-centuryness! The suspicion remains, however, that the charge has more to do with modernist scorn and political advantage than with musical analysis.

A second major shortcoming in Shostakovich's music lies in what Nabokov judges to be its 'synthetic' quality. The composer, an apparently incorrigible scavenger of musical ideas, appears incapable of creating a distinctive style. This inspired one of Nabokov's more memorable passages:

> It is as difficult to describe the music of Shostakovich as it is to describe the form and colour of an oyster ... simply because it is shapeless in style and form and impersonal in color. Yet the oyster has a very individual taste of its own which Shostakovich unfortunately lacks. For one of his chief weaknesses is absolute eclectic impersonality .... He ... borrows other people's technical inventions as if they were communal belongings. He ... imitates indiscriminately (and I believe quite unconsciously) .... (Nabokov, 1943, p. 429)

Within the *First Symphony* alone, Nabokov finds traces of Tchaikovsky, Wagner, Mussorgsky, Prokofiev, Stravinsky and Hindemith, elsewhere detecting Beethoven, Berlioz and Rimsky-Korsakov. Whilst acknowledging that the *First Symphony* is a graduation piece written by a still-young composer (and that, consequently, the thorough assimilation of influences is perhaps too much to expect), Nabokov insists that the same shortcomings exist in the mature Shostakovich. The key word in his criticism is 'impersonal': this music lacks the unique and distinctive character towards which any composer should surely aspire, and the problem is compounded by the variety of sources 'borrowed' from. There are the composers of the last century, of course, but a fondness for novelty is also apparently discernible, as for example when:

> ... satirical passages and polyphonic developments are full of the most obnoxious tricks of the *style moderne* of the twenties (dissonant superimposition of chords, 'dislocated joints' in the melodic line, and 'rhythmical paranoia' or senseless repetition of a metrical figure – all unhappy products of the 'modern' musical mind) .... (Nabokov, 1943, p. 428)[17]

Elsewhere 'jazzy rhythms of the "*Mitteleuropa*" variety' are added to this list. Worse still, 'his "tunes" are often from very ordinary sources ... imitating very common and uninteresting factory or army songs', and whereas worthier composers – Haydn, Beethoven, Stravinsky – could ennoble tunes 'from the gutter', Shostakovich is simply unable to treat such material in an original or compelling way. In short, the music employs 'tricks, devices and techniques taken from such different styles that they could not possibly lead to a unified style'.

Having comprehensively despatched any claims for Shostakovich as a composer of substance, Nabokov admits towards the end of this article to finding two positive qualities in the music, although he quickly adds that they are 'of a rather ambiguous order'. He will, first, allow that the music shows great skill, reflecting his thorough training at the 'exemplary' Leningrad Conservatory:

---

17   The piece in question is the opera *Lady Macbeth of the Mtsensk District*.

Shostakovich is undoubtedly an excellent craftsman and most of his inventiveness goes into such branches of musical craft as orchestration and efficient part-writing ... . It is not infrequent among contemporary composers that such technical strength conceals a paucity of original musical ideas. (Nabokov, 1943, p. 429)

The charge of 'mere craftsmanship' is, of course, a standard means of denigrating a body of work, of denying it the all-important honorific title, 'art'. According to widely-held conventions (which had become deeply embedded in Western art by the Romantic era and still show no sign of losing their potency), craftsmanship 'alone' can never be enough to admit a work to the status of art. The validity of these categories, 'art' and 'craft', and their relationship to one another are never questioned. Although their defining characteristics are rarely set out with any clarity, it is nonetheless essential – in terms of securing prestige within the community of the arts – to be able to demonstrate that one has the necessary skill to discriminate between the two. It is precisely because such ideas have the force of conventions – in other words, remain largely unchallenged – within the world of art music that the accusation of 'mere craftsmanship' is such a damaging one. To describe a composer as a 'craftsman' is therefore not only to deny him the prestige of the artist, it also suggests that he lacks the power to distinguish one from the other – he has, in effect, failed to notice that skill alone is never enough. Of course, by contrast, the critic's ability to discriminate is clear. This, then, is the game of status and authority that Nabokov is playing when he claims that the work of this widely celebrated composer is well-crafted, and no more.[18]

Second, Nabokov finds in Shostakovich an 'inherent optimism', which may surprise the late twentieth-century listener who is encouraged by critics to read his work as a chronicle of despair and suffering. Nonetheless, Nabokov argues that many of the works have 'gay and happy' aspects, and that, contrary to foreign characterisations of gloomy, intense Slavs, this has long been a feature of Russian music. There is, however, a problem with the optimism of Shostakovich, since 'it takes a redundant, blatant, and unconvincing form. One always feels a kind of compelling force behind it, a force of an extra-musical order' (Nabokov, 1943, p. 429). This is interesting. It appears, on first reading, to lend support to the interpretation of Shostakovich that has grown into a new orthodoxy since the publication in 1979 of *Testimony: The memoirs of Shostakovich*, the composer's purported memoirs ('as related to Solomon Volkov'). The Shostakovich of *Testimony* stood revealed as bitter, cynical, a wily survivor and implacable opponent of the system, many of whose works should be understood as coded opposition to that very system. Many writers have found this view of Shostakovich attractive and, notwithstanding the disputed provenance of the text,[19] it has since become commonplace to detect irony and

---

18   Charging Shostakovich with, effectively, the creation of a rule-bound, uninspired *academic* art, Nabokov is approaching the idea of Clement Greenberg's *kitsch*, an important element of 'Mass Culture' thinking – see Chapter 7. For an interesting discussion of the contest over the meanings of 'art' and 'craft', see Becker (1982, ch. 9).

19   See Fay (1980) who demonstrates that substantial passages have been lifted from existing Russian-language sources little known in the West. Volkov, however, gives the

subversive intent in, for example, an apparently affirmative symphonic finale. As such, it might appear 'hollow, its exultation bitterly false' (Norris, 1989, p. 14). In this vein, David Fanning – to take one example – suggests that:

> Shostakovich turned the tables not just on officialdom, but also on the 'finale problem' .... An apparently joyful conclusion, especially if the smile is prolonged into a grimace, can be an even more horrific outcome to a tragic symphony than an overtly tragic one .... (Fanning, 1993, p. 308)

At Nabokov's time of writing, however, Shostakovich's works, insofar as extra-musical meaning was considered, were generally taken at face value – that is, in the West, at least (and it is *Western* reception that is at issue here), they were considered to be straightforwardly pro-Soviet. Attitudes to this fact then divided according to the politics of the critic. If Nabokov is, here, suggesting that the optimism has a forced, or false quality to it, is he anticipating the present-day preoccupation with irony and subversion in Shostakovich? No: in fact, he draws conclusions which, far from conflicting with his view of the composer as sincere communist, confirm it:

> [This] appears to be based on the official syllogistic formula: before the revolution life was desperate, therefore art was gloomy; now the revolution is victorious, therefore art must be optimistic. It is obvious that this must rings [*sic*] like a command of the gods .... The result is that it often forces the composer into a great effort unnatural to his temperament and therefore unsuccessful. (Nabokov, 1943, p. 430)

Shostakovich, as a good communist, tries to create music which reflects the official line: by doing so, he has effectively denied himself the freedom necessary to create art. Shostakovich's 'unconvincing' optimism, far from being a subtle act of defiance which officialdom is too obtuse to detect (as post-Volkov critics tend to suggest), is a clear example of the deformation of an artist's spirit that must occur once he has allowed ideology to direct his work. It is this conception of an artist who has misguidedly followed the ideological path (to the detriment of his art) that allows Nabokov to retain, or at least profess, sympathy for Shostakovich:

> ... at times there is a graceful lyricism in his music when he forgets himself ... [which] shows us that deep behind the screen of impersonality and moral obligation there still lives an individual, a free artist, a man by the name of Dmitri Shostakovich. (Nabokov, 1943, p. 430)

In addition to the two positive qualities acknowledged by him, Nabokov's piece does in fact identify one further redeeming feature in Shostakovich, although one that, significantly, does not survive the transition to the 1951 version. In the earlier text, having set down the standard Soviet attitude to art and the role of the artist as found in

---

impression that this material – which is of an uncontroversial nature – was given to him in conversation with the composer. The implication of Fay's discovery is that the more sensational parts of the book must be in doubt. This has not prevented *Testimony* being routinely described as an autobiography, and its use as the foundation of a new conventional wisdom.

Shostakovich's published writings (perhaps one should say 'in writings published under his name'), he comments:

> Such complete devotion to the just cause of his country and its people necessarily commands respect and admiration. *The philosophy upon which it is based is morally far more solid than many other contemporary theories* ... it is free from that pernicious and amoral egocentrism from which so much music of the late nineteenth and twentieth century suffers. (Nabokov, 1943, p. 427, my italics)

He goes on to liken this attitude to 'the noble morality of the artisan-musician of the Middle Ages', with the difference that here state and the people are served rather than God and the Church. However, by 1951, when the piece was re-edited for inclusion in *Old Friends and New Music*, Nabokov had evolved from a little-known minor composer to an increasingly visible Cold War figure and it would therefore have been inappropriate for him to admire any aspect of the USSR as 'morally ... solid'. Accordingly, this whole passage was removed. In passing, it is interesting to note that something like this idea does appear two years later in the *Encounter* article, 'No Cantatas for Stalin?', but with a difference:

> ... it has to be remembered that the Russian artist has always, rightly or wrongly, regarded his work as being in the nature of a social dedication, and that this view prevails quite apart from the teachings of Marxism. The Russian artist feels that he is entrusted with a sacred duty to the community .... (Nabokov, 1953, p. 51)

Soviet 'philosophy' has here become Russian 'sacred duty', and this *national* characteristic helps explain why Russian composers turned away from experimentalism after the 1920s, 'quite distinct from the pressures to which they were subjected by the party leaders'. As such, it remains a quality that can be admired, if in more muted terms than before.

The real significance of Shostakovich

What led Nicolas Nabokov to spend so much time considering 'The Case of Dmitri Shostakovich'? The author himself provides one of the reasons. In the first place, at the original time of writing, in the pro-Soviet atmosphere of the period when only the USSR seemed to be fighting Hitler, Shostakovich was (so Nabokov tells us) something of a sensation in America. To ensure the point is taken, we learn that the *Seventh Symphony* – the '*Leningrad*' – is the most-performed contemporary work in the USA, that many of his other symphonies have been recorded 'by the finest orchestras', whilst those of other (better) composers are 'unrecorded, unpublished and unplayed'. Indeed, Shostakovich

> ... is referred to as 'the new Beethoven' or 'the new Berlioz'; he is discussed more than any other contemporary American or alien composer of the past twenty years; and as the fire-fighting hero-composer whose great symphony circled the world in bombers and transport planes, he has become a familiar figure to every American citizen who reads the newspapers. (Nabokov, 1943, p. 424)

Against this background Nabokov is at pains to demonstrate that this fame – based on political factors – is not merited by the music itself. The final section of the article, following a lengthy, detailed and overwhelmingly negative assessment of the music, makes the point very clearly. Many composers have produced far better music which yet goes unplayed

> ... because our maestros and their managers ordain otherwise .... [They] are responsible for all the uproar in this country over one or two composers for one or two seasons. They have learned how to exploit a propitious political situation ... and create a bubble reputation to relieve the stagnation of the concert repertory ... they are now doing Shostakovich [an] immense disservice by placing him in a position in which he does not belong. (Nabokov, 1943, p. 431)

Shostakovich, Nabokov tells his readers, is not as good as you think he is. There is, however, more at stake than that. If Shostakovich *is* a poor composer, what is it that has made him so, given his training and acknowledged skills? The answer, for Nabokov, is to be found in Soviet ideology as it manifests itself in relation to the arts. On the one hand a stifling responsibility to 'the people' is imposed, leading to all sorts of detailed musical prescriptions, whilst, on the other, the main currents of twentieth-century musical 'advance' are proscribed. Music, therefore, is stifled by the Soviet system, and perhaps this is done with good reason:

> Despite all the jargon about formalism, classicism, and Socialist Realism, the real fear of the Soviet government is the state of mind which may grow within a closed body of specialists .... This state of mind is *creative individualism* – which is still tied in many ways to the Western European tradition. It may lead to *political individualism*, particularly since some of the composers, with their wide national and international reputations, may feel themselves by definition outside and above the Party line. (Nabokov, 1948a, pp. 103–4)

Soviet music, in all its evident artistic poverty, serves to warn us in the West of the perils of communism, since its condition reflects Moscow's fear of where free creation might lead. Twilight sleepers among the art-loving, music-loving general public would do well to sit up and take notice.

The inarticulate music of the Soviet Union could in one sense speak eloquently: in condemnation of the system that created it. Nabokov was later to argue that there was another side to this particular coin: might not the contemporary music of the West be called on as evidence for its freedoms, as a testament to them, even? His analyses of Shostakovich and the state of Soviet music served as the foundation for this reciprocal argument, which would later come into its own as part of the rationale for the CCF's first large-scale event, the 1952 festival in Paris.

Chapter 3

Waking the Twilight Sleepers II: On Provincialism and Prokofiev

> Should not *music critics*, today, stress and defend the indivisibility of the realm of music? This century cannot afford to be provincial. Yet certain forms of provincialism are still lingering in the field of music.[1]

In 1954 Nabokov was arranging the Congress for Cultural Freedom's second arts festival, to be held in Rome. 'Music in the XXth Century' followed the Paris festival of two years earlier which, although theoretically offering a broad overview of the arts, had in practice been a largely musical affair. The Rome festival brochure laid out a rationale, based on opposition to various forms of musical 'provincialism'. It continues:

> A certain *provincialism in time* keeps 'music until 1900' on one side of the program and 'the modern province' on the other. A certain *professional provincialism* keeps, too often, the activities of composers, virtuosos [*sic*], chamber music players, opera directors and musicologists neatly separated. And some musicians even indulge in *aesthetical provincialism*: believers in one style, one method, one school – ignorant (if not contemptuous) of all things attempted or achieved along other lines. ...[2]

In itself this would be of little interest. The first became a familiar complaint of the composer in the twentieth century, the second is a routine fact of specialisation and institutional life, whilst the last reflects a perception of sectarianism and intolerance in and around the postwar New Music (and recalls the 'Atonal Trail' article that Nabokov loosed at René Leibowitz). The call is *for* contact and exchange and *against* anything defensive and parochial. The Nabokov reader, however, is likely to recognise this as one instance of a theme that frequently surfaces in the writings.

---

1   *Music in the XXth Century*, festival brochure. IACF. As the deviser and organiser of the festival, held in Rome, between 4 and 15 April 1954, Nabokov is the likely author. The italics are as per the original.

2   That this focus was apparent to those who attended is suggested by the comments of one participant, William Glock. Recalling Nabokov, he mentions the 'Festival and Congress in Rome, where half the leading composers in the world were assembled (including Stravinsky), and most of the leading critics ... the Congress had been planned as an "antidote against provincialism of every kind"' (Glock, 1985, p. 58).

It is not easy to give this theme a name. If we say he is concerned with 'provincialism'. this could easily suggest a level of analysis that is never in fact supplied. Any search for a definition or examination of the term would be in vain; rather, there seems to be an assumption that both author and readers share an understanding of its meaning and force.[3] So, to argue that 'provincialism' is a theme may be going too far. Perhaps something like 'the *effect* of provincialism on Soviet music' would better describe what Nabokov does, which is to provide an inventory of musical symptoms, whilst paying little attention to the 'disease' (provincialism) itself. Yet, this remains inadequate to describe a preoccupation whose full dimensions can only be grasped by moving beyond the comments in the Rome brochure. 'Provincialism', in that context, suggests narrowness, confinement, staleness and all that which is backward; Nabokov's festival, on the other hand, seeks to promote breadth, freedom, vitality and advanced music. Whilst this gives a reasonable summary of the public justification for that event, it would be quite deficient as a description of what 'provincialism' means if the writings are taken as a whole, since a crucial dimension is left out. Nabokov's 'anti-provincialism' is, in my view, inseparable from issues of class, and specifically concerns about the cultural influence of the middle class. These issues are arguably central to both his self-image, and his sense of cultural–political mission.

Cosmopolitan art and its enemies

We should return, first of all, to the term 'provincial', and consider its deployment in the texts themselves. We encountered the term first in the previous chapter – for example, in the description of the opera *Lady Macbeth of Mtsensk* as 'old-fashioned, provincial and unimaginative' (Nabokov, 1943, p. 428), and in the jibe about 'a half-educated student … in a provincial conservatory' aimed at particular works of Shostakovich and Prokofiev, and the language of Soviet music in general (Nabokov, nd 3, unpublished, p. 8). Sometimes the whole of Soviet art was the target, as in the speech given at the inaugural meeting of the Congress for Cultural Freedom, in Berlin, 1950:

> Little by little, this pseudo-aesthetic gave birth, throughout the totalitarian states, to a pseudo-art: a sad, grey, academic art, thoroughly outmoded, provincial and contrary to the spirit of the great Renaissance which we had undergone in the last thirty years, and which lived yet in the music of the free world. (Nabokov, nd 5, p. 2)[4]

And why is this music, this art, the way it is? Because officialdom demands it. For example, Shostakovich's 'timid … pitifully empty' scores for the films *The Young*

---

3   Nabokov clearly saw no need to define a derogatory term which was (and still is) common currency amongst the CCF's target audience of intellectuals. See also John Carey's (1992) discussion of 'suburban'.

4   I take this to have been given at the Berlin Congress since it is located in that file in the IACF papers. Indications of 'rires' and 'sourires' mark this text as a record of the speech as delivered.

Guard and *Michurin* are seen as a response to 'the provincial tastes of the middle-layer of the Soviet bureaucracy' (Nabokov, 1949a, p. 844). Nabokov felt that he had first-hand evidence of this. Serving with the US army in occupied Berlin, dealing with the re-establishment of musical life, he had had to liaise with his Russian counterparts and, years later, in 1951, wrote an account of a concert he attended as a guest of the Red Army. He records that a tenor with an 'awful provincial taste in delivery' was 'clapped and cheered furiously' by the Soviet officers and their wives (Nabokov, 1951a, p. 51).[5] Later, he was able to talk with some of the audience and performers. They admitted to admiring, but not really *liking*, the music of Shostakovich and Prokofiev, preferring the sort of music in that evening's programme, which had included Tchaikovsky, Glinka, Arensky, Rachmaninov and Borodin. Reflecting on this, he adds that:

> Later, when the music purge took place, it occurred to me how much their point of view conformed to that of the Politburo and Stalin, or rather how closely their taste and opinions in music (as represented in the edict of the Central Committee of the Communist Party) reflected the incredibly old-fashioned provincial taste of the new uneducated middle strata of Soviet society. (Nabokov, 1951a, p. 52)[6]

To help fill out the picture, it is worth considering another adjective frequently used by Nabokov, and one which seems to serve as provincialism's 'other', its opposite pole – *cosmopolitanism*. Just as opposition to 'provincialism', appearing as the keystone of the Rome festival, drew our attention to its other appearances in the writings, and suggested a larger significance, so the same function is performed for 'cosmopolitanism' by the subtitle of his 1975 autobiography: *Memoirs of a Russian Cosmopolitan*. The term seems to have three overlapping meanings, the first of which is explicit here: it is, simply, central to the man's definition of himself. The terms in which Nabokov celebrates cosmopolitanism – and, again, this is done indirectly, by reference to its fruits, rather than by consideration of the thing itself – suggests that he sees it as an outlook, an attitude of mind. It is, perhaps, best summed up as loyalty to liberal humanist ideas above country, party or race, an openness in matters of the intellect, and a striving after modernity in art – Enlightenment ideals, in short. At the 1950 Berlin meeting he announced himself to delegates as a '*musicien cosmopolite*',

---

5   The following details of the programme are given:

Kozlovsky (tenor): Arias from *Eugene Onegin* (Tchaikovsky); 'Song of India' from *Sadko* (Rimsky-Korsakov); songs by Tchaikovsky, Arensky, Glinka and Rachmaninov.
String Quartet: *Second String Quartet* (Borodin); *Andante Cantabile* (Tchaikovsky).
Piano: Twelfth Hungarian Rhapsody (Lizst); two Nocturnes (Chopin); Polichinelle (Rachmaninov).
Ukrainian singers and dancers.
Red Army Chorus: patriotic songs; WWII songs – *Broad is my Fatherland*, *The Song of the Red Pioneers*, *Red Cavalry Song*.
6   In another piece he writes: 'How often Russian officers and their families ... would politely listen and occasionally nod to me in half-hearted approval when I praised a work of Prokofieff. Now that the new decree of the Central Committee has been promulgated, they won't even have to nod' (Nabokov, 1948a, p. 103).

... a citizen of the Republic of Art, in short, a man who loves complete creative freedom, who has a horror of all frontiers, geographical and spiritual barriers and who will accept only the dictates of his own conscience, both artistically and intellectually. (Nabokov, nd 5, unpublished, p. 1)

Cosmopolitanism as *lifestyle* also works for Nabokov, given his travels from Russia to Germany to France to America, then, from 1951, the frantic international life at the head of the CCF. The 1958 synopsis of a proposed autobiography gives us some sense of this:

My life has been a multiple one. I have never been <u>only</u> a musician, nor have I been <u>only</u> a member of the international intelligentsia. In the course of these two score years I have sold newspapers, worked for a stamp collector, taught in colleges, wrote music, was involved in politics and lately became a kind of ... 'co-ordinator of cultural relations' and this, alas, on a world-wide scale. But above all, my life has been a continuous vagrancy – a constant parting and searching for a new haven. (Letter to Bessie, 3 November 1958)

His life, then, has been one of variety and breadth, we are to understand. Note, incidentally, the sense of self-importance ('... nor have I been <u>only</u> a member of the international intelligentsia'!) which is by no means foreign to the Nabokov style. He continues by pointing out that this 'vagrancy' is involuntary, and whilst this is reasonable enough – at least insofar as his departure from Russia is concerned – it does enable him to cast his life in a romantic light. This, too, is characteristic. He continues:

I have the dubious privilege and honour to belong to what one might call the <u>'Third Estate'</u> of the Twentieth Century – that vast heterogeneous multitude of men and women set into motion by various forms of intolerance and oppression: <u>The Refugees</u>. As such, my vagrancies started in 1920 and even now there seems no end to them. Shifty, [*sic*] and yet somewhere anchored in the ancient ideas of 19th Century Russian liberalism, the wave of life has carried me from exile to exile, from pre-and-post and post-and-pre wars and revolutions, through many lands and environments. And yet, as I think of it now, I loved it all ... . (Ibid.)

Second, the term 'cosmopolitan' – like 'formalism' – was frequently deployed by Zhdanov, Khrennikov and the Soviet cultural *apparat* in its attacks on artists and composers who strayed too far from orthodoxy, especially if these deviations appeared to show Western influence. In this context it functioned as a shorthand for 'anti-Soviet' – that is, anti-people. In one of his pieces Nabokov sketches a three-stage model of Soviet music history culminating in the period 1936–50, 'when all forms of experimentation were condemned by the government and declared to be cosmopolitan modernism [and] bourgeois decadence ...' (Nabokov, nd 3, p. 4). In the Cold War context the politically aware reader could be counted on to know this Soviet use of the word: for a man who became so publicly the Kremlin's antagonist it was, no doubt, attractive to wear this term of abuse as a badge of honour.

The third sense of 'cosmopolitanism' is musical. For Nabokov, musical modernism – those departures of the early twentieth century which his festivals attempted to celebrate, and whose achievements he hoped could be secured – was a movement informed by a spirit of internationalism, openness and exchange, and was, indeed, inconceivable without it. In the unpublished manuscript 'Free or Controlled Music' he writes of:

> ... the great advance or rather the great expansion of musical language involving the assimilation of dissonance ... leading ... 20th century music to new destinies. And all this was not going on in a spirit of nationalistic chauvinism or parochialism, but rather in a spirit of universal international collaboration. (Nabokov, nd 3, unpublished, p. 4)

Turning once again to the 1950 Congress speech, Nabokov summarised, for his Berlin audience, the twentieth-century advances, the 'great renaissance of Western music', and paid homage to its leading figures. He then adds:

> What was curious and novel about this renewal was that it was not confined to one country, but that, on the contrary, all of Europe participated in it ... . Music in this century was strangely free because it was distanced from politics .... We all believed, in our enthusiasm and in the free autonomy of the Republic of Music, that we had the power to preserve musical freedom. (Nabokov, nd 5, unpublished, p. 2)

This, of course, is his cue to rehearse the story of Soviet music controls, with special attention to the period since February 1948. For Nabokov, the Soviet line in general and the Zhdanov campaign in particular represented a blow struck at the shared *international* (strictly speaking, Euro-American) musical developments of the early century – one which had removed Russia from the common endeavour, to the detriment of all. The enforced production of 'provincial' art, he argued, deprived not only Soviet artists of their freedom, but also the West of a distinctive Russian contribution. After all, 'those who still remember the first two decades of this century in Paris inevitably refer to the extraordinary impact of Russian music and Russian art in general upon the Western mind at that time' (Nabokov, nd 3, unpublished, p. 4). Moreover:

> I for one refuse to consider Russian musical culture as separate from that great stream, that sublime structure of human endeavour that we call Western civilisation. ... those who are trying to separate Russian culture from the culture of the so-called Western world are doing great harm, both to Russian culture and to [that] ... of the West. ... it seems to me that control of the arts ... is a real problem and a burning issue to ... every citizen ... who is concerned with the evolution and the future life of Western civilisation. (Ibid., p. 3)

We can now enlarge our understanding of this preoccupation with 'provincialism', since it has become clear that the 'provincial' and the 'cosmopolitan' stand in opposition to one another. They constitute, in the anthropological sense, a system of binary opposites which Nabokov seems to use to classify music. That informed by cosmopolitanism will tend to be worthwhile, advanced (that is, accepting modernism and seeking to 'move on' from it) and will draw on international developments; the spirit of provincialism, on the other hand, will lead to the trivial, the backward and the parochial. If early-century modernism is assumed to be the central fact of musical life (as it certainly was by Nabokov), this device allows new music to be classified according to whether or not it meets that challenge (although of course, Nabokov was finding that others – Leibowitz, for example – located the boundary rather differently). To this must be added the political dimension since, in these writings, Soviet/Western is the ever-present subset of provincial/cosmopolitan. The latter is, in effect, a timeless, *universal* choice facing humanity which has merely been sharpened by modern communications whereas Soviet/Western represents one *instance* of that choice in one category of human life (politics), at one time (the mid-twentieth century). In the field of Soviet music Nabokov shows how these forces operate by considering its two major figures: Shostakovich and Prokofiev.

In this contest, Nabokov seems to believe, however much the state may weigh in on the side of parochialism and conformity, the impulses of musical 'cosmopolitanism' have never been quite stifled. If Shostakovich can be used to stand for the backward provincialism of Soviet orthodoxy, as we have seen in the previous chapter, another figure is required to indicate the precarious survival of a countervailing force. This is the function of Prokofiev in Nabokov's writings.

Nabokov first saw Prokofiev in 1915 or 1916 in St Petersburg, at a concert Rachmaninov was giving for the benefit of Scriabin's widow; later they were to meet and become friends in mid-1920s Paris.[7] Nabokov, by this time, knew and liked Prokofiev's music, and the friendship seems to have been a warm one: it was 'an intense relation [*sic*] of mutual musical interest'; 'there never was a misunderstanding between Prokofiev and me in all the time of our friendship, nor was there an iota of falsity about it'. He enjoyed Prokofiev's forthright and caustic views on, for example, the triviality of much French music, or the esotericism of Scriabin, and the two shared a love of the good life, both families holidaying together at the Nabokov's house in Alsace. For some time from 1930 onwards, the two composers were involved in a group called 'La Sérénade', which also included Darius Milhaud, Igor Markevitch, Vittorio Rieti and Henri Sauguet. The group 'had wealthy and fashionable patrons and its concerts were elegant society affairs with a touch of the same snobbishness that surrounded Diaghilev's ballet season' (Nabokov, 1951d, p. 111).[8]

Politically, Nabokov recalled that the older composer was hostile neither to the USSR or its official policy on music. In fact, Prokofiev was 'sympathetic to the Soviet regime [and] … had rejected the ideological position of émigré'. This is not to say, however, that he should be considered a thoroughgoing communist; indeed the picture painted recalls the well-meaning but naïve 'twilight sleepers' in the USA and elsewhere. Prokofiev, for example, saw the Soviet Union as a 'logical consequence' of the ancien régime – an 'inescapable historical necessity' – but gave 'little thought to the justice or injustice of the Soviet government'. Indeed:

> … he was a person whose political thinking never developed and who, not unlike many American artists, believed that his main job was to do his own work and leave political matters and entanglements to others. (Nabokov, 1951d, p. 132)

---

7   See Nabokov (1951d, p. 113). The chapter is called 'Srg Srgvtch Prkfv' after Prokofiev's unusual manner of signing a postcard. Like the Shostakovich chapter, it is an updated version of an earlier piece: see Nabokov (1942b).

8   Nabokov tells us that 'La Sérénade' were eight in all, naming himself, Prokofiev and Markevitch. Two photographs of the group in *Bagázh* show Nabokov with Milhaud, Sauguet and Rieti and some of their patrons, at a concert in Strasbourg, 1931.

Prokofiev also apparently welcomed some aspects of official music policy – for example, its stress on the importance of melody in relation to large-scale communication and accessibility – so that when there was a drive against 'formalist experimentation' in 1931, he

> ... welcomed the official edict as a realisation of some of his own ideas about the function of music. 'I always wanted to invent melodies,' he often remarked, 'which would be understood by large masses of people – simple, singable melodies.' This he considered to be the most important and difficult task of the modern composer. (Ibid., p. 133)

This sympathy, however, has not enabled the composer to work comfortably after returning to the USSR, it is claimed, and Nabokov describes meetings in the 1930s where Prokofiev seemed increasingly uneasy: his former confidence, the belief in the possibility of reconciling his personal aesthetic to the needs of the state now shaken. Then came the 1948 'purge' when 'Prokofiev's name led all the rest'. This is significant, since:

> ... in the eyes of those who rule the destinies of the Russian people, he is the symbol of Russia's former closer association with the modern Western world with its great emancipatory tradition and its spirit of intellectual and artistic freedom. This the tyrants of the Kremlin cannot endure. (Ibid., pp. 137–8)

Here is the essence of the 'Prokofiev problem', Nabokov argues: he is simply too closely associated with, and perhaps irredeemably corrupted by, outside influences. Earlier, in his 1949 *Partisan Review* piece, summarising the effects of the Zhdanov campaign, the case had been made even more plainly. Considering the opera *The Life of a Real Person*, Khrennikov, the head of the Composer's Union, had concluded that 'the traditions of Western modernism have captivated his consciousness', and *Pravda* questioned whether a 'composer whose work is penetrated to the core' by 'Western formalist decay' could hope to serve the people (Nabokov, 1949a, pp. 845–6). What is unique to this composer is his direct personal experience of the West in general, and his cosmopolitan modernism in particular: indeed, he is 'not a product of Soviet culture [like Shostakovich] but of pre-revolutionary Russia, a travelled man long resident in such centers of "bourgeois corruption" as Paris and the USA'. Prokofiev, then, is a living link with all that official policy sought to exclude, and even, specifically, with the excoriated Stravinsky and Diaghilev (the latter, Nabokov says, had a special villainy beyond that of the average émigré, since he had from 1905 'openly called on Russian artists to serve an apprenticeship with the modern West').[9]

Nabokov surely had a measure of identification with Prokofiev, the 'cosmopolitan composer' whose 'trials' he described.[10] Not an especially close musical sympathy,

---

9   Tikhon Khrennikov, quoted in Nabokov (1948a, p. 103).

10   According to Nabokov's résumé in the Nicolas Nabokov papers, Nabokov wrote an article titled 'The Trials of a Cosmopolitan Composer' for *The Reporter* sometime in 1949. Although the present writer has not seen this piece, it is likely to be substantially the same as Nabokov (1942b), which had altered little on its reappearance in Nabokov (1951d).

perhaps, and certainly not politically – but one rooted, nonetheless, in common experience. They shared the same friendships in the 1920s, both in the music world and the Russian diaspora; they also shared an understanding of exile and a professional relationship with Diaghilev. Most crucially, both had experienced the modernist, internationalist crucible of the arts that was Paris. Nabokov celebrated that cosmopolitan spirit, even defined himself by it, and perhaps felt that the same influences had marked Prokofiev equally. Zhdanov and Khrennikov, in the substance of their assault on Prokofiev, denounced the cultural climate that had, in his view, both made modern music and decisively shaped his own life; the attack might just as well have been directed at Nabokov himself.[11]

The class basis of Soviet music policy

Not content merely to denounce the iniquities of state direction, or what he saw as the resulting poverty of Soviet music, Nabokov was concerned to offer an analysis. The condition of Soviet music, he felt, could not be accounted for merely by the fact of control. Rather, understanding demanded an examination of the social and political background which determined the *content*, the character, of these controls. Both the analysis and the conclusions he draws are illuminating. The fullest account appears as part of a 1951 Third Programme talk, published in *The Listener* as 'Changing Styles in Soviet Music', the same piece which had had its more colourful prose tamed by the BBC's Anna Kallin (see the previous chapter). Here, the historical account is introduced by observing that Soviet music has not *always* been as bad as, according to Nabokov, it now is. Indeed:

> ... right after October 1917, Russian music became *more* experimental, *more* dissonant, *more* jazzy, and *more* mechanistic than the music of Western Europe. Composers ... even the present day master of the C major key, Dmitri Shostakovich, were writing the noisiest, the most dissonant, abstruse music in Europe ... . Today this ... music ... with all its revolutionary bravado is cited as an example of irresponsible foolishness ... . (Nabokov, 1951c, p. 599, original emphasis)

What has happened? Why has the development of Soviet music been forced into reverse? The account that follows finds an answer in social changes which had taken place largely since 1924–25 (and especially in the 1930s), but which had deep roots in pre-revolutionary Russia. In the first decade of the century, Nabokov argues, whilst the musical taste of both the aristocratic and rural labouring classes was moribund,

---

11   It is worth noting in passing, that Alexander Werth, whose *Musical Uproar in Moscow* offered a first-hand account of the 1948 events, corroborates Nabokov's analysis of the 'Prokofiev problem'. Khrennikov, says Werth, had gone 'out of his way to identify Prokofiev with Stravinsky and Diaghilev – alleging that all three represented "close to the West at any price" ideas ... it all ended in Monte Carlo, where the Diaghilev Ballet found its right mission at last – to cater to an audience of gamblers, profiteers and prostitutes' (Werth, 1949, p. 94).

that of the intelligentsia was in a condition of rapid evolution. This group produced and supported figures such as Scriabin, Prokofiev and Stravinsky who could claim to be in the forefront of music at a European level. In the background, however, profound social changes had been gathering pace since the second half of the nineteenth century. New classes – the lower middle class and the industrial proletariat – were emerging and, between them, these were creating a 'middle-brow culture': it is in this social transformation, and in the new culture it produced, that an understanding of current Soviet aesthetics must be sought.

These two groups may have been poles apart socially and economically, but in terms of musical taste they had something in common, and Nabokov is ready to coin a term for it: '*cliché-ism* ... the ready acceptance of all the worn-out formulas of low-brow western musical production'. The new influences were drawn from all over Europe, so that:

> ... in the 'pubs' of St Petersburg and Moscow, in the harbours of Odessa, the Russian factory song met with the German *Schlager* and the French *café chantant* .... The workers' and later the soldiers' songs adopted all the easy clichés of nineteenth-century musical language. The taste of the Russian lower middle classes – the *petite bourgeoisie* – on the other hand, leaned towards the world of Russian sentimental romance, of Viennese operetta, cozy Tchaikovskiana, and French importations of the Chaminade variety. (Nabokov, 1951c, p. 599)[12]

In the period following the Revolution, the influence of the modernist-leaning intelligentsia continued to grow, and this proved to be a fertile climate for experiment. But with the 'gradual extermination' of this group, and as the new Party and state bureaucracies grew in power and confidence, 'the musical habits of the old middle-stratum of pre-revolutionary Russian society began to show themselves on the bleak horizon of Soviet culture'. The Soviet middle class, for all its revolutionary politics, maintained an aesthetic continuity, with its preferences and prejudices largely unchanged. This '*petit bourgeois* taste' was shared by the leadership, and crucially, Nabokov claims, by Stalin himself:

> According to trustworthy accounts, his musical taste runs to Russian sentimental songs and famous arias, snatches of the Merry Widow, a few tunes from Tchaikovsky's operas, Red Army tunes and songs, fake night-club Caucasiana, and one or two slow movements of Beethoven's string quartets which he likes to hear performed by three quartets all playing at once. This fits perfectly the frame of reference of petit bourgeois musical habits of the time of Chekhov's short stories. (Ibid., p. 599)

In such conditions middle-class taste must prevail, and indeed great efforts had been made to extend it even to the rural population. Accordingly, older folk songs – 'modal ... ritualistic and reflective ... permeated with a profound religious spirit'

---

12   And as if all this was not bad enough, 'the revolutionary leaders, who had never cared for good music, brought the easy tunes and the march-like cadences of the western European proletarian songs with them'.

– were found to be inappropriate, and replaced wherever possible with optimistic post-revolutionary material.

Whilst this talk gives the fullest version of this analysis, aspects of it appear elsewhere. 'The Music Purge', for example, in accounting for the 1948 campaign stresses the identity of taste between leaders and middle-income officials. So Stalin enjoyed music that is 'tuneful in a conventional, easy way – that is, built around the commonplaces of 19th century semi-popular music'. As for the officials, they were likewise drawn to 'sentimental songs ... the schmaltz of 19th century Italian opera ... [and] the most hackneyed pieces of Rachmaninoff' (Nabokov, 1948a, p. 103). The outcome of this correspondence was that the middle class had been able to gain unchallenged control of the cultural field – had been able, in effect, to institutionalise its own petit bourgeois aesthetic, its 'standard tastes', behind a mask of socialist language and attacks on supposed 'formalism'.

Nabokov is describing a process in which the disappearance of the intellectuals and the rise of the bureaucracy (that is, the assumption of political and cultural power by the middle class) are merely two ways of viewing the same phenomenon. In 'No Cantatas for Stalin?', published in the first issue of *Encounter*, the focus is on the loss of the intelligentsia, and their broader, more 'cosmopolitan' outlook and concerns. This group had formerly 'set the tone of the cultural life of the nation, because it alone could understand and encourage the work of the pioneers in the arts', whereas the class that supplanted it 'was inevitably on a different plane from that of the "Westernised" intelligentsia with its intimate knowledge of all the latest artistic and intellectual developments' (Nabokov, 1953, p. 51).

In passing, it is interesting to note that Nabokov's old Dumbarton Avenue friend 'Chip' Bohlen expresses very similar views in his memoir. The original Bolshevik leaders, he writes, were educated men, very much products of 'Western European civilisation'. Stalin, by contrast:

> ... was a purely Russian-grown product. He was a Georgian and had little connection with the humane values of Western Christian civilisation, even though his education was within that framework. The Revolution drove much of the Western-oriented upper class and middle class out of Russia. Stalin's purge nearly eliminated from the Communist Party those who, in the tradition of Lenin, possessed a Western-based intellect. (Bohlen, 1969, p. 55)

Given Nabokov's emphasis on his indebtedness to Bohlen and Isaiah Berlin, any evidence of their shared views is useful, although it is hard to discern, in this instance, whether Nabokov influenced Bohlen or vice versa. It may, however, be reasonable to assume that Bohlen saw his Russian friend precisely as an example of the 'Western-oriented upper class' that had been driven out. Enough has been said here about the 'Russian cosmopolitan' to suggest that this is how he saw himself.

Nabokov's provincial/cosmopolitan model now emerges with greater clarity. More than just a means of classifying contemporary music, according to rejection/ acceptance of modernism, it is bound up with ideas about the social forces operating upon music. 'Provincialism' has a significance beyond individual choice since it describes, at least in part, the aesthetic of a class. The middle class at once embodies provincialism in its culture and constitutes the agency through which its influence is spread; the example of the Soviet Union shows where this can lead, unchecked. The countervailing force of cosmopolitanism is found principally in the values held in common by intellectuals. Only where they are allowed to thrive, as in the Western world (which, to Nabokov, appears as an unproblematic, undifferentiated realm of freedom), can the cosmopolitan spirit flourish. Only in such conditions could the 'great Renaissance' of twentieth-century music have occurred.

Soviet provincialism had musical consequences that, for Nabokov, demonstrated both the triumph of the middle class and the tragedy of middle-class taste institutionalised as state policy. It favoured a worn-out repertoire which, most glaringly, was centred on the despised late nineteenth-century idiom which modernism had hoped to have displaced. It favoured an emotional response, and all that was 'sentimental', 'schmaltzy' and 'oozy'. Having no real regard for artistic advance it welcomed the 'fake', the 'secondhand' and the 'hackneyed'. Denying all that was rigorous or challenging, its music was 'conventional', 'standardised' and 'formulaic'. Above all, it was 'easy'.

Another friend and ally – the historian Arthur Schlesinger Jr – drew on Nabokov's 'brilliant' article, 'The Music Purge', when discussing Soviet art in his highly influential book, *The Vital Center*, published in 1949. He highlights the Soviet mistrust of all that is, as he sees it, 'difficult' in art:[13]

> The totalitarian man requires apathy and unquestioning obedience. He fears creative independence and spontaneity. He mistrusts complexity as a device for slipping something over on the régime; he mistrusts incomprehensibility as a shield which might protect activities the bureaucrat cannot control. ... The paintings of Picasso, the music of Stravinsky are strangely disturbing. They reflect and incite anxieties which are incompatible with the monolithic character of 'the Soviet person.' Their intricacy and ambiguity, moreover, make them hard for officialdom to control ... Complexity in art further suggests the whole wicked view of 'cosmopolitanism' .... (Schlesinger, 1949, pp. 78–9)[14]

Schlesinger goes on to borrow a favourite quotation of Nabokov's, drawn from 'a famous anti-Tsarist satire by Saltikov'. Looking through a philosophical manuscript, a police inspector concludes: 'What I don't understand is undoubtedly dangerous to the security of the State.'[15] The Soviet state appeared to share the view of Saltikov's

---

13   I should point out that I regard 'difficult' not as a simple, neutral, term, but as one whose meaning needs to be contested. See also 'provincial', 'suburban', 'mere craftsmanship'. It is crucial that these terms be questioned. In whose interests are they deployed? When used, who and what is being elevated, who and what is being marginalised? Such questions of cultural power will form the core of Chapter 8.

14   Peter Coleman, historian of the CCF, describes this book, along with *1984* and Koestler's *Darkness at Noon*, as pivotal in their influence upon a postwar liberal Left rapidly distancing itself from communism. Schlesinger's commendation must have been welcome, appearing where it did, and issuing from a man who became one of the most highly regarded American intellectuals. Nabokov's own intellectual credentials were, after all, not universally respected.

15   Originally quoted in Nabokov (1948a, p. 103). Other appearances of this quotation occur in Nabokov (1949a, p. 851) and Nabokov (1951c, p. 598). In the latter it is attributed to Saltykov-Shchedrin.

inspector. Certainly, their actions suggested it. If this was the case, if Soviet officialdom feared the 'difficulty' and 'complexity' of modern music, could it somehow be enlisted as a weapon in the struggle against communism? Nicolas Nabokov felt that it could and, in 1951, as the newly appointed secretary-general of the CCF, he devised a plan to do just that.

Chapter 4

'A Very Popular Fiasco':
The 1952 Festival in Paris

'Masterpieces of the XXth Century' ... has spilled such gallons of captious French newspaper ink, wasted such tempests of argumentative Franco-American breath, and afforded, on the whole, so much pleasure to the eye and ear that it can be safely called, in admiration, an extremely popular fiasco. (Flanner, 1952b, p. 74)

After the 1951 Berlin meeting, and the decision to create to carry the work forward, Nabokov and Josselson, installed in a Paris office, had to decide how to launch the CCF as an ongoing organisation. This they achieved in extravagant style with the 1952 Paris festival, 'L'Oeuvre du XXème Siècle'. Against the background of a Western Europe still marked by postwar austerity this event, in terms of its scale, its ambition and its glittering roster of artists, was remarkable enough. In its anti-Soviet aims, and specifically as an overt fusion of the cultural and the political, the festival may have been something unique. However, as Janet Flanner (the *New Yorker*'s 'Gênet') suggests, it also proved extremely controversial.

'Masterpieces of the Twentieth Century' (Nabokov's only slightly less audacious English title for the event) spanned the entire month of May, opening on 30 April and holding its final closing concert on 1 June. Events took place almost every night: 12 orchestral or choral concerts, five performances of opera, eight of ballet, and seven concerts of chamber music. In addition to the 'star' of the festival, the Boston Symphony Orchestra, it also boasted the Vienna Philharmonic and the Orchestre de la Suisse Romande; opera companies were represented by the Vienna State Opera and Covent Garden Opera; and a particularly high profile was given to George Balanchine and the New York City Ballet.[1] According to Flanner again, 'in a Paris spring season more lush with varied entertainment than any other since the peace, the American exposition ... dominated the scene by its very weight', a force that undoubtedly owed as much to quality as quantity. Ansermet, Böhm, Walter, Markevitch, Monteux and Munch conducted, whilst Britten and Stravinsky directed their own works; soloists included Geza Anda, Arturo Benedetti Michelangeli and Joseph Szigeti. As the festival's French title suggests and, as reinforced by its supporting literature, the programme was intended as a survey of the best, and most significant of twentieth-century music. The works of 62 composers were performed, including Bartok, Satie,

---

1   All programme details from the *Masterpieces of the XXth Century* festival brochure (Paris: Congress for Cultural Freedom 1952), IACF.

45

Stravinsky, Boulez, Hindemith, Ives, Dallapiccola, Messiaen, Milhaud, Tippett, Varese, Thomson, Webern, Schoenberg, and Berg to choose only a few of the more celebrated.

And yet, in theory at least, this was *not* a festival of modern music: it was never described as such by its organisers, inside or outside the CCF, and it should have been a broad arts festival. Those of Nabokov's colleagues who doubted the wisdom of his appointment as secretary-general, and who had questioned the political efficacy of a strategy centred on the arts would, no doubt, have been that much more concerned at the idea of a festival of modern music only; in the event, however, this is effectively what 'Masterpieces of the Twentieth Century' became. Yet, even as late as December of the previous year, Nabokov was describing the festival as having five parts: '1 – a literary program; 2 – an art exhibit; 3 – a musical program; 4 – a film program; 5 – a dramatic program' (Nabokov, 1951e, unpublished, p. 2). In the same progress report the last two items are described as 'discussed ... [but] not yet ready for presentation', and doubts are expressed about the practicalities of achieving the theatre component: as it transpired, both these elements were abandoned. The literary and art components as they finally appeared were severely diminished versions of their December selves. 'Six to eight lectures and four to six forums on the novel and poetry of this century' became a single 'large meeting' followed by four 'study groups before limited audiences'. Curiously, this literary programme, whilst described in the festival brochure as concerned with 'the literary trends of the XXth Century', makes no specific references to any such, announcing instead themes of 'isolation and mass communication', 'revolt and human fellowship', 'diversity and universality' as issues pertinent to artists in general (Masterpieces of the XXth Century brochure). Whilst the various references to the respective temptations and threats of mass culture and totalitarianism would no doubt have found approval with the *Partisan Review* crowd, it is perhaps apprpriate to question whether such a pitch would appeal to writers of more literary than political inclination. Visual art in the festival was represented by one exhibition; tellingly, art and literature *together* occupied one page of the festival brochure – following the seven devoted to music.

Reviewing the festival for *Commentary*, Herbert Luethy drew attention to the lopsided nature of the event. Praising the 'splendid' art exhibition at the Musée d'Art Moderne, he nonetheless described the literary discussions as 'exactly what ... [these] could be expected to be when improvised as "poor relations" of the other arts – just to show that the organizers had taken care to include everything'(Luethy, 1952, p. 72).[2] Moreover, he was in no doubt that 'L'Oeuvre du XXème Siècle' – an ill-advised, 'pretentious' title – was essentially a music festival, albeit an extraordinary one: 'incomparably rich and varied ... perhaps never had that large a public been made so intensely interested in modern music.' If Nabokov's programme invited the charge of parochialism – being too musical, and insufficiently 'cultural' – other critics (and, for the secretary-general, more dangerous ones) held that the festival was *merely* cultural, that it avoided the political issues which were the CCF's entire *raison*

---

2   On the subjects chosen for the literary discussions – 'diversity and universality', 'revolt and communion', and so on, he added that these were 'highly general ... about which everybody can say everything and nothing in a twenty minute speech'.

d'être.[3] Ironically, Nabokov had anticipated both arguments and set out to defuse them in his December progress report to the American Congress for Cultural Freedom (ACCF), opening his summing-up as follows:

> The exposition is not intended to become just another music festival of which there are already too many in Europe, nor is it intended to be a kind of 'cultural fair' aimed at amusing and entertaining the Parisian snobs and international tourists. The fundamental aims of the exposition are cultural and political. (Nabokov, 1951e, p. 7)

In fact, as we shall see, the event attracted criticism on both the above grounds, and others besides.

Background to the festival

Whilst CIA sponsorship of the Congress for Cultural Freedom has been public knowledge for over 30 years, until recently little has been known about the detail of the relationship. The fact of the CIA connection had the effect of raising questions about Congress's policies, whilst simultaneously ensuring that these were impossible to resolve. For example, was the idea for a major arts festival born from within Congress, or foisted on it from outside? Peter Coleman, author of the first book-length study of the CCF writes:

> The idea for the massive 1952 Paris cultural festival ... did not emerge from discussions within the CCF, which had never previously discussed such an idea. It surely reflected the concern of the US administration that America was losing 'the battle of the festivals' to the Soviet Union. (Coleman, 1987, p. 313)

The implication is that the Paris Festival concept was imposed from CIA headquarters in Langley. Nabokov's own autobiographical account recounts otherwise. Having agreed to serve as the secretary-general of the CCF and after working out his notice at Peabody Conservatory, he set out on the eleven-hour flight to Paris on 23 May 1951:

> ... I started formulating my first proposal to the cultural committee. I wanted to start off its activities with a big bang and in the field of twentieth-century arts. At that time contemporary art and music were the victims of Stalin's and Zhdanov's most odious repression, just as they had been a decade earlier in Hitler's Germany. I felt that we had to reaffirm our belief in their values and that the time had come to draw an inventory of their achievements in the first fifty years of this century. Thus was born ... the general outline of my first ... festival. (Nabokov, 1975, p. 243)

Stonor Saunders supports this claim (although she differs on the dates).[4] In her

---

3   This internal debate over the cultural strategy will be considered more fully in Chapter 6.

4   My research also supports this. An undated proposal, found in the IACF papers states that the decision was made *earlier*, at a meeting of the CCF Executive Committee on 15 May 1951. This document – 'not for publication' – is headed 'Masterpieces of our Century

account, Tom Braden – 'running' the CCF for the CIA's International Operations Division – had already secured approval for Nabokov's plan (which Josselson had passed up the line) by the end of April (Stonor Saunders, 1999, pp. 113–17). All agree that concerns were soon being expressed – especially by members of the Congress's American affiliate, the ACCF – that the emerging festival plan was inappropriate, a diversion from more properly political activity. Less than two weeks after Nabokov's departure for Europe, an ACCF Executive Committee meeting discussed his proposal. Whilst the minutes record 'general approval', the essence of the opposition to an arts-centred strategy is already clear in the views of Eliot Cohen and Sidney Hook. Cohen complained that the 'primary aim of the Congress in Europe is not to mobilise the works of artists', whilst Hook urged that 'the proposal as it stands needs much more sharpening. People in Paris don't lack opportunities to hear modern music, see modern art, etc. If we sponsor such presentations it should be with a political direction or point ... .'[5] On the same day Nabokov wrote to James Burnham, the highly influential author of *The Managerial Revolution* and ACCF member, seeking support for his ideas: the festival (or something like it) would, he argued, do more for the Congress than 'fifteen public meetings and one thousand public speeches' (letter to Burnham, 6 June 1951).

Nabokov was not, however, without supporters in New York. The historian and author of *The Vital Center*, Arthur Schlesinger Jr, wrote on 18 June attacking the 'neurotic' and 'extreme' nature of leading elements of the ACCF (letter to Nabokov, 18 June 1951). Nabokov's reply sympathised with Schlesinger's frustration, commenting that 'some of our friends have veered so far to the right that soon it will be hard to talk to them'. He goes on to sketch his plans for May 1952, which are receiving 'enthusiastic reactions ... from all sorts of quarters', and then echoes earlier rhetoric: the festival will, he says, 'have much more retentissement than [one] hundred speeches by Arthur Koestler, Sidney Hook and James Burnham about the neuroses of our century' – in effect, it will have more impact, be more memorable (letter to Schlesinger, 15 July 1951). Here, Nabokov uses the same argument as in the Burnham letter: this festival will do more political good than tired old speechifying. However, in confidence, and to a friend, the argument can be made more pointed by contrasting the exciting potential of the festival with the dreary methods of *particular* CCF 'hawks' – and, for Nabokov, opponents – such as 'Field Marshal' Hook (as Nabokov described him when recalling the Waldorf action (Nabokov, 1975, p. 234)), Koestler, whose abrasive style had alienated some at the Berlin Congress (Coleman, 1989, p. 34), and Burnham himself.

In retrospect, the reservations of Nabokov's fractious colleagues in the ACCF were, of course, immaterial, since larger forces were in play: now that CIA had given its approval, the festival would go ahead. Indeed, arrangements were already in place

---

(tentative title): A retrospective Festival of the main artistic achievements of the first half of this century.'

5   From the minutes of a meeting of the Executive Committee of the ACCF, dated 6 June 1951, IACF papers. Unfortunately the proposal supplied by Nabokov cannot be positively identified: a comparison with the 'Progress Report' (1951e) might have been instructive. It is possible, however, that the document referred to in note 4 – an outline of the thinking behind the festival under a 'tentative title' – may be that considered at this meeting.

for the covert funding of 'Masterpieces' via a dummy trust – the Farfield Foundation (incorporated 30 January 1952) – set up specifically for that purpose, but sustained afterwards as the principal conduit for funding the CCF. This was a favourite device of the CIA's, and the Farfield, although the chief means of routing money to Congress, was only one of many used for this and other purposes. The Foundation's President – and its apparent benefactor – was Julius 'Junkie' Fleischmann, a Cincinnati yeast and gin millionaire. Fleischmann, a director of the Metropolitan Opera in New York and fellow of the Royal Society of Arts in London, was known for his interest in the arts, as well as his wealth. As such, he was an ideal 'front man' for the operation. His 'duties', however, were nothing but window-dressing: all Fleischmann and his fellow directors had to do was attend board meetings every other month, and go through the motions of approving payments to Congress – payments over which he had no influence whatever. All the while, the fiction of private philanthropy was maintained, and not just in public. In December 1951, just pre-Farfield, Fleischmann, just back from a trip to London and writing to Nabokov, who had expressed his wish to have the Boston Symphony Orchestra at his 'dream festival' says:

> Now as to the Boston [Symphony] ... I decided not to go to 'Billy Budd' but to return on the *Mauretania*. I told our sad story to a 'guy' who got interested. The result was that the day after we landed he called me up and said that he had raised $65,000 for the express purpose of getting the Boston to the Exposition. I had to promise to withhold his name and I don't even know the names of his associates. (Letter to Nabokov, 13 December 1951)

Even to Nabokov, the cover story had to be maintained. The creation of the Farfield Foundation simplified Congress funding; it meant no more ad hoc subsidies from the International Ladies Garment Workers Union (ILGWU)[6] and no more gifts from mysterious 'guys' in mid-Atlantic. Now the CCF could be sustained by an apparatus that was both long-term and publicly convincing – and so it proved for 15 years. Whatever the rumours about the Congress's real backers – and there were many – until the *New York Times* revelations in 1966 they remained just that.

Political rationale

The task confronting Nabokov was to create a grand arts festival that was credible within Congress at a *political* level. In addition to the usual logistical, contractual and financial demands of a large-scale event, this plan presented the secretary-general with major communications tasks on two fronts. Ultimately a restricted public was the target for the festival in terms of its political objectives – the 'artistic milieux' and

---

6   The ILGWU had been the ostensible source of funds for Americans for Intellectual Freedom's Waldorf-Astoria action in 1949: see Nabokov (1975, p. 233). Nabokov recalls that he approached its leader, David Dubinsky, on Hook's suggestion, adding, with no discernible sense of irony: 'the astonishing thing was that, *as if by a miracle*, the suggestion of the need for an agitprop apparatus of our own produced one' (p. 234, my emphasis). The broader utility of the ILGWU to the CIA is set out in Braden (1967, p. 14). See also Stonor Saunders (1999, pp. 46–55).

youth. First, though, it was necessary to win over the CCF's own supporters. However little influence the wider membership may actually have had over policy, the Paris leadership's concern – and surely the Agency's too – was to sustain and build the Congress as an anti-communist force. This implied a paramount need for internal unity, if at all possible. Reference has already been made to the doubts of the ACCF about the direction the organisation was taking, and to Nabokov's letter of 20 December to Pearl Kluger. In it he responds to worries apparently expressed in an earlier letter of hers, and acknowledges that 'the American Committee is profoundly disturbed by the absence of political orientation in connection with the festival ... the Committee believes that preparations must be made now to carry out the political aspects of the festival'. 'This is being taken care of,' he continues, 'but the American Committee will have to be patient with us in this connection because if we start making speeches and propaganda now, we will put the whole ... Exposition in jeopardy' (letter to Kluger, 20 December 1951).

The 'Progress Report' (Nabokov, 1951e, unpublished), which Kluger also received, represents an attempt by the Paris leadership to create a rationale that would pacify its internal critics. Following on from a synopsis of the festival is a four-page account of their aims in producing it. The event will establish the CCF on the world stage, Nabokov argues, attracting new members from the ranks of European and American intellectuals. If the plan appears grandiose, this is because circumstances demand the utmost ambition: the new organisation must aim for no less than 'an influence comparable to that of the Communist Party in the Western world'. Noting the extent of the communist 'hold' over intellectuals – especially artists – a counter-strategy is then laid out. First, the festival will make an impressive presentation of the most important works of twentieth-century art, and stress at every opportunity that this rich and varied culture could only have come about in free societies. These 'fruits of freedom' can then be compared to 'the sorry output of writers, poets, painters and musicians living under tyranny, stifled by their rulers to sycophancy and conformism'. In short, the festival will 'prove' that communism is inimical to true creativity, and establish the Congress as the friend of the artist, ever vigilant against threats to the freedoms without which art is unthinkable. In addition, one final aim is to:

> ... counteract the traditional European misconception of the United States as a country lacking in culture – a misconception consistently exploited by Communist propaganda; show, on the contrary, that the culture of the United States is inseparable from the culture of Europe and that American artists have contributed their share to the cultural edifice of our time. To this end, the Congress for Cultural Freedom has invited American artistic organisations of the highest standing to participate in the exposition. (Nabokov, 1951e, unpublished, p. 7)

This piece of the jigsaw was given a distinctly lower *public* profile: Nabokov felt that European sensitivity over American propaganda – a sensitivity especially acute among the liberal left target audience of the Congress – dictated caution in handling this issue. Nevertheless, this issue did undoubtedly play a principal role in the whole enterprise, and this question of the US image will be considered in the following chapter.

The last section of the 'Progress Report' represents perhaps the clearest statement of the rationale for the arts-centred strategy. It commences with Nabokov's intention that this will *not* be 'another music festival'; the scheme has, on the contrary, been carefully wrought around a core of 'cultural and political' aims, and will firmly establish a worldwide reputation for the Congress as a defender of freedom. Traditional political methods such as meetings (and perhaps also the 'little magazines' favoured by ACCF intellectuals) only preach to the already converted, whereas the urgent need is to reach *beyond* the existing supporters, to join battle with the communists in the wider intellectual sphere. For it is here – among the 'middle-of-the-road intellectuals' – that the Soviets' propaganda has been most pernicious and most alarmingly successful: here the Congress must struggle to regain the sympathies of those

> ... who have lost confidence in our culture ... [and] have allowed themselves to become dupes and used as fronts ... [those] who accept the thesis that the world is divided into two antagonistic, imperialistic camps of which the United States is the most belligerent and the country most lacking in culture. ... This influence has created an atmosphere of fear and paralysis which inhibits the desire of the individual to take a stand on our side. (Nabokov, 1951, unpublished, p. 8).

Acknowledging that some of the Congress's friends may see this as a 'frivolous' project, Nabokov restates the conviction of the Paris leadership that 'the arts [at] present in Europe – mainly in France and Italy – are one of the richest fields for our political activity'. One reason for this belief is the sense that the Congress can only gain in stature and influence from being seen to care about the arts, and not merely indulging in 'fruitless polemics with the other side'. Finally, there is an outline of a tactical approach to communications: the publicity campaign will be progressive, with the initial stress on the content of the festival, but later increasing emphasis on the political meaning 'inherent in the program'. To make doubly sure that this meaning is not lost, a public meeting of the Congress will form a postscript to the proceedings: 'Thus, the exposition and the Congress immediately following will represent two phases of a trial – the first, producing the evidence, the second, reaching the verdict.'

The brochure *L'Oeuvre du XXe Siècle: 1* contains an adapted version of this rationale, intended for the festival-going public. Alongside a series of specific articles on opera, ballet, American music and so on is an introduction by Nabokov, which begins with some general observations on the course of music in the twentieth century (Nabokov, 1952a). It is immediately clear, he begins, that modern music embodies a spirit of experimentation and innovation, and the observer may be struck as much as anything by the dramatic diversity of the musics produced in the two decades after 1900. In this field of dynamic, varied music, however, one major fault line can be distinguished, dividing contemporary composers over essentially harmonic issues. The division is one of 'expression' versus 'construction', the former 'neo-classical' group being concerned broadly with known diatonic materials, whilst the latter have developed a new and radical chromatic method. Having sketched a great divide in the world of music, however, Nabokov urges that this situation is nothing new in itself: the question of chromaticism has led to strong differences before, sometimes to much more divisive effect (here, he offers the curious example of Gesualdo and Palestrina) than is currently the case. Second, the world of music is much more united and coherent than it would appear. For one thing many composers do not fit neatly into either 'camp', but freely use the 'discoveries' of both. But beyond that, Nabokov suggests that *rhythm* has moved to centre-stage at this point in musical history, following the long period in which harmony was of prime importance, and before that, melody: it is exploration of the possibilities of rhythm which have given the music of the period 1900–25 its 'physionomie particulière'. In addition one can identify a shared sense of reaction against a romanticism drained of its former potency, leaving a music 'superficially exciting but profoundly conventional', tied to academic and essentially nineteenth-century procedures.

Needing – in terms of his political objectives – to demonstrate unity behind the confused facade of contemporary music, Nabokov's piece moves towards consideration of those extra-musical factors which are of more importance to the purpose of the festival itself. The first concerns the nature of twentieth-century life, with the growth of a larger public for symphonic music through larger halls, via the gramophone and via radio, and with the new possibilities presented by developments in travel. Musics are no longer isolated: significantly, Nabokov cites, on the one hand, the growing awareness in Europe of *Russian* music ('... around 1910, Russian music ... came to be seen as a major piece of the musical jigsaw ...') and, on the other, the impact of a 'remarkable school [which began] to bring to the two Americas its original synthesis of European tradition, American and exotic influences'. More broadly, creative personalities of the first rank began to appear from areas in Europe which had previously appeared musically marginal. He concludes:

> Everywhere we find exchange and mutual influence. The hobbling spirit which had, more than once, led musicians towards the national, or even the nationalist, in the nineteenth century has, like it or not, given way to universalism. (Nabokov, 1952a, p. 5)

Contemporary music, then, is an international undertaking whose multiplicity of styles conceals an essential unity. All modern music, in Nabokov's view, begins with the liberating departures of the early-century modernists, and proceeds via a common refusal of all restraints on free creativity. The stylistic diversity is evidence not of a riven practice – atomised, fractured, confused – but, rather, the fruits of an art founded on innovation and freedom.

In essence we have returned to cosmopolitanism, although here described more grandly (and more tendentiously) as universalism. The specific examples of musics – Russian and American – which owed much to the new cosmopolitanism are carefully chosen. Reminded of the comparatively recent arrival of Russian music (which, Nabokov implies, is of great worth), the reader will supply his own lament for its present sorry condition; the claim of American music to the respect of European audiences being less firmly established, and subject to the prejudices of anti-Americanism, its value and contribution to Western culture must be asserted whenever possible. Identifying the 'universalism' of modern music therefore becomes an opportunity to subtly attack Soviet culture and elevate that of America.[7]

---

7   This was not the only time Nabokov mentioned Soviet and American musics 'in

If the cosmopolitan spirit and the technical possibilities of the modern world have opened new horizons for composers, have facilitated music's own dynamic, innovatory impulses, have catalysed a period of unprecedented musical production, the riches of which will be amply displayed in the month of the festival, it only remains for Nabokov to call attention to those forces which threaten creativity. Notwithstanding the talent – even the genius – of the composers, he argues, this work was all predicated upon a climate of *freedom*:

> Freedom to experiment, freedom to express oneself, freedom to choose one's own *maîtres* and make one's own decisions, to choose irony or naïveté, the esoteric or the familiar. In the coming festival … there is scarcely a piece that does not owe its character, its soul even, to the fact of being the music of men who know the value of freedom. (Nabokov, 1952a, p. 5)

And, today, we are that much more aware of its value, he continues, because we see, 'in several corners of the world', powerful states where these rights, along with others, 'material and spiritual', are denied. Whilst concentrated power is nothing new,

> … only in the twentieth century have we seen politicians setting themselves up as Professors of harmony, composition and aesthetics … covering great artists in insults whose vulgarity is only exceeded by their stupidity, and imposing on music a 'party line' of servile texts, predictable style and ground rules for the creation of 'national' and 'progressive' art clearly designed to induce despair of the human race and artistic progress. (Nabokov, 1952a, p. 5)

Ultimately, if a festival of modern music has any value, it must be to fight against despair, for no totalitarian ideology can diminish the great masters, 'who speak not only for themselves, but for the whole of civilisation'.

Nabokov wrote other material for the festival, including a short preamble in its brochure. Whilst this adds little to the account above, it does serve to confirm the sense of the event as nothing less than an inventory of cultural achievement – 'all the abundant riches which the mind of free man has created' – in the first half-century. This ambitious undertaking (which is probably without precedent, he modestly continues) is intended to inspire young artists, affirm the CCF's faith in Western culture, and underline the essential connection between great art and freedom. The second piece is an article by Nabokov which appeared in the May 1952 edition of *Preuves*, the Congress's French journal (Nabokov, 1952b). As its title – 'Élégie Funèbre sur quatre notes' – suggests, the piece is a four-part lament, with a connecting thread that can be broadly described as 'wrongs done to composers by society'. Section I, '*L'Atlantide* de Manuel de Falla', dealing with the Spain of Franco, is the only instance known to me of Nabokov's complaining of censorship by a

---

the same breath'. In his introduction to a book by friend and CCF supporter Virgil Thomson (*American Music since 1910*), he refers to 'two important, unconnected and contradictory events that occurred in our century.' These are, once again, the Soviet Union's 'brutal suppression of musical freedoms' and the 'rise to full maturity of American music'. In connecting these 'unconnected events' the writer's political intent is clear (Nabokov, 1971, p. xv). This was Vol. 1 of the Twentieth Century Composers series, edited by Nabokov and Anna Kallin. For more on Kallin, see Chapter 2; for more on Thomson's *Four Saints in Three Acts*, see Chapter 5.

contemporary *right-wing* regime.[8] According to this account, after the exiled Falla's death in Argentina in 1946, his sister brought the score of *L'Atlantide* back to Spain, since when nothing had been heard of it. The various efforts that were made to see the score, let alone arrange a performance, met with no success. Dismissing suggestions that the composer's will forbade its performance, Nabokov alleges that the real reasons are political, connected to Falla's use of a text by the Catalan poet Jacinto Vordaguer, and he closes on a note of high outrage: '... the score of *L'Atlantide* is withheld from us. The cover-up is complete, impenetrable, scandalous: without doubt one of the most shameful events of our era' (Nabokov, 1952b, p. 8).

In the Section II, 'The Misfortunes of *Lady Macbeth of Mtsensk*', Nabokov returns to familiar ground. Shostakovich's successes and reversals from 1932, the time of the opera's completion, are set out: initial success and performances abroad, then the *Pravda* attack of 1936, rehabilitation with the *Fifth Symphony* and wartime celebrity followed by further disgrace in 1948. Significantly, Nabokov does not take the opportunity to revisit the doubts about the composer that he expressed only a year before in *Old Friends and New Music*. There, the music was 'shapeless in style and form ... impersonal in colour' (Nabokov, 1951d, p. 206), and general worries were expressed about the dangerous trends which Shostakovich might represent. Now, such comments are conspicuous by their absence. Curious? The answer lies in the political point Nabokov wished to make, which is here less to do with Soviet *aesthetics* than Soviet *censorship*. Consequently, the piece builds to the continued ban on performances of *Lady Macbeth*, and the author's efforts to obtain a score for the present festival (only one copy was found, and that of a concert suite extracted from the larger work). Downplaying any criticism of the music now makes complete sense, since Shostakovich is being held up not as an exemplar of the Soviet aesthetic, but as a victim of Soviet control. The reader is more likely to share Nabokov's concerns if the censored works are *great* works; thus Shostakovich's *Lady Macbeth* is now, somewhat surprisingly, 'a work of real merit ... [which shares] the fate of de Falla's *L'Atlantide*. Another work sequestered, forbidden. Another victim of the appalling intolerance of our century' (Nabokov, 1952b, p. 10).[9]

---

8   However, there are, it is true, some glancing references to Nazi Germany and, of course, the frequently employed term 'totalitarian' could imply even-handedness: generally, however, the context indicates that Nabokov is referring to the present – that is, to the postwar, post-Nazi world – and his choice of examples makes it clear that, in practical terms, the term refers *only* to the communist countries.

In this, Nabokov is no more than the typical Cold War partisan. A balanced observer – even one unprepared to look outside Europe – might arguably have considered the situation in Greece, which in the period 1944–49 suffered a period of civil war in which the British and, later, the Americans were actively involved. Artists were not exempt from the associated repression, and the imprisonment and torture of the composer Mikis Theodorakis is well documented, along with his problems later, after the Colonels' coup in 1967. See Giannaris (1972) and Holst (1980).

9   As we saw in Chapter 2, Nabokov was not always so generous in his assessment of this work: rather, his critical opinion seems to bend according to the political purpose at hand. Thus, *Lady Macbeth* can be a good or a bad piece depending on whether the target is Soviet censorship or Soviet music.

The article concludes with the juxtaposition of two lengthy passages reproduced from the writings of Soviet musicologist Boris Asafiev (writing here under the pseudonym of Igor Glebov): here aesthetics *are* the matter at hand – specifically, the manner in which the Soviet regime controls aesthetic questions, leading to farcical reversals of earlier opinions. The two passages, from 1936 and 1948, offer sharply contrasting views of Stravinsky. Nabokov allows them to speak for themselves, contenting himself with asking, in mock innocence, 'How can we explain such a radical change of heart? … What can have happened in Glebov's mind?'.

There is one more section: 'In Memoriam: The Death of Béla Bartók', an oddity in Nabokov's written output. This is a brief account of the composer's difficult circumstances between leaving Europe in 1940 and his death in the USA in 1945. Nabokov sketches Bartók's poverty and declining health, the American public's lack of interest and his neglect by members of the musical world (with a few honourable exceptions): by contrast, his posthumous reputation has only climbed. At first sight, this third note in the 'Élégie' sits uneasily with its companions: the theme of unacceptable state power which runs through the pieces on de Falla, Shostakovich and Glebov, if not absent, is indirect in that Bartók's problems in exile occurred as a consequence of the totalitarianism that caused him to flee. There are some references here to Soviet criticisms of the composer's work – of the 'formalist, decadent' kind – and yet the thrust of the piece is to draw attention to Bartók's neglect by the very society in which he sought freedom; indeed, it could even be interpreted as an example of just that American disinterest in high culture which the CCF was at pains to deny. Ultimately, and largely because of the inclusion of this section, the impression left by the 'Élégie' is unclear. If it suggests anything, it may be that the position of the contemporary composer is a precarious one: when not prey to the appetites of over-mighty governments and the interference of *apparatchiks*, he is yet insecure, vulnerable, adrift in the free markets of the West, where the public is fickle and the subsidies are small.

Reception

So much for the public and private rationale behind the 'Masterpieces of the XXth Century' festival. We now turn to the question of how this event, and its carefully prepared political message, were received at large. Both Janet Flanner and Herbert Luethy offered overviews of the festival as a political–cultural phenomenon, Flanner, in her regular guise as the *New Yorker*'s 'Gênet' and in a second piece for *Freedom and Union* and Luethy in a substantial article for *Commentary*. Between them, they describe an artistic success which, in *political* terms, must be considered well-meaning but ultimately counter-productive. For Luethy, the festival was 'dazzling' and 'brilliant', and mention has already been made of his high praise for it as a festival of contemporary music (he singles out the Paris première of *Wozzeck* as its finest moment). Flanner's more mixed view – that many of the 'Masterpieces' were no such thing, that the good and the mediocre sat alongside the excellent – is perhaps tipped in Nabokov's favour by her lavish praise of particular events. She identifies the New York City Ballet in Jerome Robbins' *Pied Piper* (based on Copland's *Clarinet Concerto* of 1948), Stravinsky's *Oedipus Rex* with staging and narration by Jean

Cocteau, and the Boston Symphony Orchestra – the 'magnificent, mellifluous star of the festival'.[10]

Politically, the intention of 'Masterpieces' was not lost on either commentator, and both offer potted versions – Luethy at somewhat greater length. Both suggest that, in propaganda terms, the festival seems to have been not merely ineffective but actually negative. Clearly, the event *was* seen as an American affair, despite the CCF's professed status as an international organisation, and these writers suggest that the Americans' staging of a cultural festival in Paris, and on such a large scale, only served to aggravate French concerns about their nation's reduced status in the postwar world, touching issues of national pride, political and cultural leadership that, to some extent, crossed the political spectrum. Luethy selects a particular quarrel which, notwithstanding its own special sectarian bitterness, brings out the general point. Serge Lifar, master of the Paris Opéra ballet, had attacked the festival in *Combat*, a paper of the intellectual Left, for daring to include Balanchine's New York City Ballet at the expense of his own troupe. Lifar concluded thus: '… on the plane of culture, of civilisation, of the spirit, France does not take counsel from anyone: she teaches others!' (1952, p. 74).[11] This may be ridiculous, Luethy argues, but it reflects the wider reaction of the Paris press: 'The "American" festival, too rich, too lavish, and its publicity often lacking in modulation and tact, provoked an outburst of embittered and small-minded chauvinism of the worst kind – of cultural chauvinism.'

Beyond any single event or editorial, these writers argue that the festival was permeated by a sense of bad feeling, a malaise which can be traced back to its too-transparent nature as foreign – worse – *American* propaganda. Flanner has perhaps the most colourful phrase: in a letter to a Nabokov clearly irritated by her *New Yorker* piece, she writes: 'There was a kind of gypsy curse on the 20th Century exposition. It hurt you, Fleischmann, M. Munch even, it hurt many of us in different ways though we all had the best of intentions' (letter to Nabokov, 7 August 1952).[12] Both attested to the sense of French affront, provoked by what were perceived as lectures on the value of Western civilisation from a nation which had taken little part in its making; both stress that the enterprise offended against the host nation's belief in the centrality, even the superiority, of its own culture. According to Luethy, the French intellectual elite considered 'its own civilisation to be the one unique and universally valid civilisation extant' whilst, for Flanner, the situation is summed up by an 'intelligent, candid' young Frenchman:

---

10   For the full programme of the Festival, see the Appendix.

11   In passing, the author points out the irony of Lifar, 'who had collaborated so shamelessly during the Occupation … [now] mounted on the stuffed horse of French patriotism' and takes *Combat*, 'once a great newspaper of the Resistance' to task for affording him this opportunity. Incidentally, Nabokov had met both Lifar and Balanchine when Diaghilev's ballet produced his *Ode* in 1928. See Nabokov (1975, pp. 151–60). *Bagázh* does not mention Lifar's intervention.

12   Flanner apologises for 'wounding' Munch, conductor of the Boston Symphony Orchestra, by mentioning, in her *New Yorker* piece, that 'in 1946 he had been harshly treated as a supposed collaborationist'. She points out that she was merely referring to *allegations* – by others – that are a matter of fact, and repeatedly stresses her own positive attitude to the festival.

All we French have left, he said, after the physical, military collapse of 1940 is our unshaken belief in our civilised, cultural superiority ... 'Modern contemporanean art [*sic*], modern contemporanean music were born in Paris ... our mental climate gave them birth, even if some of their fathers were foreigners. Now you bring their works back to us ... on a golden salver we can not afford. We are not the logical people Descartes thought we were. ...' (Flanner, 1952a, p. 7)

If the difficult reception of the festival can be attributed in part to French – or, more particularly, Parisian intellectual – attitudes to culture, Flanner argues that contemporary political developments must be considered in equal measure. *Combat*, she says, provided the best analysis of the 'extremely popular fiasco', as she styles the festival (Flanner, 1952b, p. 74), in a series of articles which highlighted the immediate political context – namely the plan for German rearmament, the arrival of the controversial General Ridgway to head NATO (trailing allegations of bacteriological warfare in Korea) reports of atrocities in the Koje prison camp in Korea, and an alleged leaked report to the US National Security Council (later proved to be spurious) suggesting that world war was inevitable before 1960. Flanner agrees with *Combat*'s assessment that, in this highly-charged situation, the 'American festival' effectively fed the anti-American sentiments which existed across the political spectrum, exacerbating 'Europe's great fear'. Nabokov seems to have hoped that observers would coolly assess the Western cultural heritage on offer, and reach an appropriate political conclusion. Even assuming, however, that one accepts his argument that the works somehow speak for the 'free world' (and Luethy, as we shall see, did not) this seems to presuppose a level of dispassionate analysis that the Cold War atmosphere tended to undermine. If 'Masterpieces' was indeed the 'trial' of Western civilisation, to pick up Nabokov's metaphor, the 'evidence' was considered by a polarised and partisan jury. Ultimately, Luethy concludes, 'the most absolute art was mixed up with the most realistic politics, and far too many people wondered whether their approval – or disapproval – would be entered to the account of Arnold Schoenberg or General Ridgway' (Luethy, 1952, p. 75).[13]

Before turning to some retrospective views, it is worth noting some of Luethy's personal comments on 'Masterpieces', relating to its rationale and also to the character of Nabokov's programme. In terms of the former, he starts with the conventional wisdom that art and politics do not mix. According to Luethy, 'there is no committed art, for commitment would make it cease to be art at all', and he continues: 'that is why there is something disturbing in any ideological mobilisation of culture.' If the art works of the festival cannot, by definition, embody or express any political position, can they really function as part of an acknowledged political scheme? He doubts it, although his view is not entirely one-sided. On the one hand, the festival may have helped reinforce the idea of a civilisation worth defending, helped counter the 'chatter about the "decadence of the West" ... Perhaps even the truth needs a Barnum', he muses. Then again, he questions the sense in which any

---

13   General Matthew Ridgway arrived in Paris in May 1952 to take command of NATO forces. According to the communist press, Ridgway had ordered the use of bacteriological weapons in Korea and should be considered a war criminal: street demonstrations over Ridgway's presence left one dead and 200 wounded. See Kuisel (1993, pp. 48–9).

art work can be considered to advertise the social conditions in which it was made and, tellingly, points to Bartók and specifically to Nabokov's *Preuves* account of the composer's last years. Bartók's works – or Berg's, or any other artist who died unappreciated – do not advertise Western society *except* in the limited, but crucial, sense that that society preserves the 'vital minimum of freedom' – the freedom to die of hunger in pursuit of an artistic vision. This, though essential, is all the West can claim. It is, however, *not* a matter of generosity and does *not* occasion self-congratulation: witnessing fashionable Parisian society at the festival, Luethy sensed 'some terrible misunderstanding', as if this world sought posthumous credit for the achievements of Bartók and of Berg.[14]

'A festival of Western civilisation? One could with equal justice have called it a Russian festival.' This comment of Luethy's is perhaps surprising in view of the wide range of nationalities represented, and his own observation that one-third of the composers featured were French (this was a matter of 'politeness rather than merit', he adds). Nonetheless the claim is made, not perhaps entirely convincingly, that the proceedings of May 1952 were dominated by the legacy of Diaghilev. Certainly, Luethy is able to make a number of connections: Stravinsky, of course, with a concert performance of *Rite of Spring* and the New York City Ballet dancing the *Firebird* with Chagall's original décor; Prokofiev's *Prodigal Son*, with Roualt's original sets; Balanchine, Diaghilev's protegée, and not forgetting Nabokov himself, whose first success came when the Ballets Russes presented his *Ode*. All in all, Luethy suggests, this was a 'rearguard' festival, a thing of nostalgia for the Parisian 'good old days', a 'museum of masterpieces' whose very graphic identity (an image uniting a lyre, olive branch and star) embodies an 'obsolete "1900" symbolism'.

Certainly when viewed today, in terms of the conventional wisdom of current music history, much of this rings true. For all its inclusion of the key early modernists (Debussy, Bartók, Stravinsky, Schoenberg), the second Viennese School (Berg, Webern), as well as the more maverick figures important to later experimentalists (Ives, Varèse, Messiaen, Satie) and even a key postwar radical, Boulez, there is perhaps too much that runs 'against the grain' of twentieth-century music, at least in so far as this is generally perceived. All of which is not to suggest that anyone staging a musical event in 1952 could be expected to choose only what is *later* judged to be significant, especially someone whose avowed aim was unashamedly to take stock of the first half-century rather than indicate the likely course of the second. Nonetheless, here is one contemporary observer who clearly felt that the proceedings were too backward-looking, and what we know of the organiser's own tastes may lend weight to this view. Nabokov's admiration for Stravinsky – both the man and his music – was reflected in the performance of nine of his works in Paris and the presence of the composer himself, who conducted five (next came Ravel, with five performances, followed by Bartók and Debussy with four apiece). This took place just at the point when influence, among the younger generation of composers, was shifting decisively away from neoclassicism and towards the twelve-tone school, and especially Webern (two pieces). Nabokov, however, could not follow even his most admired friend

---

14   Luethy notes wearily that '*Elle* had devoted a whole number to the question: "How to dress for the Festival of the 20th Century?" '

Stravinsky into the serial universe. Two years later, when Nabokov was organising his 'Music in the Twentieth Century' festival in Rome (co-sponsored by the CCF), Stravinsky would once more take a high profile. At this point, an acrimonious falling-out occurred between Pierre Boulez and Nabokov: in an astonishingly colourful and acidic letter Boulez damned the whole enterprise, chiefly on account of its competitive element (see Chapter 8). It is worth speculating whether a conflict of taste – Boulez the radical against Nabokov the conservative (and, perhaps gallingly, a conservative who could evidently command substantial resources) may have contributed to this quarrel.

In retrospect

If even politically well-disposed contemporary critics saw the enterprise as worthy but misguided, posterity has hardly been kinder. Indeed, few have paused to consider it at all. By the early 1960s there had been four festivals: Rome was followed in 1958 by the Venice conference on 'Tradition and Change in Music', and then by the large-scale Tokyo 'East–West Music Encounter' of 1961 (plans for a later festival in Rio de Janeiro came to nothing[15]). In addition, as we shall see, the CCF had assisted the exiles Enescu and Panufnik, contributed towards Igor Markevitch's Salzburg-based 'Mozarteum' youth orchestra project, and played a major role in setting up the Philharmonia Hungarica after the 1956 revolution. Consider for a moment: the secret service of the world's largest superpower covertly funded a series of festivals and conferences attended by some of the leading composers, performers and academics of the day, deploying art music in pursuit of its own geopolitical objectives. This is surely a remarkable cultural–political undertaking, and yet one searches musical scholarship in vain for even the briefest reference to it. The Congress's musical work was perhaps most notably overlooked by Arnold Perris in his *Music as Propaganda: Art to Persuade, Art to Control* of 1985.[16] Perris devotes a chapter each to the regimes of Stalin, Hitler and Mao, as well as one to 'The Contemporary Composer as Social Critic' but leaves the Congress entirely untouched – an extraordinary omission. Other writers who touch more briefly on 'music and politics' cover the same restricted ground – generally the Soviet situation on the one hand, and Western Marxist composers on the other. This leads, by a process of steady accretion, to the impression

---

15   In 1961 Nabokov visited Rio, confidently expecting to stage a festival there: this was not to be primarily Western classical music-based, but a triangular 'rencontre noir' between the cultures of Africa, North and South America. This was partly in line with the interests that had led to the 'East–West Musical Encounter' of that year, and would surface later in Berlin, and partly to circumvent the inevitable criticisms of 'no Soviet involvement'. Nonetheless, by this stage, experience suggested that opposition was to be expected, 'except that here it will probably be more vociferous and more violent' (letter to John Hunt, 13 November 1961).

16   Reviewing the book, Joseph Blum found that 'the focus is further narrowed by the author's willingness to accept the most banal popular stereotypes ... I can only conclude that [he] is unaware of how one-sided his ideas appear in print' (Blum, 1988, pp. 152–3).

that the political use of music, in the postwar world at least, is a thing uniquely of the Left.

And yet, we have seen that the political rationale for the Paris festival was absolutely public and unabashed (except for the issue of the USA's cultural elevation, which *was* largely tacit); we know that much of the ensuing frank debate centred precisely on questions of music and propaganda; and we know that the role of the CIA in the Congress had been public knowledge – at least in broad outline – for over 30 years. Finally, Nabokov himself, however marginal in terms of his role as composer, had a considerable profile within the world of music (and beyond), being well-connected to a degree that is hard to overstate. His next career move, to the Berliner Festwochen in 1963 – another highly charged political context after the building of the Berlin Wall two years before – only increased this visibility. Scholarly neglect is indeed surprising.

Away from music, the publication in 1989 of Peter Coleman's *The Liberal Conspiracy: The Congress for Cultural Freedom and the Struggle for the Mind of Postwar Europe* caused a small flurry of comment. Coleman himself devotes little space to the arts side of the Congress's work, commenting only that whilst Nabokov may have been 'more an impresario than an intellectual' (Coleman, 1989, p. 44), the 1952 festival nonetheless put the CCF 'on the map'. Reviewers were divided in their views of Nabokov and his festivals. William Phillips, one of *Partisan Review*'s founders and co-editor with Philip Rahv from 1946–55, took a negative view which, as we shall see, matches the contemporary objections of *Partisan Review* and the ACCF. Ultimately he dismisses the CCF as:

> ... a bureaucratic enterprise pretending to be an intellectual one. I was particularly put off by a musical event created by transporting the Boston Symphony Orchestra to Paris at a cost, it was rumoured, of half a million dollars. It was made fun of by the French, who described it as the greatest Parisian couturier's ball. ... so much money was wasted on this impresario's dream ... inspired by Nabokov, himself a composer. (Phillips, 1990, p. 11)

He does, however, concede that, in retrospect, *something* like the CCF – with all its faults – was necessary to counter the real influence of the communists, especially in Paris, and especially at that time. *The New Leader*'s John P. Roche, however, returns to the basic point:

> Nicolas Nabokov suggested that the Congress organise cultural fetes to convince the European masses that Western culture was superior to Stalinist and thereby wean them away from the huge French and Italian Communist parties ... This struck me as hilarious. ... (Roche, 1989, p. 19)

This is a little disingenuous. The project is surely less derisory when one appreciates – as Roche surely must have done – that the target audience was decidedly *not* the 'masses', but rather the European intelligentsia. In contrast, John Muggeridge, whose father Malcolm had been a CCF supporter, whilst not commending the specifics of the policy, nonetheless suggests the larger scheme was timely and right. 'The greatest virtue of the Cold War', he wrote in *The American Spectator*, was that:

... it turned ... [the] obligation to innovate into a patriotic duty. By 1945, with atom bombs exploding, concentration camps giving up their ghastly secrets, and avant-gardes having nowhere else to advance but to nihilism, the whole modernist-progressivist project of the last two hundred years seemed to be in jeopardy .... Then, providentially, an international crisis arose which necessitated renewed commitment to modernity and progress in the name of saving Western civilisation. (Muggeridge, 1990, p. 35)

It is left to music critic Samuel Lipman to offer a rare positive assessment of the 1952 festival itself. Coleman, Lipman argues, unfairly neglects the artistic aspects of the CCF in favour of the political and the interpersonal; however, from what he *does* say, we may infer that he is of the same mind as:

... those figures, like Hook and Koestler, who found literary and artistic endeavours a waste of time because they had no immediate political payoff. But another judgement is possible. This writer ... attended the Paris Festival, and found in the performance of music by, among many others, Stravinsky, Shostakovich and Prokofiev, a synoptic refutation of the Soviet dictatorship that wished these works buried. (Lipman, 1989, p. 64)[17]

And the CIA: did they feel their money – $166,359 just to pay for the Boston Symphony, according to Stonor Saunders – had been well spent? This is still unclear, though one important source, in his public statements, has tended to defend the undertaking. Tom Braden, as the first head of the CIA's International Operations Division, was charged with overseeing the activities of Congress. If the disclosures of 1966 caused profound dismay among at least some of the CCF's former supporters, this was only aggravated by the appearance, in the spring of the following year, of an article in the *Saturday Evening Post* entitled 'I'm glad the CIA is "immoral"'. The author? Thomas W. Braden. He describes how the Division was formed in response to the success of the various communist 'front' organisations. Through the successful use of fronts the Soviets had 'stolen the great words' ('Peace, Freedom and Justice'), had thrown a 'great spell' over many of the world's intellectuals, and were generally securing the services of many who would not knowingly have supported the Kremlin. When Braden set out to describe the 'solid accomplishments' of the first three years' work, he began thus: 'I remember the great joy I got when the Boston Symphony Orchestra won more acclaim for the US in Paris than John Foster Dulles or Dwight D. Eisenhower could have bought with a hundred speeches' (Braden, 1967, p. 12). The significance of this example is not just that Braden offers it – presumably to prove that an expensive and covert operation was money well spent – but that *it is the first example he gives*. It seems hardly likely that Braden would have opened with this if he considered the arts festivals to have been an irrelevant waste of money. Also interesting is the favourable comparison of arts festivals with political speech-making: we may recall Nabokov's use of the same device in his 1951 letters to Schlesinger and Burnham. Nabokov claimed not to have known of the CIA funding, and yet we find that he and the CIA chief responsible share the same phraseology on

---

17   Symptomatic of Coleman's disinterest in the arts, Lipman suggests, is his tendency towards factual error, for example, the translation of Pierre Monteux and Charles Munch into composers, and the mis-spelling of Virgil Thomson's name.

this important issue. This is interesting but inconclusive, as one could propose several possible explanations. Was the phrase passed down the line, as it were, from Braden via the Agency's CCF agent Michael Josselson, to Nabokov, who adopted it as his own? Or was it a phrase devised and habitually used by the secretary-general, in the course of arguing the case for the Paris festival, which worked its way back to Langley and stuck in Braden's mind? All we can do is note that a certain phraseology employed by Nabokov to sell the idea of arts festivals, was used 16 years later by the CIA chief responsible for funding those festivals to justify the project. At the very least, it seems that the CIA was not dismayed.

Much more recently, Braden has resurfaced to fill out his views on the whole affair. In a TV interview in 1995 he argued for the operation in very familiar terms. On the one hand, the operation had genuine cultural objectives in terms of the aesthetic danger of totalitarianism: 'the idea that the world would succumb to a kind of fascist or Stalinist concept of art and literature, music, that this was to be the wave of the future ... if you look back on it, even now it's a horrifying concept.'[18] And, he claimed, highlighting the cultural threat of communism could only be good, politically:

> We wanted to unite all those people who were writers, who were musicians, who were artists, and all the people who follow those people ... to demonstrate that the West and the USA was devoted to freedom of expression and intellectual achievement without any rigid barriers as to what you must write and what you must say and what you must paint – which was what was going on in the Soviet Union.

And he added: 'I think we did it damn well.'

---

18   Braden, Thomas, interviewed in *Art and the CIA*, directed by Frances Stonor Saunders (Fulmar Television for Channel Four, 1995).

Chapter 5

Filling the Gap: The CCF as Surrogate Ministry of Culture

In the eyes of intellectuals and artists in the US and abroad, Washington has been for a long time the center of political power and not the symbol or the home of artists and intellectuals. In other words, in America and all over the world there was a feeling of alienation of the cultural community from Washington and from the White House. ... (Letter to Jackie Kennedy, 23 February 1961)

Nabokov's 1961 letter to Jackie Kennedy succinctly expresses the conviction underlying a major aspect of CCF strategy: namely, that the USA was widely perceived, at best, as insufficiently committed to legitimate culture and, at worst, as the prime source of cultural corrosion. He goes on to suggest something like an informal honours system – a way of conferring presidential approval for outstanding intellectual or artistic achievement – thus sending a message to this community that 'the White House is a cultural center concerned with the life of the mind and the arts, and that in fact it is their home where they are appreciated, invited and honoured'. The following year his suggestion – this time, made through the good offices of Arthur Schlesinger Jr – was more specific: that the president and Mrs Kennedy should host an anniversary dinner for Stravinsky – which they did (Nabokov, 1975, p. 178).[1]

The date of Nabokov's appeal is significant: February 1961, a mere month after Kennedy's arrival in office. Perhaps sharing the perception of 'most intellectuals ... [who] wanted to believe that Kennedy cared deeply and thought profoundly about the cultural life of the nation' (Lasch, 1965, p. 312).[2] Nabokov had apparently moved quickly to capitalise on the possibilities of the new era. However, if the prospects for changing the image of the USA appeared brighter at the dawn of Camelot, this task in itself was nothing new to the secretary-general of the Congress for Cultural Freedom. In practice, the aim of changing perceptions of the USA had been closely tied into the CCF project from the outset, and the record shows that Nabokov believed music –

---

1   Robert Craft's account of the dinner can be found in Craft, (1972), pp. 150–2. Of the birthday toast offered to Stravinsky by the President, Craft writes that 'the speech is short and, because an American President is honoring a great *creative* artist – an event unprecedented in history – it is moving' (Craft's emphasis).

2   No evidence was found in either the Nabokov or IACF papers of a similar appeal to the previous residents of the White House.

particularly in the form of the great American symphony orchestras – could represent a powerful weapon in this struggle.[3]

CIA chief Tom Braden's glowing praise of the acclaim 'won for the US' by the Boston Symphony Orchestra has already been noted. Nabokov himself had put the case quite explicitly to H.E. Cabot, President of the Board of Trustees of the orchestra, in the course of securing their participation in 'Masterpieces of the XXth Century':

> I may assure you that the frame works [*sic*] in which the Boston Symphony Orchestra will appear will be of the most imposing ones [*sic*] for the Festival which we are planning has the idea of presenting to Europe the highest achievements of American art. (Letter to H.E. Cabot, 27 June 1951)[4]

Much the same argument was presented the following year when Nabokov and Michael Josselson (the CCF's executive director – and CIA agent) suggested to Fleischmann that the Farfield Foundation might fund a European tour in 1954 by the Philadelphia Orchestra under Eugene Ormandy. Nabokov wrote:

> I firmly believe that a tour of a first-rate American orchestra in Europe *does more towards American prestige* and the cementing of friendly transatlantic relations *than any other artistic event of its kind*. (Letter to Fleischmann, 22 May 1953, my emphasis)[5]

Similar thinking is presented in a letter to the (US) National Music Council on the subject of the Paris festival, but with the important rider that European sensitivities – the danger of inflaming anti-Americanism – require the American component to be kept within bounds. After listing the 'native American' composers included in the programme for May – Copland, Barber, Piston, Thomson, Schuman and Ives (not to mention those who are 'American by adoption') – the letter continues:

> One of our aims is to bring about a better understanding between American and European culture, and in order to achieve this we have had to limit the American participation in the Festival to the works of the composers mentioned above, in order not to give the impression here that we are trying to impose something which the Europeans do not want. All this is a matter of tact ... (Letter to NMC executive secretary, 25 February 1952)

---

3   This reflects the view that the USA had become – in the words of the critic David Ewen – 'the musical center of the world.' Quoted in Horowitz (1987), p. 253.

4   Nabokov was in no doubt about the quality of the orchestra: 'it was one of the most perfect symphonic ensembles ever put together; an instrument of extraordinary beauty and precision, the result of careful selection, daily practice and decades of a tradition of stringent discipline' (Nabokov, 1951d, p. 188).

5   A second letter, of 9 June, adds that whilst Josselson had previously considered that the CCF should *not* be mentioned in connection with the tour, further discussion had produced agreement that a Congress-sponsored tour – to Holland, Germany, Italy and Austria – should indeed take place. In the event, Fleischmann's reply – rejecting the idea – was already on the way to Paris (dated 8 June). All letters in IACF. It is interesting to note in passing that Nabokov the composer had connections with both the orchestras he turned to as the CCF began its cultural campaign: Koussevitsky had commissioned *La Vita Nuova* and *The Return of Pushkin* for the Boston, whilst *Studies in Solitude* was produced for Ormandy and the Philadelphia. See Nabokov (1975, p. 234).

What emerges from these letters, especially if taken together with the *internal* rationale, as discussed in the last chapter, is that we can see Nabokov presenting different parties with different justifications for the Congress's musical activities. Not in themselves contradictory, these accounts nonetheless demonstrate a highlighting of one or other part of the overall rationale at the expense of the rest. So, whilst, internally, the promotion of American high culture is acknowledged as one aim among others in the Paris festival Progress Report of December 1951 (Nabokov, 1951e, p. 7),[6] in correspondence with Cabot this is the only part of the rationale that appears (and note also the flattering tone of the extract). Again, when arguing the case with Josselson and Fleischmann that the Farfield (in effect, the CIA, as we now know) should support an orchestral tour, this is the part of the argument than Nabokov draws on – but now with an important addition. Here, 'presenting the highest achievements of American art' does not close the matter, it is, rather, the means to a larger political end – the increase of American prestige and an improvement in transatlantic relations. For the National Music Council, American *composers* are the major issue, but, again, with no mention of any extra-musical scheme.

Politics, then, seems to be reduced to the issue of promoting the USA in Nabokov's correspondence with musical institutions, and yet, in truth, politics are rarely mentioned at all in his negotiations with artists and orchestras towards the various festivals. This might seem to lend weight to those voices – found not only among his contemporary detractors in New York – suggesting that the whole supposed political framework for this activity was bogus, little more than a window-dressing required to facilitate his own pet projects. Hugh Wilford, in *The New York Intellectuals: From Vanguard to Institution*, acknowledges that the theory espoused by Paris – that is, that 'cultural' activity offered better prospects than a head-on political approach – was 'based on a realistic assessment of the intellectual mood in Europe and further afield'. He goes on to argue that, in practice: 'it also provided a convenient excuse for European NCL (Non-Communist Left) intellectuals to spend CCF monies on cultural projects that did not possess much relevance to the political conflict between the U.S. and the USSR' (Wilford, 1995, pp. 208–9). Even a close and valued friend of Nabokov's – Isaiah Berlin – has cast doubt on the festivals' political dimension, stating that any such rationale must be seen as 'artificial' (Berlin's view of the enterprise was not, however, without approval, as we shall see below). Whilst acknowledging the force of Berlin's evidence in itself – coming as it does from a source friendly to both Nabokov and the CCF – the broadly non-political nature of the musical correspondence does not, in my view, lend it convincing support. It seems, rather, to call to mind Peter Coleman's description of Nabokov as the *impresario* – trimming his phrases to fit the needs of the moment, offering whatever arguments and flattery are required 'to get the show on the road'. Berlin aside, those of his opponents whose natural milieu was not the performing arts (and the New York Intellectuals – a locus of criticism in the CCF's American affiliate – were largely a literary and

---

6   It is probably not without significance that this is the *last* of the reasons listed: Nabokov would have known that the ACCF, whilst not unsympathetic to the idea of boosting US prestige and promoting its cultural achievements, needed a more directly anti-communist rationale. Despite this, they remained sceptical, at best.

political group, as the next chapter will show), may have taken this somewhat slick, salesman-like quality – not to mention the charm, the ease with stories, the evident delight in the company of the rich and celebrated – as evidence of insincerity. Equally, these very social and entrepreneurial skills may have been exactly what Michael Josselson (and the Congress's secret service sponsors) considered was needed to facilitate the political work. Indeed, Nabokov's continued occupation of his post suggests just that.

The 'musical correspondence' tended, if anything, to highlight the promotion of American culture at the expense of the sharper arguments about freedom and totalitarianism, but in more public settings the position was reversed. Research in the Nabokov and IACF papers has produced only one example of his broaching the former issue in public, in a February 1952 speech to the Anglo-American Press Club in Paris (Nabokov, 1952c, unpublished). Following on from a statement of the basic public justification for 'Masterpieces', Nabokov argues that 'this will be the first positive effort by the West to answer the growing weight of propaganda which has been directed against our decadent, degenerate, "cosmopolitan" culture'. Significantly, whilst the reference is to 'the West', the principal examples produced to refute the charge are 'American':

> We shall present to European audiences for the first time the Boston Symphony Orchestra ... which, in the so-called 'uncultured' United States, plays 47 weeks of concerts each year ... also the New York City Ballet of George Balanchine (and Lincoln Kirstein), a native American ballet which was born and grew up in the City of New York ... consisting almost entirely of native American born dancers ... we also hope to be able to present the remarkable opera of Virgil Thomson and Gertrude Stein, written here in Paris during their famous collaboration ... and to be performed here ... by an all negro cast – 'Four Saints in Three Acts.' (Nabokov, 1952c, unpublished)

Having presented as the prime evidence for the 'defence' three transatlantic imports, Nabokov hastily adds 'But this is far from being an American show. Our part in the exposition will be small when compared with the contributions from other countries', and goes on to cite specifically the Covent Garden *Billy Budd*, the Wiener Staatsoper *Wozzeck*, the Hallé with Barbirolli and the Sheffield Chorus, and – rump of the proposed 'dramatic program' – 'a series of dramatic readings [by] a selected group of English and French stage personalities' (of which only the operas would survive into May). Nabokov's dilemma is revealed starkly: on the one hand, the Congress intended to amend what it considered European misconceptions of American life and culture (and in truth, the polarised Cold War atmosphere made this essential if support for communism was to be reduced); on the other hand, to stand revealed as American propagandists would fatally weaken an organisation the very foundation of whose appeal was its purported independence. And so, within a single speech we find Nabokov's instincts leading him to offer a specifically *American* defence against the attacks on Western culture, whilst having – almost in the same breath – to deny that the festival will be an 'American show'. If the CCF was to achieve anything, its assertion of autonomy – intellectual, financial and institutional – had to be credible: Nabokov wrote in 1951 that 'constant efforts should be directed towards proving to European intellectuals that the CCF is ... not an American secret service agency' (letter to James Burnham, 6 June 1951). In the Cold War climate, however, this requirement conflicted massively with the goal of elevating the cultural image of the USA, and in fact it is clear that the Congress *was* widely perceived as having official American links *of some sort*, whatever its protestations to the contrary.

Isaiah Berlin believed that the CCF festivals were able to 'present America in a liberal and cultural light',[7] and there is some evidence that the pursuit of this goal involved something more then merely ensuring a significant US presence – that, in fact, at least some of the *detail* of the programme's American element was considered with this end in view. The example of Virgil Thomson's *Four Saints in Three Acts*, performed in Paris by the American National Theater and Academy, is illuminating. The USA's treatment of its black population, especially in the South, represented a real Achilles' heel in its cultural Cold War – a vulnerable point on which it was frequently attacked by just the liberal-left intelligentsia the CCF sought to influence. The Paris festival was no exception: Herbert Luethy, referring to a *Combat* editorial on the 'Festival of NATO', remarked (rather too dismissively, we may feel) that 'of course, much reference was made to poorly educated barbarians from Alabama and Idaho, and to lynched Negroes in the South' (Luethy, 1952, p. 74).

Against this background Thomson's *Four Saints*, if performed as originally intended with an all-black cast, could have an importance beyond its purely musical and dramatic virtues. In November 1951 Albert Donnelly (who, as festival secretary, assisted Nabokov) wrote revealingly to Fleischmann. After proposing 'a certain negro singer', Leontyne Price, for the cast,[8] he continues:

There is a strong feeling that for psychological reasons the entire cast of *Four Saints* should be American Negro: to counter the 'suppressed race' propaganda and forestall all criticism to the effect that we had to use foreign negroes because we wouldn't let our own 'out'. The case for a 100% American *Four Saints* is very strong, I think. (Letter from Donnelly to Fleischmann, 15 November 1951)[9]

---

7   Sir Isaiah Berlin, interviewed by the author, 11 June 1997.

8   Price was a special favourite of Nabokov's. He had already been arguing her case to Thomson himself, writing 'Please don't forget my little negro girl Leontyne Price. She can sing much better than she did the other day ...' Letter from Nicolas Nabokov to Virgil Thomson dated 18 October 1951. IACF.

9   At the 1950 Congress the CCF had also seemed more concerned with countering 'suppressed race propaganda' than with the reality of life for blacks in America's South. Two papers had been delivered in Berlin on just this issue, one – by a George Schuyler – entitled 'The Negro Question without Propaganda'. This extract gives a little of the flavour: 'In the vicious propaganda campaign of lies and distortions to which ungrateful totalitarian slave states have subjected the United States of America (which saved them from Hitler), the treatment of its Negro citizens has been held up as a horrible illustration of the weaknesses and failures of democracy ... Actually, the progressive improvement of interracial relations in the United States is the most flattering of the many examples of the superiority of the free American civilisation over the soul-shackling reactionism of totalitarian regimes.' All this on the eve of the Civil Rights era. Typed manuscript, IACF.

Another instance of political factors weighing in on details of programming is provided by a letter of January 1952 from Nabokov to Leopold Stokowski. Nabokov hoped that Stokowski would agree to conduct the closing concert of the festival. After stressing that every aspect of the festival is 'part of a carefully worked out whole,' he adds that 'what I chiefly wanted to avoid is that this last concert should become a vehicle for anything which might be interpreted as American propaganda.' This means that care must be taken not to include little-known US composers lest this give rise to charges of favouritism, and Nabokov rejects the idea of commissioning one Hall Johnson on this basis. As for Randall Thomson and Howard Hanson: 'Neither of [these] ... are very well known here, and when known, ... not as pioneering spirits in the domain of contemporary music' (letter to Stokowski, 25 January 1952, p. 1). In terms of the festival's purposes, Stokowski would be better advised to choose from the works of Yves (*sic*), Thomson, Harris, Schuman, Barber or Copland and, if the latter, Nabokov suggests that 'in the light of what I said before' (presumably about avoiding the propaganda charge) he would prefer *El Salón Mexico* to the *Lincoln Portrait*.

On the same issue – maintaining the appearance of autonomy – external relations were even more important than details of programming: in particular it was crucial for the CCF's purposes that it should have no apparent links to the US government or official agencies. In 1952 the Boston Symphony Orchestra was due to undertake a German tour following on from its appearance in Paris, funded by the US High Command in Germany (HICOG). Nabokov writes to Shepard Stone, of that organisation, that this tour:

> ... should be announced under the auspices of HICOG, and that the name of the CCF, for reasons understandable to you, should not be used in connection with HICOG ... we believe it would be advisable to say that the orchestra is coming [to Europe] under the auspices of the Congress but that the German tour is entirely under the auspices of HICOG. (Letter to Stone, 13 February 1952)[10]

All of which is not to say that the military could be of *no* assistance and, indeed, in December 1951 we find the organiser of the 'Festival of NATO' writing to NATO itself. Interestingly, the CCF here is described, unusually, as 'an organisation of anti-Communist intellectuals' rather than – less specifically but more positively – an organisation formed to defend and promote freedom. The phrase 'anti-Communist', with its right-wing associations, was generally avoided by Nabokov and used sparingly by the organisation as a whole, since the Congress, as Peter Coleman has described it, 'felt itself to be of the Left and on the Left' (Coleman, 1989, p. 12) and certainly wished to speak *to* the Left. Nabokov hoped that NATO might agree to pay the costs of artists coming from within its area; in addition, the organisation could perhaps use its influence to help obtain funding and the best artists. He adds:

---

10   An indication of the exchange of personnel in this area is given by the fact that Stone would later head the Congress after the 1966 'disclosures' and the name change to the International Association for Cultural Freedom.

You will understand that because of its political implications such a project cannot be allowed to become 2nd rate. To do so would be to put into the hands of the Communists a new propaganda weapon which they could be counted upon to exploit. (Letter to Parsons Jr, 28 December 1951)

NATO's response is not known.

The CCF as surrogate Ministry of Culture

The perceived relationship of Congress to the USA was merely problematic during the years of its greatest activity and influence: ultimately, after the 1966 disclosures established the fact of CIA funding, it was to be fatal. But whilst the CCF's enemies saw it confirmed as an arm of the CIA, one strategy open to supporters was to acknowledge that, whilst it may have been acting on behalf of, and in the interests of, the US government, it should more accurately be seen as an American Ministry of Culture, something which would have been politically impossible to establish openly. As such, they argued, its purpose was benign: if criticism was due, this should be directed towards those Congressmen whose antideluvian attitudes towards modern art made the subterfuge necessary.[11]

This was the view taken by Nabokov's friend Isaiah Berlin – namely, that the Congress was merely doing for the USA what the British Council did for the UK. For those of like mind, the real source of the funding (which may have been suspected for many years) was immaterial: the CCF was simply undertaking good works on behalf of the USA, which the democratic log-jam on Capitol Hill did not allow; that the CIA made this possible is evidence not of perfidy but of wisdom. Yehudi Menuhin, another friend of both Nabokov and his organisation, anticipated this view when he agreed in 1961 to sign a letter rebutting allegations about its funding, adding that 'as a matter of fact, I would think much more of the CIA if it did associate with "people like us" '.[12] Likewise, six years later, when the facts were no longer in dispute, George Kennan, the highly influential diplomat and Soviet specialist (and another old friend of Nabokov's dating back to the agreeable Bohlen soirées of the early 1940s) would write that 'the flap about CIA money was quite unwarranted ... This country has no

---

11   An alternative defence was that the fact of CIA *funding* should not be equated with CIA *control*: in short, that the intellectuals of the CCF did nothing that they would not have done anyway, that secret service patronage merely allowed them to do it more easily and more often. This is also the position taken by Hugh Wilford, a historian broadly sympathetic to the 'New York Intellectuals' who made up the core of the CCF's American affiliate. For Wilford, the question is: 'academic ... The important point is that the Intellectuals recognised the Cultural Cold War as *their* cause ... the principle on which the American propaganda effort was founded, that is cultural freedom, was exactly the one they themselves had been defending ever since the 1930s' (Wilford, 1995, p. 199).

12   Yehudi Menuhin to unknown respondent, dated 14 May 1961. IACF. The 'people like us' are presumably the liberal, centre-left constituency of the CCF, but perhaps Menuhin also had in mind the artistic community.

ministry of culture, and [the] CIA was obliged to do what it could to try and fill the gap' (letter, Kennan to Stone, 9 November 1967).

Samuel Lipman's 1989 defence of the Paris festival gave some of the background to this case: 'It was a time', he wrote, 'when it seemed at least plausible to associate intellectual activity itself with the Communist threat' (Lipman, 1989, p. 14). Ten years later, at the time of Nabokov's letter to Jackie Kennedy, sociologists were beginning to document a transformation in American public attitudes to the intelligentsia, so that, as Christopher Lasch argues, Kennedy's projection of himself as an intellectual surrounded by intellectuals was astute. In the McCarthyite 1950s, however, things had been different: 'The intellectual's cosmopolitanism [seemed] ... un-American, his sophistication snobbery, his accent affectation, his clothes and his manner the badge, obscurely, of sexual deviation ...' (Lasch, 1965, p. 314). In this general atmosphere, and with Senator Dondero's noisy public campaign against abstract art, the point of covert support was more to deceive the US Congress than the beneficiaries, Lipman suggests, recalling 'many musicians associated with the 1952 Nabokov festival quite confidently ascribing this funding to the US State Department'.

Towards the end of the Eisenhower decade, the sociologist and CCF supporter Edward Shils argued that conditions in the USA did indeed present special difficulties for intellectual life and what he termed 'superior' or 'refined culture'. In his view, whilst one can overstate the intellectualism of European ruling elites, it remains true that in the UK, France, Germany or Italy the aristocratic, patrician element provides 'an external gloss of intimacy with high culture'. By contrast, 'the political elite [of the US] gives a preponderant impression of indifference toward works of superior culture' (Shils, 1964, p. 10).[13] The economic elite is scarcely any better, the great collectors notwithstanding. Seeking to account for this, Shils calls special attention to the Puritan legacy of hostility against 'self-indulgent' artistic expression, and a certain 'provincial' distrust of (high) culture as inherently suspect because of its associations with an anglophile upper class. This is one symptom of a divide between 'newer' and 'older' Americans, and the difficulties it creates for cultural life are, if anything, exacerbated by political and economic elites who 'feel little obligation to assume a veneer of refined culture' (Shils, 1964, p. 21). Shils's views were given some support by the historian Richard Hofstader, who argued, in 1962, that American attitudes were founded on a perceived opposition between intellectuals who were:

> ... effete, impractical, artificial, arrogant, obeisant to European models of learning and manners ... [and those following other] long-standing American mores ... [such as] pragmatism, efficiency, masculinity, spontaneity, unpretentiousness, restless energy [and] quick decisiveness. (Horowitz, 1987, p. 250)

---

13   Note: the original seminar on which the book was based was held in June 1959. This seminar and the associated collection of papers features a number of key 'liberal anti-communists' from the CCF orbit, notably Irving Kristol, Sidney Hook, Hannah Arendt, Daniel Bell and Arthur Schlesinger Jr. Arthur Berger (one of the founding editors of *Perspectives of New Music*) also spoke on 'the plight of the American composer'.

The background to the idea of the CCF as a surrogate US ministry of culture can be summarised as follows: American art was not only first-rate but possessed of a real political potential;[14] this potential, however, could only be realised by side-stepping American prejudices which could be found in a concentrated form in some elements of the legislature. The key players – Nabokov, Josselson and Braden – would in fact go on to offer retrospective defences in very much these terms. Nabokov's autobiographical treatment of the Congess period is disappointingly sketchy (his later idea for a book – *Les Riches Heures du CIA* – came to nothing[15]), but in dealing with the scandal that broke over it in the mid-1960s he bemoans what he sees as the lack of imagination and courage that led to 'puny' and 'unwilling' federal arts funding, and prevented the job being done *openly* – as 'a kind of Marshall Plan in the domain of the intellect and the arts' (Nabokov, 1975, pp. 243–6). Josselson and Braden also defend the CCF, although one can discern something of the conflict – inherent, perhaps – in the idea of a culture ministry – the conflict between political and purely artistic ends. Defending the CCF's tarnished legacy to a dismayed Stephen Spender, Josselson writes:

> We can all deplore that there has never been, and is not now, and is not even in the offing an American ministry of culture … in the absence of such a body, or of sufficient European or American sources of funds, the alternatives then, as you know, were to do nothing or take the money and do freely what we felt was right with it. (Letter, Josselson to Spender, 23 April 1967)

And 'what was right' involved more than just shabby *realpolitik*:

> When the Congress supported arts festivals, from *Masterpieces of the XXth Century* to the festival in India with Yehudi Menuhin – do you think that this was just some kind of window-dressing? … Into these and other like activities the Congress put all its money, and nobody can say that this was done for American propaganda. (Ibid.)

Shortly afterwards, Tom Braden began on similar lines, arguing that 'back in the early 1950s, when the cold war was really hot', open funding had simply not been an option, since 'the idea that Congress would have approved many of our projects was about as likely as the John Birch Society's approving Medicare' (Braden, 1967). Braden, as we have seen, professed concern at the implications *for art* of the 'Stalinist concept', the dire aesthetic threat which the CCF helped confront; equally, and as one would expect from the man who had to win Agency support for an ambitious, innovative and expensive programme, he is not afraid to talk straightforwardly in terms of propaganda value. Thus, from his 1995 interview:

---

14   According to Hugh Wilford, this is the key to understanding an 'American cultural cold war effort [which] valorised the cultural over the political and the high over the popular' (Wilford, 1994).

15   In a letter to Nabokov dated 21 December 1976 Isaiah Berlin advised against this. NN.

It's very easy to talk about culture, but talk about culture doesn't really have an influence on the public. For example, the CIA paid for the Boston Symphony Orchestra to go over to Europe and make a tour, and I think that the Boston Symphony – the impact of that tour, the people who said 'Heavens! the Americans, *look what they do!*' – the impact was much stronger than four presidential speeches by Dwight D. Eisenhower about culture and democracy. (My emphasis)[16]

One senses that, for Braden, this is indeed a straightforward matter, that the goals of art and the USA were, and still are, congruent. On the basis of the available evidence there is every reason to suppose that, for Braden, supporting freedom of artistic expression was identical to supporting the USA. Others, in 1966 and after, have been less sure.

The case of France

Internal CCF documents, together with the records of Nabokov's private correspondence, show that the CCF's cultural strategy (within which music was of particular importance) was not merely pro-'freedom' and anti-'totalitarian', but intentionally and actively pro-American. At the same time, the organisation was faced with the impossible task of improving the image of the USA whilst appearing to be politically independent. The problems facing the Congress's strategy, however (and we have seen that some contemporary observers had grave doubts over its political wisdom), were a function not only of its own contradictions, but of the social, political, and cultural context(s) into which it was launched, and any assessment of that strategy must consider the latter. Partly for the sake of containment (to invoke an appropriate Cold War term) in the face of what was a major international operation, the present study must work within some self-imposed limits. The situation in France was seen as particularly alarming within Washington foreign policy circles, leading directly to the establishment of the CCF office in Paris and the opening 'big bang' to which we have given so much space, France has, therefore, a special claim to our attention. There is no doubt that Nabokov shared this perception of a particular 'French problem.' In a 1951 article surveying the European music scene, he identifies a mixture of fear and ignorance in European intellectuals' attitudes to America: fear of losing their cultural pre-eminence, and an ignorance typified by the French, who have:

> ... a frozen image of the United States based on a set of worn-out symbols of the early 1920s. America is still to them the land of skyscrapers, gangsters and the 'Revue Negre' .... Their incomplete or incorrect image has been formed by biased reports, by irresponsible journalism, and, last but not least, by anti-American Communist propaganda. (Nabokov, 1951b, p. 58)

---

16   Braden, Thomas, interviewed in *Art and the CIA*, directed by Frances Stonor Saunders (Fulmar Television for Channel Four, 1995). Note, once again, the appearance of this 'speeches' device, which has now featured in two letters by Nabokov in 1951, in Braden's 1967 article and in his 1995 interview.

Equally, there is little doubt that Nabokov and Josselson saw an arts festival such as 'Masterpieces of the XXth Century' as a political weapon ideally suited to the French context. After the festival, Nabokov wrote to Sidney Hook of the ACCF:

> Yes, I think despite what it may have looked like to people reading the French press, the festival was a psychological success in the complex and depressingly morbid intellectual climate of France. Of course, in any other country we would have had a finer press reaction ... . I still believe it was the *only* kind of action we could have taken here in Paris which would have established the Congress as a positive, and not only a political, organization. (Coleman, 1989, pp. 56–7, my italics)

France, then, was seen as representing an especially severe case of a Europe-wide disease, and if France was bad, Paris – the 'world capital of fellow-travellers' – was worse. The phrase belongs to Peter Coleman, historian of the CCF, who added Arthur Koestler's comment that, from Paris, 'the Communist Party could take over France with one telephone call' (Coleman, 1989, p. 7). His, however, is very much an account centred on the Congress's internal dynamics, paying little special attention to any particular local context. Richard F. Kuisel's work, concerned with the issue of the 'Americanisation' of postwar France, gives much more local detail, stressing that, in considering French attitudes to the USA, one must distinguish between underlying factors and contingencies of the Cold War. On the latter, Kuisel acknowledges the postwar attraction of the PCF (Parti Communiste de la France) to intellectuals that so alarmed the Americans – indeed the Party liked to see itself as the '*parti de l'intelligence*' (Kuisel, 1993, pp. 40–42). Describing the variety of relationships between this loose group of literary and artistic figures and the PCF, Kuisel argues that they tended to share a respect for it based on its proven anti-fascism and record in the Resistance, as well as for its strategic strength as the largest party of the Left. In terms of their attitudes to the superpower across the Atlantic, anti-Americanism was certainly widely present in their writings, but Kuisel stresses that this was by no means the sole preserve of the Party and the *compagnons de route*, or indeed merely a thing of the Cold War moment: suspicion of the USA and what it might represent, whilst by no means universal (the question of America was 'contested territory', he suggests), had broader appeal and deeper roots. In its most strident, political manifestations, French Cold War anti-Americanism may have been a thing of leftist Paris, Kuisel argues, but key concerns that had become apparent in the interwar period were shared by a larger constituency. Surveying French writing about America from the 1920s and 1930s, he concludes that:

> ... a smug tone of ... cultural superiority marked this reporting about the New World. In its most extreme form America was denied a civilization of its own ... as one commentator noted, whereas Americans showed tourists the Chicago stockyards, the French instinctively escorted visitors to the Louvre and Notre Dame. (Kuisel, 1993, p. 11).

The 'postwar stereotype' of American culture was already in place by 1930, he suggests (rather confirming Nabokov's view of 1951) and its key characteristics are ideas of standardisation, conformity and materialism. Americans themselves are vigorous and dynamic but – in dramatic contrast with the fine-tuned discretion which is the special attribute of civilised France – they prefer action to thought; their growing influence threatens to promote the replacement of the latter by the former. Likewise, American culture (essentially escapist and adolescent, brutal and commercial) is regarded as invasive, part of a larger social, economic and cultural model which, driven by the process of 'Americanisation' threatens a dystopian future. In this process, France, with its unique importance and value to the world in terms of civilised, humanist values, had more to lose than most. So, for the French Left, added to their political opposition to the USA as the fountainhead of capitalism was what amounted to a *mass culture* critique of American society that operated in very similar terms to that proposed by the core of New York Intellectuals associated with the CCF (see Chapter 7). Where the two groups divided was over the implications of this shared mass culture analysis for allegiance in the Cold War: whilst the French regarded the danger as chiefly American-born, the New York group saw it as part of a broader phenomenon, arguing that the fight against mass culture and the fight against Stalinism were international, and inseparable. According to Kuisel, a much more general and pervasive cultural attribute was also held in common between the two nations:

> ... it has been said that France and the US clash because they are the only two Western nations that harbour universal pretensions. They are certain that other nations want to imitate them. Americans believe they possess the secret of freedom and prosperity and the French believe they are the champions of *civilisation*. Inevitably the pretensions, or egocentrisms, of these two cultural imperialisms, will conflict. For most of those writing about America [in France] during the cold war this rivalry had two dimensions. The mission of the Parisian intelligentsia was both to project a revolutionary critique and as gatekeepers to export and guard *civilisation* as well. America in the 1950s represented counterrevolution and mass culture. France represented revolution and *civilisation*. The stakes in the debate were immense. (Kusiel, 1993, p. 127)

We may recall that, considering Parisian reaction to 'L'Oeuvre du XXème Siècle', both Janet Flanner and Herbert Luethy drew attention to just the sense of French universalism that is described here, showing how, in practice, it presented the CCF's cultural programme with great difficulties. Kuisel, however, shows that to deep-rooted cultural anxiety and an extraordinary sense of national self-importance we must add a whole series of contingent political factors in accounting for this. There were trade issues: the USA insisted that France remove barriers to imports but maintained its own (then as now, film represented a particularly sore point, with Hollywood access to the French market insisted upon as a condition of the Blum-Byrnes loan); aid issues (the French regarded the UK as having received preferential treatment); the rebuilding, and – from 1950 – re-arming of Germany; military worries over the war in Korea; the nuclear build-up and the US military presence in France; and general concerns over what seemed to be American ideological zealotry, personified by Joseph McCarthy.

From one perspective, this suggests the potential difficulties facing *any* American-inspired campaign seeking to influence French intellectual opinion. Equally, from the American Cold War perspective it could been seen as underlining the scale of the problem and the urgency of the need for redress. In particular, as Irwin M. Wall has observed, the USA remained 'puzzled and bothered' by the resilience and continued internal strength of the Communist Party in France (and Italy). Although elections, such as those of June 1951, might not always give them a strong showing, the Party could yet become a serious candidate for power and presented real practical problems in the present. For example, the existence of a strong and resilient PCF was thought to exercise a debilitating effect on the government, in terms of a reluctance to confront Moscow, whilst an alleged permeation of the bureaucracy by communist sympathisers worked against the sharing of state secrets and military technology (Wall, 1991, p. 212).

A 'cultural and informational campaign to redress America's image' in France was launched in tandem with the Marshall Plan in 1948. Kuisel lists its objectives as establishing that America wants peace and freedom and respects French independence whilst presenting American achievements in science and art and the benefits of its way of life in general. The means were various: press releases, radio programmes and documentary films, organisations such as the *Association France–Etats-Unis*, the French service of Voice of America, academic exchanges, journals and Fulbright scholarships. The advent of the CCF in 1950 is set against this background, and the establishment of the Paris office and Nabokov's plans for the 'big bang' coincides with Truman's creation, in 1951, of the Psychological Strategy Board (PSB), a subcommittee of the National Security Council. This structural innovation was designed to oversee the propaganda campaign, and produced, accordingly, 'Plans for the Reduction of Communist Power' in France and Italy, and a special 'Psychological Operations Plan for the Reduction of Communist Power in France'. Wall, whose work records the establishment of the PSB, notes that numerous meetings in the autumn of 1951 were devoted to the implementation of these plans, codenamed Project Cloven and later called Project Midiron, adding that almost all detail remains classified. The membership of the committee – the under-secretary of state, Deputy Secretary of Defense and the Director of the CIA – should be enough to convince us that the Paris festival formed part of a much larger, centrally coordinated operation (Wall, 1991, pp. 213–14).

In October 1952 a memo from Vincent Kaplan, an American information officer based in Paris, reveals that the propaganda campaign employed 70 Americans and several hundred French, and a United States Information and Education (USIE) report on the six months to 31 May 1952 gives further indications of the scale of the operation. According to this, 4 760 000 people had seen documentary films in 34 000 showings; a USIE radio programme attracted 1–1.5 million listeners; 56 French 'leaders' had received grants to visit the USA; 30 teachers of English received grants to study there; 38 Fulbright lecturers arrived; and so on.

Just as the work of Kuisel and Wall indicates aims and motivations for the larger US campaign that are by now familiar to us from the rationale given by Nabokov for his activities, so their evidence suggests that Americans working on the campaign in Paris shared Flanner's and Luethy's scepticism as to its likely success. Reviewing the operation in September 1952 Ambassador James Dunn 'concluded that its effectiveness varied in proportion to its "unobtrusiveness"; the French did not like to be "told" anything' (Wall, 1991, p. 217), a judgement which must surely bear on the distinctly obtrusive festival of only four months before. And, in a gloomy assessment from the point of view of the CCF and its sponsors in Langley, Information Officer

Kaplan gave the opinion that even if minds *were* changed in relation to the American way of life, political orientation would not necessarily follow, concluding that the cultural offensive was 'largely a waste of time and money when not actually harmful' (Kusiel, 1993, p. 26).

We have seen, then, that presenting the USA in a 'liberal and cultural light' formed an important part of the mission of Nabokov and the Congress, and that this was inherently problematic in practice, conflicting with the image of functional autonomy and independence of mind upon which any success would have to depend. We have also observed that this aim would be elevated retrospectively by the CCF's apologists, turning it into a veritable culture ministry, undertaking – in exceptional circumstances when the stakes were high and the need great – the sort of external image-building work that is readily, and openly, subsidised in many other countries. Finally, we have examined this aspect of the work in relation to the context of early Cold War France, seen how those circumstances influenced the perceived need for some sort of programme, the inevitability of resistance to any such activity, and glanced at the larger operation of which 'Masterpieces of the XXth Century' formed a part. Having discussed, in this chapter and the last, the rationale for a 'cultural strategy', the festival which was perhaps its most dramatic manifestation, and the nature of its reception in France, we should now examine the *internal* debate. How were the issues portrayed within the CCF?

Chapter 6

Paris/New York:
Congress Divided

> The Congress sponsored in 1952 a comprehensive exposition of music, painting, sculpture, and literature. The festival was the brainchild of Nabokov, who played the leading role in it. Although there were efforts at desperate rationalisation to show that all of these activities had something to do with the defense of the free world, actually it did more to further Nabokov's career and reputation than to further cultural freedom. (Hook, 1987, p. 445)[1]

New York University professor of philosophy, Sidney Hook, was a key figure in the American Committee for Cultural Freedom, the CCF's US affiliate, and his comments are characteristic of ACCF attitudes to Nabokov's 'cultural' strategy. Chapters 4 and 5 have suggested that this was indeed widely criticised, even – perhaps especially – from within the secretary-general's own 'side'. Journalists and diplomatic insiders who were, in general, favourably disposed towards aims such as opposing the influence of the Soviet Union, and raising the cultural profile of the USA, nonetheless voiced doubts as to the efficacy of the CCF's approach. However, some of the severest critics were to be found *within* the organisation itself and, in terms of the various national affiliates of the Congress, the ACCF was very much the first among equals. Chapter 1 described the genesis of the CCF in Americans for Intellectual Freedom, an ad hoc group set up to oppose the Soviet-sponsored Waldorf conference of 1949: those individuals would go on to dominate the new ACCF, set up in 1951, and exert considerable influence on the larger CCF. The relationship with the Paris Secretariat, however, became fraught, with the New Yorkers hopeful and exasperated, pleading and hectoring by turns.

Yet the ACCF remained 'more equal than others'. The key role of the AIF nucleus at the outset may have produced a sense of a special right to intervene (and perhaps a corresponding nagging feeling of obligation on the part of Paris). Furthermore, the American Committee was comprised of Americans. This had several consequences. First, Congress was, as everybody knew, funded from the USA: without the generosity of American foundations it would not exist. Second, the desire to change attitudes to the USA and American culture was an important subtext to the whole venture. Third, there was the widespread view that the USA was the only real bulwark against communism. For many Americans this was a particular instance of a more

---

1   Hook's description of the festival as 'comprehensive' is something of an over-statement, as we have seen.

general truth – that America was exceptional, uniquely free, and therefore endowed with a historic gift and mission. Especially strong in the Cold War years, this was, and is, a deep-rooted part of the American myth. For all these reasons the ACCF was a special case within Congress. We should now, therefore, turn to the American Committee as a specific locus of dissent which created considerable problems for the parent organisation in the years of its highest profile.

The ACCF had a very particular character in that it was largely a subset of that group which has come to be known as the New York Intellectuals, and we need to consider that group, in terms of their history, preoccupations and political evolution, to provide a context for the emerging row with Paris. This dispute (which, even in the case of Hook, is less straightforward than the opening extract might suggest) can then be considered in more detail. It is perhaps ironic that the New York group opposed Paris despite being centrally concerned with the content of, and prospects for, the 'high culture' which was also central to Nabokov's concerns, so some explanation must be sought for their growing frustration with a CCF strategy which might be thought to have effected a neat marriage between this and their other key interest – anti-communism. The dispute, however, was very real and, whilst it is possible to argue that Nabokov and the New York group shared important underlying concerns, this will be the subject of the next chapter. For now, let us examine the 'New York Intellectuals'.

If the moment at which a section of the New York intellectual community became – at least, for the purposes of literary and political historians – the 'New York Intellectuals', is difficult to pinpoint, the consensus of most scholarship is that they are identifiable as a group from some time in the late 1930s, and its core is not hard to identify. Sidney Hook is there, as is fellow philosopher and author of *The Managerial Revolution*, James Burnham. Key figures in the *Partisan Review* circle included Phillip Rahv and William Phillips, both co-founders, and co-editors in the period 1946–55, along with associate editors Delmore Schwarz and William Barrett. Eliott Cohen launched *Commentary* in 1945, with Clement Greenberg and Irving Kristol as associate editors. The art critic Clement Greenberg wrote a series of influential articles for *Partisan Review* in the late 1930s and would go on to champion Jackson Pollock and the abstract expressionists in the 1950s; Kristol would later become a co-editor of the CCF's London-based *Encounter*. Daniel Bell's name will forever be associated with *The End of Ideology*, the book which crystallised a key idea for both the New York Intellectuals and the CCF as a whole. Another influential book of the period, *The Vital Center*, was written by the historian Arthur Schlesinger Jr, who would later become a speechwriter for John F. Kennedy. The critic and political maverick Dwight Macdonald founded the short-lived journal *Politics* in the mid-1940s; Mary McCarthy was associated with several of his endeavours, including the Europe–America groups, which can be seen as a precursor of the CCF. Melvin Lasky worked for the *New Leader* in the 1940s, later producing a US-sponsored journal in occupied Berlin, *Der Monat*; despite apparently being prevented from joining the Paris leadership by the CIA, Lasky was an important figure in the CCF and would later become co-editor of *Encounter*. Other names included James T. Farrell, Lionel Trilling, Leslie Fiedler, Irving Howe and Robert Warshow.

At this point – the late 1930s – they were leftists, mostly revolutionary in inclination, yet with a hardening opposition to the shape of Stalinist Russia and the official Communist Party of the USA. A number had moved away from communist orthodoxy (with the purges and show trials of 1934–37 being a particularly decisive moment in the process), most towards some sort of Trotskyist position – that is, regarding the Soviet Union as a basically progressive social structure usurped by a repressive and self-perpetuating clique. They had also rejected the Comintern policy of a Popular Front uniting the communists with other social democratic and Left forces in a broad anti-fascist coalition. At this stage, individuals were finding new political homes among the splintered factions of Trotskyism – the Socialist Workers Party, the American Workers' Party, the Workers' Party and the like.

Reactions to the outbreak of the Second World War were varied but, hardened by the Nazi–Soviet pact of 1939, the group maintained a uniform opposition to Stalinism in stark contrast to the pro-Russian feeling widespread after Hitler's invasion in 1941. With the onset of the Cold War there began a gradual, but inexorable, drift to the Right with the struggle against capitalism gradually abandoned in the face of a perceived need to support the USA as the chief bulwark against a ruthless, expansionist USSR. As the 1940s drew to an end, members of the group were moving to centre-stage in the intellectual theatre of the Cold War. Key events in the next part of their story have been rehearsed in Chapter 1: it was the period of the Soviet-sponsored 'peace conference' at the Waldorf-Astoria (1949), the inaugural Congress for Cultural Freedom in Berlin (1950), and the establishment of the CCF as an ongoing force (1951). In all these undertakings, and indeed throughout the 1950s, the New York Intellectuals were prominent.

For our present purposes we need not follow the group into the next decade, although suffice to say that their drift to the Right continued. During the 1960s the New York Intellectuals remained mute as the CIA's Phoenix programme systematically disposed of the Vietnamese opposition; they were equally quiet during the overthrow of Mossadegh in Iran (1953) and Arbenz in Guatemala (1954). The intellectual shock troops of liberty and democracy stood by as US-trained and financed armies erased liberty and human rights in an archipelago of what have been called 'subfascist' client states (Chomsky and Herman, 1979). By the 1980s, unsurprisingly, a number of key figures declared themselves supporters of Ronald Reagan.

Oriented chiefly towards literature and politics, the group saw itself, unapologetically, as an elite: critical, independent, distanced from institutions, unafraid of confrontation. Such a stance requires opponents, but by the 1950s capitalism itself was no longer under fire, leaving a distinct shortage of domestic antagonists. To be sure, there were still the remnants of American communism, then the object of Senator McCarthy's attentions, but the Intellectuals' self-image demanded a contest which would set them at odds with society. This was accomplished by taking a cultural turn and developing a critique of mass society, with special emphasis on the values and preferences of the middle classes. Throughout the period, the key institutions for the group are the small journals – the so-called 'little magazines' – which it founded itself, especially *Partisan Review*, but also *Commentary*, *Politics*, *New Leader* and *Dissent*.[2]

2　There are numerous studies of the New York Intellectuals, and scholarly interest

Accounts of the group typically stress its sense of marginality, of addressing society from some point on the periphery. Social and ethnic origins come into play here: largely the children of Eastern European Jewish immigrants, raised in ghetto areas in the second and third decades of the twentieth century, they undoubtedly faced major social and economic barriers in the process of acquiring any sort of valued position and status in American society. In the 1930s the combination of the Depression and academic anti-Semitism made it difficult to obtain the teaching work that many felt themselves qualified for. Hugh Wilford argues that the dissenting character of the group, its feeling of outsider status, was grounded in the real-life experience of at least some of them, and contributed to their oppositional stances in both politics and culture. As their revolutionary politics became Trotskyist in orientation they were rendered doubly marginal, at odds with both the surrounding society and the pro-Moscow Communist mainstream; at the same time there seemed to be 'startling correspondences between the suffering and loneliness of the alienated modern artist and their own experience of marginalisation' (Wilford, 1995, pp. 1–3). It is worth noting, in passing, that the New York Intellectuals were by no means all Jews and, even to the extent that they were, the fact of being bright, aspiring and Jewish is not enough in itself to explain the particular phenomenon of the group; after all, as Alan Wald reminds us, 'upwardly mobile Jews comprised a disproportionate number of intellectuals in *all* radical movements in New York in the 1930s' (Wald, 1987, p. 9).[3]

The political journey of the New York Intellectuals

Because of their ethnic and socioeconomic background, their politics and aesthetics, the New York Intellectuals found themselves outside the mainstream and, crucially, they tended to make this a virtue. Condemned to the political fringes they might be,

---

shows no sign of abating. For my purposes, the group, whilst important, is very much ancillary: their orientation, their ideas are of interest only insofar as they form a context for Nicolas Nabokov's policy at the CCF. Consequently my researches in this area have been kept within bounds. I have nonetheless tried to maintain some balance in the outlook of the texts which constitute this limited frame of reference. Hugh Wilford, in *The New York Intellectuals: From Vanguard to Institution* (1995), is a sympathetic observer, emphasising continuity between the earlier and later phases of the group. By contrast, Alan M. Wald (1987) is concerned to expose what he sees as the 'political amnesia' of those in the group who sought to downplay their previous revolutionary convictions, or to assert what he sees as a bogus consistency. From a non-Marxist standpoint, Richard H. Pells is also critical, in *The Liberal Mind in a Conservative Age: American Intellectuals in the 1940s and 1950s* (1985). Finally, I also draw on two writers who have touched on the group in considering the CCF itself, coming to opposing conclusions: Peter Coleman, the former editor of the Congress's Australian journal *Quadrant*, is sympathetic in *The Liberal Conspiracy: The Congress for Cultural Freedom and the Struggle for the Mind of Postwar Europe* (1989), whilst Christopher Lasch, writing in the wake of the CIA funding disclosures, is ruthless in his essay 'The Cultural Cold War: A Short History of the Congress for Cultural Freedom' (1968).

    3   Wald is questioning the thesis of Alexander Bloom in *Prodigal Sons: The New York Intellectuals and their World* (1987). According to Wald, Bloom simplifies the phenomenon by reducing it to a question of ethnicity.

but should they not recognise and guard their *autonomy* – the opportunity for truly free critical thought – that this afforded? Alienation, for them, was the precondition of independent creation and, if this held some dangers, the group should respond by 'cultivating ... [its own] standards and norms, by resisting the bourgeois incentives to accommodation, and perforce making a virtue of its separateness from society' (Phillip Rahv, quoted in Wilford, 1995, p. 3). The means by which this could be accomplished, the key to the group's sense of itself as a community, was the 'little magazine', and *Partisan Review* in particular. Founded in 1934 by the communist-affiliated John Reed Club, an independent *PR* was relaunched in 1937, establishing a broadly left-wing, pro-modernist character. Journals of ideas in this mould, most famously *Encounter*, would be central to the *modus operandi* of the CCF internationally. The other side of the alienation coin was a resistance to, even a fear, of institutions – typically stigmatised as 'bureaucracies': in practice this meant academia, publishing and the state – those areas that could conceivably use the Intellectuals' skills (and, increasingly, in the Cold War era, did), and whose blandishments might lead to incorporation. The threat was one of dilution, of neutralisation: as it seemed to them, 'the institutions were capable of taking "anything", no matter how "extreme or serious" and rendering it "palatable"' (William Phillips, quoted in Wilford, 1995, p. 13). Self-styled political vanguard *and* cultural elite, the New York Intellectuals saw themselves as caught up in projects far larger than themselves: maintaining their precious autonomy was raised to an obligation – a matter of responsibility to both the Future and Art.

With stakes this high, it follows that this mission should have been pursued in a militant style, with what often seemed like a relish for confrontation, and – in the 1950s as in the 1930s – there could be no question of neutrality. As Richard Pells puts it: 'The identity of the combatants had now changed, Russia having supplanted both the "bosses" and the Nazis as embodiments of everlasting villainy. But the intellectuals' frame of mind remained the same' (Pells, 1985, p. 97). This frame of mind could brook no compromise, so that:

> Often, their supreme enemy appeared to reside less in Moscow than in western Europe. The Party hacks were a minor nuisance compared to the sceptical and nonaligned intellectuals of Paris, Rome and Berlin. In the view of Americans like Barrett, Hook, William Phillips, and James Burnham, the truly unforgivable sin of the early 1950s was not Stalinism but neutralism. (Pells, 1985, p. 124).

Events had, they believed, established beyond doubt that a simple choice existed between totalitarianism and freedom: indeed, the horrors of the mid-twentieth century exposed 'the end of ideology' (the phrase made famous by Daniel Bell's 1962 book of the same name), which became a key idea for the Intellectuals,[4] or alternatively – as Christopher Lasch prefers to describe it – a 'polemical staple'. Ideology was over in the sense that no-one – unless sentimental or wilfully blind – could equivocate between East and West, or hold up the shortcomings of American society as reasons

---

4   Coleman, incidentally, suggests that the phrase had already been used by Edward Shils, in *Encounter*, and by Raymond Aron in *L'Opium des Intellectuels*. See Coleman, (1989, p. 54).

to withhold support. The starkness of the situation, which appeared to them in such clarity, led to the conclusion that:

> 'Man stands at a crossroads ... which leaves only the choice of this way or that.' At such moments 'the difference between the very clever and the simple in mind narrows almost to vanishing point'; and only the 'professional disease' of the intellectual, his fascination with logical subtleties and his 'estrangement from reality,' kept him from seeing the need to choose between slavery and freedom. (Arthur Koestler at the 1950 Congress in Berlin, quoted in Lasch, 1968, p. 325)

Peter Coleman argues that this 'end of ideology' should be seen in the context of a CCF project which genuinely celebrated the 'irrepressible pleasures of universal curiosity ... the central importance of the critical, free-thinking spirit'. The CCF intellectuals had, he argues, rejected 'the dogmas of both Communism and anti-Communism', preferring to rely 'on the critical resources of free tradition' (Coleman, 1989, pp. 54–5). This, however, suggests a sort of non-alignment, a willingness to turn one's fire in either direction, and a quality of open-mindedness which, whilst it may hold true for some of those associated with the Congress (one thinks, perhaps, of Bertrand Russell) is surely quite foreign to both the style and the substance of the New York group's thinking. Indeed one could argue that even as the group moved rapidly to the Right, it nonetheless retained the traditional vices of the Left: rancour, intrigue, factionalism and dogma.

Notwithstanding any political shift, most observers seem to agree that the group's essential character – the obsession with intellectual independence, the militancy, the sense of mission – was retained with it from the 1930s into the Cold War 1950s. So far as the interpretation of the group's political evolution in the same period is concerned, unanimity dissolves, since the postwar period – particularly after 1950 – finds the former revolutionaries sharing common cause with the US government in the fight against communism, and becoming increasingly unwilling to find fault with either the fundamentals of capitalism or the actions of the state. Continuity or apostasy?

The defence sometimes argues that there *is* an unbroken thread here: opposition to Stalinism. Peter Coleman makes exactly this point – that those who formed the CCF had held to their principles. And this was admirable:

> Even when the Soviet mythos was strongest, there had always been dissenters on the intellectual Left ... [but they] remained a very small minority and had no significant organisation, national or international, remotely capable of overcoming the Stalinist and fellow-traveling hegemony. They lived in an intellectual no man's land. (Coleman, 1989, pp. 2–3)

Coleman is describing the CCF milieu as a whole, but the argument applies equally to the *Partisan Review* group: against the resources of the Comintern, the legions of left-liberal 'fellow-travellers' and a public widely sympathetic to the Russian peoples' wartime sacrifices, they had maintained a principled opposition to Stalinism, functioning (so they thought) as a small reservoir of truth and clearsightedness. According to this view, the New York Intellectuals are to be seen as consistent throughout the 1940s, rewarded at the end of the decade by the belated arrival of government in the anti-Stalinist ranks. This was an outcome for which they also deserved some credit.

Hugh Wilford also argues for continuity although, like Coleman, he has to be somewhat selective about the group's principles in order to make the case: specifically, the inconvenient issue of their youthful revolutionism has to be overlooked. The apparent contradiction of independent radicals turned government-sponsored cold warriors hides significant correspondences between the two phases, he suggests. Specifically, there is the fact of their independence, linked to a sense of cultural authority, and what he sees as a long-standing defence of intellectual freedom[5] (which would later mesh with US Cold War slogans of 'cultural freedom'); in addition, he cites their elite or vanguard role in both cases and a particular sort of aggressive, confrontational and masculine rhetoric (Wilford, 1995, pp. 23–4). Above all, for this writer, the Congress and its supporters could never reasonably be described as right-wing. Franco, Salazar, Peron and Sukarno were their targets along with the communists, he argues, along with Joseph McCarthy on the domestic front (other writers, incidentally, would severely question this); they maintained a distance from political conservatives and had few links with anti-communism in the Church and private business. Coleman agrees, the Congress:

> ... appealed to intellectuals, a class of people for whom, as Raymond Aron observed, 'anticapitalism is an article of faith.' For them even to agree to debate the possible merits of the free enterprise system, Aron said, would be an emotional and philosophical surrender .... The basic hallmark, in short, of the Congress's anti-Communism was that it felt itself to be of the Left and on the Left. (Coleman, 1989, pp. 11–12)

In the opposite corner, Alan Wald finds the continuity thesis to be bogus and – since it has been advanced by the protagonists themselves – self-serving. It is a myth, he suggests, which obscures:

> ... the profound difference between *anti-Communism* (originally, opposition by revolutionary Marxists to Soviet Communism, after the rise of Stalin, as a deformation or perversion of socialism) and *anticommunism* (in the United States, an ideological mask for discrediting movements for radical social change and supporting the status quo by amalgamating these movements with Soviet crimes, expansionism and subversion). (Wald, 1991, p. 7, my italics)

Wald's standpoint is a Marxist one, and the idea that the New York Intellectuals deployed their anti-Stalinist views as part of a stratagem to defend the vested interests of capitalism is too far-fetched to be credible. On the contrary, the Cold War seems to have been a genuine, even a passionate, motivation for them. The basic point, however, is simple and well-made: in the 1930s the majority of the New York Intellectuals had indeed been revolutionaries, whilst in the Cold War era they largely accepted the political and economic underpinnings of capitalism, with what Wald calls 'a sprinkling of criticism to salve their consciences' (Wald, 1991, p. 267).

---

5   On intellectual freedom, however, one recalls that Sidney Hook argued in 1953 that 'members of the Communist party and similar groups' should be excluded from teaching in schools and universities. See Wald (1991, p. 4).

Richard Pells also suggests that the Intellectuals' *volte-face* cannot be disguised:

> Even as they continued to treasure their radicalism and their sense of alienation, they
> were becoming – however inadvertently – the champions of existing institutions and
> the defenders of American power abroad ... for all their intellectual acrobatics ... the
> contributors to *Commentary* and *Partisan Review* evolved during the postwar years into
> articulate exponents of a new orthodoxy on foreign affairs. Despising all forms of
> mass conformity and total politics, they found themselves supplying the philosophical
> ammunition for the cold war. (Pells, 1985, pp. 72–6).

Criticism of the West remained, he continues, but this represented more an
undercurrent of unease than anything resembling the thoroughgoing dissent of their
former selves. Finally, Christopher Lasch, whose early attack on the Congress and its
milieu stung enough to draw an equally trenchant response from Sidney Hook in his
autobiography 20 years later, has a perspective that describes a desertion of the Left,
whilst acknowledging one element of continuity that will prove useful to the present
study: he argues that a strong antipathy towards liberalism is exhibited by the group
in both its earlier and later incarnations. This has already been touched upon in the
reference to Koestler's assault on the irrelevance of liberal intellectualism in the face
of the totalitarian enemy. More generally, liberalism is excoriated as fatally flawed,
and having allowed communism to gain ground:

> Anti-communism ... [for these men] represented a new stage in their running polemic
> against bourgeois sentimentality and weakness, bourgeois 'utopianism,' and bourgeois
> materialism. That explains their eagerness to connect Bolshevism with liberalism – to show
> that the two ideologies sprang from a common root and that it was the softness and
> sentimentality of bourgeois liberals which had paradoxically allowed communism –
> liberalism's deadly enemy, one might have supposed – to pervade Western society in the
> thirties and early forties. (Lasch, 1968, p. 326)[6]

In contrast to liberal weakness, the New York Intellectuals – forming what Lasch
has elsewhere called 'the cult of the hard-boiled' (Lasch, 1965, p. 308) – prided
themselves on their toughness of mind, immune from communist contagion partly
because of their own youthful exposure to it. Since the debilitating softness,
sentimentality and naivety of liberalism were so widespread, their own qualities were
that much more to be valued, giving them – in their own eyes, at least – a vital role.
'The student of these events,' Lasch continues:

> ... is struck by the way in which ex-Communists seem always to have retained the worst
> of Marx and Lenin and to have discarded the best. The elitism which once glorified
> intellectuals as a revolutionary avant-garde now glorifies them as experts and social
> technicians ... these reflections lead one to the conclusion ... that intellectuals were more
> attracted to Marxism in the first place as an elitist and undemocratic ideology than as a

---

6   Other writers also note the persistent *anti*-liberal strand – for example, 'To
describe them as "liberal anti-Communists" during this period is mistaken. Indeed, their Cold
War anti-Communism contained strong traces of anti-liberalism, a residue of their radical
past ...' (Wilford, 1995, p. 194).

means of analysis which provided, not answers, but the beginnings of a critical theory of society. (Lasch, 1968, p. 338)

For our present purposes, the important points here are the elitism of the group and the denunciation of liberal 'sentimentality'. Both of these will become relevant when, in the next chapter, we consider the cultural turn taken by the group in the 1940s and 1950s, and return to Nicolas Nabokov.

The New York/Paris schism

So much for this brief introduction to the character and history of the 'New York Intellectuals' who formed the backbone of the American Congress for Cultural Freedom. We have already touched on the ACCF's early worries about the direction being taken by the Paris office as evidenced by 'L'Oeuvre du XXème Siècle', and should now pick up that story before seeking to assess it in a broader context. By the end of the 1952 festival in Paris there was already deep suspicion in New York of the Secretariat, as well as considerable scepticism over the part music and the arts might play in the struggle against communism. We have looked at the exchange of letters between Paris and New York in which Nabokov sought to win the ACCF over; recall, also, *Partisan Review* editor William Phillips' retrospective assessment of the festival as 'a bureaucratic enterprise pretending to be an intellectual one ... the greatest Parisian couturier's ball ... this impresario's dream ...' (Phillips, 1990, p. 11). Sidney Hook took a similar view in the autobiography *Out of Step*, an extract from which opened this chapter. On the 1950 negotiations designed to secure a permanent Congress, he has this to say of the selection of Nabokov as secretary-general:

In Nabokov's favour were his European origins and experience as a Russian exile, his linguistic abilities, his status as an intellectual and musical composer in his own right, and his claim, somewhat exaggerated, to be acquainted with almost everybody worth knowing in the literary and cultural world of Europe. It turned out to be a perfect job for Nabokov but unfortunately, in my view, not for the Congress. (Hook, 1987, pp. 444–5).

From this point, the CCF headed sharply in the wrong direction, according to Hook. Although careful not to give Nabokov *all* the blame, in that the secretary-general was subordinate to the Executive Committee, he suggests that, since this committee was comprised of busy people who were dispersed and met infrequently, Nabokov was in practice largely responsible. The substance of Hook's criticism is this: the Paris office was simply too scared of antagonising the 'anti-anticommunists', of provoking non-political or neutralist European intellectuals by standing revealed as unabashed Cold War protagonists. Desperate to win over all possible well-wishers and equally desperate not to upset the middle-ground waverers, the resulting policy, purged of political content, could only be anodyne. This was emphatically *not* what the Executive Committee had intended:

When ... [they] voted to set up the international festival, it was assumed it would all be ancillary to the ideals and values of the Freedom Manifesto. What Nabokov did was to turn his back on this. Most of his efforts went to win over well-wishers for the Congress ... by dazzling them with artistic delights after the high cultural season in Paris was over. (Hook, 1987, p. 445)

In practice, all that the enterprise produced was an enormous enhancement of its organiser's reputation, a 'junket tour for hundreds', and a burdensome bureaucracy. Hook goes on to argue that what premise there was for the enterprise was misguided: after all, 'since art has flourished even under political tyrannies, there was nothing the festival presented that could not have been offered to the world under the aegis of an enlightened despotism'. This, of course, flatly contradicts the rationale which Nabokov had tried to present – that art *cannot* thrive in the absence of freedom, at least if we understand thriving or 'flourishing' to include quality, dynamism and modernity as well as quantity, and that his festival would make that case. (Nabokov might have replied that, yes, dictatorships produced much art, even nurtured it, but what *sort* of art?) In addition, the inclusion in the programme of Shostakovich's *Lady Macbeth of Mtsensk* (along with the troubled history which Nabokov was eager to provide) provided the proof that art certainly could *not* be said to 'flourish' in the dictatorship which consumed the greater part of the CCF's attention (strangely, Hook refers to the performances of banned works by Shostakovich and Prokofiev at the festival, but does not appear to sense any self-contradiction). Nabokov's approach may or may not have been valid, but it looks as though Hook has not really done it justice.

There is an interesting, if confusing, postscript to this issue. Contemporary letters exist from Hook to Nabokov that seem to show the relationship in quite a different light, and which are hard to reconcile with the views expressed in the Hook memoir: indeed, taken together, they form a striking contrast. For example, here is Hook writing in June 1952, immediately after the festival:

> My impression ... is that the Festival was a success, that it was the only kind of thing that was possible in France at least, and indeed it was the only event that didn't turn out to be a psychological defeat for the cause of freedom. I am particularly pleased, too, because my confidence in your judgement and leadership has been vindicated. (Letter, Hook to Nabokov, 12 June 1952)

How are we to reconcile this with the later account? As the encouragement of a friend and colleague in the early stages of a new and unprecedented undertaking, generously suppressing doubts which, later, would prove to have been well-founded? Possibly, but, if so, the doubts were still well suppressed when Hook wrote three years later in March of 1955. At this point, Nabokov's second festival, 'Music of the XXth Century', had taken place in Rome, and one might assume that Hook's exasperation would – certainly by this time – be apparent. But, instead, he writes:

> Don't be so defensive about some of the small people who have no notion of the situation abroad and whose combined efforts weigh much less than yours in the struggle for the Congress's program. You have strong friends here and the documents I brought back and Mike [Josselson] sent gave them ... a healthy respect for the work you are doing. Although one or two try to discredit what I say on the grounds that I am a partisan of yours ... [most] recognise that ... I am in a better position [than anybody] to give an objective account of

things. Don't worry about the American Committee. Preserve the amenities so that no false issues arise but save your energies for the tough job ahead. (Letter, Hook to Nabokov, 31 March 1955)

The most glaring contradiction here of the picture painted later, apart from the personal warmth and approval, is the apparent acceptance that special political circumstances *do* apply in Europe, and that, in this light, the Nabokov–Josselson policy is not only appropriate, but meeting with some success. What are we to make of this? Is there perhaps a sense that, since the festival was widely held to have failed (at least at a political level), and later seemed 'hilarious', that it then became hard to mount a retrospective defence and easier to join in the ridicule?

The relationship between Paris and New York is further complicated by an exchange of letters in 1954 and 1955 in which the very American Committee which objected to music festivals is seen attempting to introduce an *extra* musical element into the programme of the Congress: namely that it should sponsor a European tour of the early music group New York Pro Musica Antiqua, under the direction of Noah Greenberg. Sol Stein, the American Committee's Executive Director, wrote to Michael Josselson in January of 1955, suggesting that as Pro Musica Antiqua already had a tour arranged for the near East and southern Europe, could the CCF set up dates:

... in Paris, London, Berlin and wherever else ... it might be appropriate to show America's interest in early European music as evidenced by these brilliant performers ... a group which I am sure I need not rave to you about. (Letter, Stein to Josselson, 20 January 1955)

Paris's response, however, was in the negative. Nabokov's reply once again shows how reluctant he and Josselson were to do anything that might attract the charge of 'American propaganda'. Moreover he points out that there are a number of European groups of the same stature, so it would definitely be a mistake to break with the existing policy of *not* supporting tours of *particular* artists or organisations, in favour of Greenberg's group (letter to Stein, 1 February 1955). Interestingly, an approach of this sort had apparently been made earlier, in late 1954 and by Sidney Hook himself! Given what we know of Hook's dismissive approach to the utility of the arts in the anti-communist struggle – at least as described in *Out of Step* – this is again surprising. Josselson wrote to Hook in December of 1954 thanking him for a folder giving details of Pro Musica Antiqua, but declining in the same terms as Nabokov's later response to Stein (letter, Josselson to Hook, 17 December 1954).[7]

It seems, then, that the ACCF on at least one occasion tried to contribute to the CCF policy of foregrounding the arts, despite the real doubts harboured by many of its leading members, only to meet with a rebuff. Of course, the feeling of frustration over this issue was mutual, and it appears that the Paris office, for its part, had questioned the direction of the American Committee. Indeed, the Pro Musica Antiqua proposal may have been an attempt to meet this criticism: in a letter of September 1954 to Michael Josselson, the ACCF's Sol Stein refers to Josselson's view that 'the American Committee, unlike the rest of the Congress, concentrates on activities that

---

7   Hook's letter was dated 6 December: the present writer was unable to find this in the archives.

are "political" rather than "cultural" ' (letter, Stein to Josselson, 1 September 1954). He goes on to ask exactly what sort of cultural activities they are expected to engage in given their limited funds. There is a real sense of frustration here: not only do Nabokov and Josselson mount glossy festivals in Paris and Rome, which seem to many in New York to divert from the political struggle; they have the nerve to suggest that the ACCF should follow their lead, without providing the means to do so. The Pro Musica Antiqua proposal can, perhaps, be seen as a response to Paris which tried to show an interest in, and concern for, the arts side of Congress policy *without* creating any financial implications for the straitened ACCF.

Significantly, it also involved a group led by someone that the New York Intellectuals could consider 'one of them.' In his letter to Josselson, Sol Stein added: 'As you may know, Noah Greenberg, who is Director of the Pro Musica Antiqua, is a close friend of many members of the committee here' (letter, Stein to Josselson, 20 January 1955). As a member of the Workers' Party, Greenberg had, in fact, been immersed in very much the same political milieu as many members of the ACCF. The Workers' Party was formed in 1940 by Max Schactman as a result of a split in the Socialist Workers' Party. One faction, led by James P. Cannon, held to the view that the rulers of the USSR constituted a caste who had taken control of a socioeconomic structure that could, and should, be defended; Schactman and his followers (who included prominent ACCF members James Burnham, Dwight Macdonald and Clement Greenberg) argued that the Soviet Union was ruled by a new class, and that therefore the whole structure needed to be replaced (Wald, 1987, p. 166). In retrospect, given what we know about the political journey of the New York Intellectuals, this fits neatly into the trajectory that took them from revolutionaries to cold warriors. To return to Greenberg, Wald tells us that:

> A number of rising young scholars and artists passed through the ranks of the Workers Party during the 1940s, but few became integrated into the organisation or remained for any length of time. One of those who did was Noah Greenberg, who carried out devoted party work in the seamen's union for a number of years before becoming a world-famous specialist in medieval music. (Wald, 1987, p. 303)

The connections go further, since Greenberg went on to organise choirs for the International Ladies Garment Workers' Union (see Haskell, 1988, p. 109). This is significant because the ILGWU played a very special part in the CIA's network of compliant organisations. Tom Braden has described how Jay Lovestone and Irving Brown of the ILGWU set up an anti-communist trade union in France – *Force Ouvrière* – and how the CIA later took over financial responsibility for the project (Braden, 1967, p. 14). Furthermore, of course, when Nabokov, Hook, Macdonald and the others had organised their protest against the Waldorf-Astoria 'peace conference' in 1949, it was ILGWU leader David Dubinsky who had acted as a conduit, enabling the CIA to bankroll proceedings. The point in all this is not to suggest that Noah Greenberg was a CIA agent, merely to demonstrate his position in a web of connections linking the anti-Stalinist Left to the Agency. The proposal that *his* group should represent the Congress in Europe was, therefore, far from fortuitous.

The split between the CCF and the ACCF came to a head with an ACCF memorandum of January 1955 which set out the causes of their disaffection with the

Secretariat's policy, as well as making proposals for change. The introduction gives the background, and includes comments on the festivals in Paris and Rome. There were, it says, real doubts about the wisdom of the considerable cost of the Paris festival, given that an event of this sort would be unlikely to have more than 'very indirect influence' on European neutralists. Whilst the Hamburg Congress on Science and Freedom was approved, 'the Rome Congress on music ['Music in the XXth Century'] engendered an unfavourable reaction'. The document continues:

> It is superfluous to say that no one has any objection to art and music festivals as such; rather we believed that the Congress for Cultural Freedom had responsibilities more urgent than sponsoring international meetings of composers, performers and music critics ... . We were perfectly aware of the Communist cultural offensive in Europe and of the need of persuading Europeans that the Western world's freedom is more conducive of cultural growth than the restricted and exploited culture under Communism. But it seemed that little of this sort of persuasion was planned or produced, in Paris or in Rome. When one considered the political atmosphere in Europe and the lack of resolve in the face of the Communist threat, *the Congress seemed to be holding arts festivals in Rome while Europe burned.* (Executive Committee, 1955, unpublished, p. 2, my italics)

The statement goes on to criticise the undemocratic internal structure of Congress and air various grievances relating to communication, membership and the financial relationship between the parent body and its national affiliates. The thrust of the argument, however, concerns what they see as the 'lack of relationship of some of CCF's major activities to its principal purpose: opposition to all forms of totalitarianism, with especial awareness that Communist totalitarianism is the greatest present threat to cultural freedom'. This loss of focus derives from a mistaken analysis of the political atmosphere in Europe and Asia, which is not likely to present an unabashed anti-communist programme with the level of antagonism that the Secretariat seems to expect. This mistaken fear has led the Congress to 'hide behind "cultural" undertakings so deeply as to lose all effectiveness in the political struggle against Communism', and as evidence they cite 'its activities, including "Encounter", "Preuves", the Paris and Rome festivals, the Rosenberg statement, etc.'[8] In fact, however, the ACCF adds that even if this assessment of the European situation was accurate, the resulting policy would still be in error, since to adopt any position which fell short of thoroughgoing opposition to communism could only encourage neutralism and anti-Americanism, 'third force' concepts and notions of 'co-existence'. As we have seen, all such ideas were anathema to the New Yorkers.

---

8 Elsewhere the draft statement argues that *Encounter* has failed to adopt a thoroughgoing anti-communist policy, instead publishing 'primarily literary material, often of questionable merit' (Executive Committee, 1955, p. 2). Congress's response to what the ACCF predictably considered the 'Communist' campaign on behalf of Julius and Ethel Rosenberg is also deemed inadequate (pp. 2–3).

High culture and politics

Richard Pells has argued convincingly that the US government saw American intellectuals as vital assets in the Cold War, particularly if they could combine anti-Stalinism with left-wing credentials: this the New York Intellectuals, who formed the core of the ACCF, could quite eminently do. In the battle for the hearts and minds of overseas intellectuals, official policy was to take a cultural, rather than a political, approach, and to stress *high* culture at the expense of popular culture: this the CCF was doing. In terms of the CIA's objectives, these two groups, the ACCF and the CCF, seemed full of promise – and yet there existed this stubborn disagreement between the two over the 'cultural policy' of Nabokov and Josselson. It was not as if the New York group was indifferent to high cultural issues; on the contrary, it was highly exercised by what it saw as the threat posed to 'legitimate' culture by 'mass' culture, and – as the following chapter will show – tended increasingly to see anti-communism and the defence of high culture as two aspects of the same struggle. Why then should they have become *so* opposed to the strategy of Nabokov and Josselson, which appeared to be based on just that premise?

The arguments directed across the Atlantic at the Paris office should not, of course, be lightly dismissed. ACCF members were hardly alone among contemporary observers in suspecting that the Paris festival had been of little political value, and that, despite all Nabokov's and Josselson's caution, it was widely regarded as an American propaganda enterprise anyway. The fact that historians have tended either to pay the Congress's cultural undertakings scant attention, or to hold them in small regard, seems to bear out this criticism: posterity lends its weight to the sceptics.

It may well be that the Congress was simply too timid, on the one hand, or indeed just plain wrong in holding to the argument neatly summarised by the poet and editor of *Encounter*, Stephen Spender, in his response to the ACCF's 1955 attack. Spender argued that:

> ... *our politics should be the implication of our interest in culture* ... rather than the other way round ... we should do everything we can to get hold of artists, writers, scientists and so on, and help them in an interested way with their work and try to show them that ... the question of freedom, the struggle, fighting for freedom is involved. (Quoted in Wilford, 1994, pp. 317–18, my italics)

This encapsulates the CCF's policy as carried out by Nabokov, as overseen by the CIA's man Michael Josselson, and as defended by Tom Braden, the architect of the policy back in Langley. For their critics, however, placing the focus on 'cultural' activities was a mistake, and, moreover, one which laid Congress open to exploitation by those for whom the anti-communist struggle was something less than a top priority. We have seen that Sidney Hook's assessment (at least as offered from the vantage point of the 1980s) spoke of 'junket tours' and stressed the benefits reaped by Nabokov personally from the festivals he organised under the auspices of the CCF. Hugh Wilford, the historian of the New York Intellectuals, leans toward this view. Although he argues that the CCF's policy was based on a realistic reading of the mood in Europe, he believes that it did, arguably, allow European intellectuals to appropriate the organisation for their own pet cultural projects. (Ironically just this accusation would later be levelled at the New York Intellectuals themselves, especially in the light of the 1966/7 revelations of CIA funding.)

The New Yorkers, then, were not without potent arguments: yet it is surely strange that this group, with its strong self-image as a high-cultural élite, should feel *such* resentment towards a policy which foregrounded high culture. Might other factors have been at work? Thomas Bender's history of intellectual life in New York includes a perspective on its culture in the mid-twentieth century, which may cast the dispute in a new light. In looking to the 1930s and 1940s for the roots of the city's present-day intellectual and artistic pre-eminence, Bender argues that one must consider a broad series of developments covering painting, sculpture, photography, architecture, music and dance. These were reflected in a series of new journals such as *Modern Music* (1924–46), *New Theatre* (1933–37) and *Dance Index* (1944–49), as well as in the criticism of writers such as Virgil Thomson and Edwin Denby in the *New York Herald Tribune*. The writers gathered around *Partisan Review*, however, had little interest in those arts outside the stockade of literary modernism and, according to Bender, 'shared an almost puritanical fear of the seductiveness of the aesthetic pleasures of the ear and the eye' (Bender, 1987, p. 324).[9] What he describes is a distinct fissure in the intellectual life of the city, between what he calls the 'literary intellectuals' – that is, the New York Intellectuals – and another group which he terms the 'civic intellectuals'. Including figures such as Virgil Thomson, Lincoln Kirstein (New York City Ballet), the architect Philip Johnson and Alfred Barr (of the Museum of Modern Art), this latter group was opulent – distinctly 'uptown' – comprising not only intellectuals and artists but also patrons of the arts, and with links to the 'world of vast wealth' sustaining the Museum of Modern Art. These were – Bender takes the phrase from Virgil Thomson – 'the eye and ear people,' and quite distinct from the 'literary intellectuals'. For one thing, the social milieu was of a different order; here was talent and intellect, but also *resources* and *connections* and, as such, something quite at odds with the treasured periphery of *PR* and *Commentary*. A subtext of Parisian links also exists: the composers – Thomson, Carter, Copland – who studied with Nadia Boulanger; and Balanchine, the protegée of Diaghilev, who in turn influenced Lincoln Kirstein. Furthermore, he argues that the civic intellectuals were distinct in terms of their contacts with black culture (recall that Thomson's *Four Saints* had a black cast) and that, because they refused to accept the rigid polarities of the avant-garde/kitsch, high/mass culture distinctions maintained by the literary group (see Chapter 7), they retained a breadth which made them, ultimately, more forward-looking and more influential.

Here, then, is an analysis that may help resolve the issue of the divide between the ACCF and the CCF over the 'cultural' policy. For what was this policy but the promotion of the 'eye and ear' arts, under the control of an 'eye and ear' man – a composer chiefly noted for his contribution to the ballet? Nabokov's festivals foregrounded cultural fields in which the New York Intellectuals had little interest – worse still, fields in which they could claim no expertise. If, as Richard Pells has suggested, the subtext of their engagement in the Cold War was the desire to

---

9   Bender describes *PR* as an 'afterglow of an older vision of intellect,' based around importing and consuming European politics and literary modernism (Bender, 1987, p. 321).

demonstrate their own indispensability, this development threatened to sideline them just at the point when government seemed to have come round to the resolute anti-Stalinism that they had pursued so doggedly and for so long – and also just at the point where recognition, resources and influence might have begun to seem attractive after years of virtuous, penurious life on the margins. If Bender is right to discern, in the New York of this period, two groups separated by a gulf of understanding, it may well have been galling for the *PR* writers to look across the gulf and see composers and ballet-masters, hitherto undistinguished in the fight against the totalitarian enemy, suddenly appearing in Paris in the name of the Congress *they* had created. Assured by Nabokov that Virgil Thomson, Aaron Copland, Eliott Carter, Roger Sessions and Lincoln Kirstein – or at least their works – were suddenly in the frontline of the struggle, the pique is perhaps understandable. The campaign against Stalin, they had reason to think, was *theirs*. As for the new recruits, lacking training, appropriate firepower, battle honours and with no evidence of a real will for the fight, they could never be equal to the task ahead. Most alarmingly of all, the call-up suggested that 'General' Nabokov had no real idea how or where to engage the enemy.

Nabokov himself may reasonably be seen as someone who crossed the boundary between the worlds of the literary and civic intellectuals, between the smoke-filled room and the salon. Whilst it is fair to argue that he was, at heart, one of the 'eye and ear people,' his knowledge of literature – as suggested by his work at St John's College, and confirmed by Isaiah Berlin – was substantial. His political engagement must be considered sincere: the evidence of his disillusionment with Allied policy in Berlin, the polemics in *Politics* and *Partisan Review*, the involvement with the Dwight Macdonalds Europe–America Groups and the Waldorf-Astoria action with AIF – all these pre-dated the CCF and any real possibility of self-advancement. He would appear, then, to have had credentials which could conceivably have satisfied the literary–political faction and, with experience of *both* worlds, he was – as Sidney Hook acknowledged – potentially a great asset to the Congress. As it turned out, however, he was unable to find a strategy which could unite both groups effectively in a common cause.

Chapter 7

One End Against the Middle: Intellectuals Behind the High Culture Stockade

Art and the American Left in the 1930s

For the New York Intellectuals, the journey to an anti-Stalinism which, for all practical purposes, denied and erased their earlier anti-capitalism, was accompanied by an increasing preoccupation with the cultural life of their own country. This group became powerful advocates of mass culture theory; in turn, the CCF served as a vehicle for the transmission of a body of ideas which held considerable appeal for mid-twentieth-century intellectuals. Interestingly, prominent members of the New York group saw this cultural campaign not as a displacement of their anti-Stalinism, but as contiguous with it. In this world-view Western 'mass culture' and communism became linked, Hollywood and the Kremlin met: twin symptoms of forces of dehumanisation and control which must be resisted. Nabokov's campaign – from the articles of the 1940s and on into the Congress period – involved making links between the world of art music (and, specifically, the cosmopolitan world of contemporary music) and the anti-communist cause. Stalinism, for him, was a danger to artists, and therefore to art, and therefore to humanity. His focus was very much on the deformed high culture of the USSR, with little surface interest in the culture mills grinding away on Madison Avenue and Broadway. Yet it remains true that, in his position as the Congress's secretary-general, he moved in circles much taken up with fears of the new mass culture. So, how does his project appear when viewed in this context?

The origins of the New York Intellectuals' preoccupation with what came to be known as 'mass culture' must be sought in the 1930s, and the politics of the disintegrating American Left. In 1935 the Comintern – Moscow's apparatus for controlling the international communist movement – had adopted a 'Popular Front' policy, under which communists were expected to seek alliances with liberals, socialists, social democrats – in short, with all anti-fascist forces. This contrasted dramatically with the previous 'ultra-leftist' period, when the official Moscow line had been a hard line, and careless associations could lead otherwise blameless and obedient fellow travellers to be branded 'social fascists'. For those supporters who found their loyalty strained by this reversal, there was much worse to come – the purges, the show trials, and finally the non-aggression pact signed between Molotov and von Ribbentrop in 1939. On all of these issues the Communist Party of the USA defended the Soviet Union. All of this led to much desertion: as we have seen, favoured destinations for many of the New York Intellectuals were the various smaller Trotskyist parties.

For writers and artists of the Left, the split also had an aesthetic dimension, for in the Popular Front period Communist parties opposed experimentalism and the avant-garde in favour of realism and naturalism: they demanded accessible, comprehensible (and, of course, socialist) art. As Christopher Brookeman puts it:

> Avant-garde abstract art was seen as negative and pessimistic and ... therefore potentially counter-revolutionary. The popular front consciousness which dominated the arts in America during the 1930s when radicals of all persuasions buried their differences and united in a common struggle against fascism, created an affirmative mood in which the experimental disruptions of modernism seemed out of place. (Brookeman, 1984, p. 47)

The Party was also at pains to stress its Americanism, to argue that, far from being a foreign import, it should be seen as in the traditions of the country's founders. Consequently, art was required to be *Americanist*, as well as socialist and readily understandable. Music was no exception and, in tune with this mood, we find Aaron Copland, writing in 1935, arguing that European modernism had lost its relevance: 'It is no secret that many of the young composers who had taken one or the other of these two older men [Schoenberg and Stravinsky] as their models have now thrown in their lot with that of the working class' (quoted in Brody, 1993, p. 172). For composers who did so, a new approach was required. Arthur Berger recalls that:

> ... artists were being supported [by the Works Progress Administration] to carry out projects with Americana as their subject matter. You can easily understand that the mannerisms and devices coming out of Vienna were too remote for this purpose ... . Curiously enough, Americanism at that time went hand in hand with political leftism – not the breast-beating Americanism, but the American liberalism that had spawned the WPA. Now it should be obvious that the demands of a proletariat music required greater accessibility than could be vouchsafed by the type of music emanating from Vienna. (Coppock, 1978, p. 49)

Berger also testifies to the confusion felt by a composer of the Left at the changes in the official line. Composers who had at one stage been encouraged to include the new techniques in workers' songs – to create, as Henry Cowell said, 'a music that is revolutionary in form and content' (Lee, 1992, p. 123) – now found that these should be 'like Tschaikowsky [*sic*], like traditional folksong. One had to bring the message of the new order to the people in a language they could understand' (Coppock, 1978, p. 49). The same issues emerged in the Composers' Collective of New York City, formed in 1932, where Cowell argued for modernism against his co-founder Charles Seeger, who offended against every tenet of modernism when he insisted that:

> ... the composer must learn to know this audience [i.e. the workers], to study its musical needs and requirements and fashion their work so that it may fit these requirements. It is obvious that throwing off certain habits and traditions of thought that have been moulded exclusively by production for the needs of the bourgeois concert hall ... is no easy task. (Quoted in Lee, 1992, pp. 86–7)

Seeger believed that eventually a 'people's style' would emerge, in which 'advanced' musical trends and proletarian content would combine: in the short term, however, composers should bend to the needs of the proletariat. Gradually, however, such debates were stifled as the Party imposed its line and narrowed the definition of socialist realism. Seeger went on, in 1938, to become the director of the Federal Music Project, reinforcing Berger's link between the New Deal liberalism responsible for such projects, and 'political leftism'. This overlap created a powerful impetus for a sort of cultural nationalism which extended into the patriotic war years. The avant-garde, naturally, were dismayed. Looking back to the period, Eric Salzman distils the later modernist orthodoxy (and disdain) when he writes of 'the rise and fall of musical populism [and] the great retreat into social usefulness and tonal comprehensibility ... [the] clarion calls for a music within the listening grasp and performance capabilities of the musically unwashed' (Salzman, 1964, pp. 16–18).

This sort of reaction was shared by a number of contemporary artists and writers who felt that the Popular Front had led to an intellectual dilution in the cultural organisations of the Left (as Irving Howe put it, 'the poets were gone ... the journalists remained'), and already in the 1930s a counter-attack emerges. First of all, the Moscow line was confronted in the field of art theory. Trotsky himself wrote to *Partisan Review* in 1938, stressing the opposition of 'true intellectual creation ... [to] lies, hypocrisy and the spirit of conformity. Art can become a strong ally of revolution only insofar as it remains faithful to itself ' (quoted in Brody, 1993, p. 176). This presented an opening for anti-Stalinist intellectuals seeking to affect a reconciliation between the Left and the avant-garde. However, as their active interest in revolution subsided, this shaded into support for a detached, depoliticised art. Two intellectuals in particular spearheaded the counter-offensive: Clement Greenberg and Dwight Macdonald. Macdonald's influential analysis of mass culture, begun in *PR*, continued in the pages of his own *Politics* (1943–49). Greenberg outlined a binary opposition between 'avant-garde and kitsch' in his famous 1939 article of that name and, significantly, he argues that the avant-garde must remain critical – *but of itself, not of society* – this, and only this, being the determining mark of quality in a culture threatened by the monstrous twin banalities of popular culture and the Popular Front.

By the end of the 1930s, then, Trotskyism had become the home of dissent and intellectual independence on the Left. The cultural turn found them attacking not only popular culture, but what they saw as the 'sub-intellectual lives and tastes of Communists' (Ross, 1989, p. 22). In the polemics of Macdonald and Greenberg, these Left intellectuals found the theory they needed: an analysis of the new enemy – mass culture – that had replaced capitalism, and a defence of a hermetic artistic elite. It may seem paradoxical that out of the 1930s fracture in the revolutionary Left, there grew an invigorated, unapologetic and *apolitical* American avant-garde. As Greenberg later remarked, 'Some day it will have to be told how anti-Stalinism which started out more or less as Trotskyism turned into art for art's sake, and thereby cleared the way heroically for what was to come' (quoted in Guilbaut, 1992, p. 239).

Post-war: the appeal of Mass Culture theory

Born in the immediate prewar era, the group's preoccupation with mass culture had, by the 1950s, became central. It filled the vacuum left by the critique of capitalism, the belief in a transformed, socialist future, and can arguably be seen as displaced radicalism: Richard Pells, for example, argues that the mass culture critique allowed postwar intellectuals

> ... who no longer assailed their traditional enemies – the capitalists, the political bosses, the labor barons, the military chieftains ... to preserve a little of their radical heritage ... [by concentrating on] the popular tastes and values of their countrymen. (Pells, 1985, p. 218)

From within the orbit of the ACCF, Daniel Bell agrees. For Bell, the intellectuals – traumatised as they were by the experience of the 1940s, living in an era dominated by the external communist threat – turned inwards to their own society, finding despair, anomie and alienation. The mass culture that was held responsible also allowed them to maintain their self-image, so that 'though in the 1950s there was a burning out of the radical political will, this radical will – the distancing of self from the society – was maintained in the culture and through cultural criticism' (Bell, 1979, p. 45). Bell and Pells agree that they *saw themselves* as having remained radical. It remains an open question, however, whether, in real terms, their postwar cultural concerns can be said to weigh equally with their earlier revolutionism. Bell seems to think so; Pells, however, is more sceptical (note, in the above extract, his crucial qualification 'a little').

The mass culture theory newly adopted by this group had much in common with its earlier, conservative incarnation. In his influential *Culture and Anarchy*, Matthew Arnold had warned of the influence of the new forms catering for a cultural market enlarged by the growth of literacy. In the face of this unsettling situation, it fell to the educated few to preserve the 'sweetness and light' of high culture from the surrounding 'anarchy'. In the mid-twentieth century, F.R. Leavis powerfully amplified and developed these ideas. His perspective was a pessimistic one: catering for the mass market involved a 'levelling down' process, unleashing a flood of trivial 'standardised' cultural products, characterised by their 'deliberate exploitation of the cheap response', their 'surrender ... to the cheapest emotional appeals'. The greater problem was not, however, the inherent worthlessness of mass cultural products, but rather the threat that it represented to the survival of high culture by undermining its traditional authority. Mass cultural products tended to exploit a hunger for self-improvement and education, thereby pretending to a quality they did not possess. Such claims of quality might seem to be reinforced by the sheer scale of production, a fraud which the poorly educated mass audience was not equipped to expose. The net result was an alternative scale of value which consistently placed worthless products in the glow of art, at the same time implicitly challenging those who retained the power of discrimination:

> Here we have the plight of culture in general. The *landmarks* have shifted, multiplied and crowded upon one another, the *distinctions* and *dividing lines* have *blurred away*, the *boundaries* are gone. (Leavis, 1994, p. 14, my italics)

This is a key mass cultural idea, and one retained by the intellectuals around the ACCF and CCF. Once-accepted boundaries between high and low culture have been, or are being, broken down, with ominous portents for the former. A second important theme follows from this. Leavis argued that only a very small public was 'critically adult' – still able to discriminate 'amid the smother of new books'. This educated few therefore bore a heavy responsibility: it fell to them to guard all that was truly valuable in art and hand it on, intact.

Much of this is retained by the New York group, despite all the social and political distance between *Scrutiny* and *Partisan Review*. In his influential essay 'A Theory of Mass Culture', Dwight Macdonald argues that mass culture has eroded the once-clear distinction between folk culture and high culture. Parasitic upon high culture, it nonetheless competes with – and is corrosive of – both; easily understood and enjoyed, it drives out the good everywhere. Moreover, Macdonald borrowed from his *PR* colleague, Clement Greenberg, the idea of 'kitsch': academicised art with a 'built-in reaction', which Greenberg had said 'predigests art for the spectator and spares him effort, provides him with a shortcut to the pleasures of art, that detours what is necessarily difficult in genuine art'. Mass culture is dynamic, indeed *revolutionary*, and, echoing Leavis, Macdonald warns that it is 'breaking down the old barriers of class, tradition, taste and dissolving all cultural distinctions' (Macdonald, 1994, pp. 30–32). Even high culture is not immune, prey as it is to the immobilities of academicism (and with composers like Elgar providing 'kitsch for the elite'): only the avant-garde refuses to compete, in 'a desperate attempt to fence off some area where the serious artist ... [can] still function'.

How could culture be saved? Macdonald identifies two strategies. First, there is what he calls the 'liberal' approach. This is essentially the 'democratisation of culture', an attempt to raise the level of culture as consumed by the mass audience, to drive out kitsch by means of an educational mission. It will not be easy, since kitsch is narcotic, addictive. The alternative, 'aristocratic' solution would involve rebuilding class walls and aesthetic distinctions, reviving the intellectual elite in order to provide a sanctuary for *real* art – demanding, progressive, individualist. Either way, the prospects, he warns, are poor, since 'the engine ... shows no sign of running down'.

Mass culture theory, then, appealed to the Right – to Eliot, Nietzsche, y Gasset and Leavis – as well as to the Left-but-rapidly-heading-Right *PR* set. Crucially, however, it answered different questions for each group. Whilst the Right sought an explanation for a perceived cultural decline, a lost age of deference and excellence, the Left needed to account for the collapse of their revolutionary hopes. What could explain the quietism of the proletariat and the resilience of bourgeois structures? Capitalism must have developed some mechanism unforeseen by Marx, some means of disabling the historical forces which should have led to socialism. Mass culture gave some sort of explanation, seeming to block a future utopia. These ideas found powerful expression in the analyses of the Frankfurt School theorists (exiled in New York by the 1940s), and particularly in those of Theodor Adorno.

Adorno's model of mass culture, and the products of what he called the 'culture industry', proceeds via a focus on the specific example of music (in practice, this meant the Tin Pan Alley songs and the popular swing music of the 1930s – he never felt moved to revise his views in the light of the emergence of bebop or rock). Adorno identifies two key features of popular music: standardisation, and what he terms 'pseudo-individualisation'. The former represents the central distinction between serious and popular music which operates, he insists, according to set formulae both in terms of *form* – the 32-bar AABA song, a few dance types, the limited subject matter of lyrics – and *detail*, which is reduced to a 'veneer' of predictable 'effects' (Adorno, 1994, pp. 202–3). This freezing of music into a few standard moulds has come about through the competition within the culture industry, since all producers must imitate what works – that is, what sells – and so no deviation from the 'natural' (conventional) language of music is allowed. Very much like Greenberg and Macdonald, Adorno takes the category 'art' as given (in his case, the benchmark is the Austro-German art music tradition of the eighteenth and nineteenth centuries), and assumes that good art presents some sort of challenge to the listener – that it requires some *effort*. Since popular music can be reduced to a few set formulae, no such effort is required, and, indeed, 'the composition hears for the listener'. This standardised music is designed to produce standard reactions, 'a system of response mechanisms wholly antagonistic to the ideal of individuality in a free … society'.

The manipulation of the audience goes further, however. In order to guarantee continued sales, popular music needs to guarantee stimulation and novelty; it must, in short, appear to be always *departing* from convention, whilst simultaneously upholding and *reinforcing* the conventions themselves. This is achieved, Adorno argues, through the process of pseudo-individualisation, the appearance – it is no more than that – of differentiation among the products of the culture industry. It may take the form of 'so-called improvisation' (creating a myth of 'pioneer artisanship') or nebulous variations in style between performers. By such means, 'cultural mass production [is endowed] with the halo of free choice'. In reality the circle is complete, and the obedience of the audience is total: standardisation creates standard reactions, so that their listening is done for them, whilst pseudo-individualisation ensures that the process of control goes unseen. This manipulation can only proceed in tandem with concealment, Adorno argues: 'Concentration and control in our culture hide themselves … unhidden they would provoke resistance.'

Adorno's version of mass culture theory therefore provides an explanation for the quiescence of the working class. Popular culture functions as a distraction from the fear, insecurity and sheer meaninglessness of work under capitalism. The tragedy for working people is that the music they run to for relief only reproduces, in the cultural sphere, the obedience of the workplace. Furthermore, popular music not only provides a diversion from the real source of workers' problems, but functions in a way that retains their attention: once diverted, they remain so. The masses seek novelty, to escape the monotony of their lives, but in turning to the easy release offered by the culture industry they must quickly become bored again, leading to more consumption of more popular music. Combining temporary stimulation with addiction, popular music for Adorno is a narcotic which saps the vitality of the working class.

Listeners are of two types, corresponding to a broad division into dance music on the one hand, and sentimental music on the other. The 'rhythmically obedient' listener is expressing, through his response to music and, by following the unvarying dance rhythm, a desire to *obey*. The 'emotional' listener wants to be allowed to weep – to weep for their own lack of fulfilment, a desire which can be temporarily assuaged by sentimental music. These listeners turn to late Romanticism and 'Slavic melancholy'. Such emotional release holds no fears for the power structure: 'it is catharsis for the masses, but catharsis which keeps them all the more firmly in line. One who weeps does not resist any more than one who marches.' In this way Adorno draws the admirers of Rachmaninov and Tchaikovsky into his theory along with the foxtrotting fans of Paul Whiteman and the Lindy hoppers of Harlem. All are found to have been shaped by the culture industry; all are marked by apathy and unthinking obedience.

The 'middlebrow' idea and its political uses

These, then, are some of the recurring themes in mass culture theory as taken up, and developed, by the New York Intellectuals of the ACCF. We have also argued that its appeal must be seen in terms of their political journey from 1930s revolutionaries to Cold War 'radicals', engaged in a restless, uneasy accommodation with American society. In order to return to Nicolas Nabokov, it only remains to consider a development of this theory, and one particularly associated with the 'anti-communist liberals' of the 1950s. This is the idea of a middlebrow culture. Joan Shelley Rubin, in *The Making of Middlebrow Culture*, traces the emergence of the term. It was called into being, she argues, by a real and unprecedented cultural movement which in the three decades after the First World War encompassed a wide range of activities all aiming to make the fruits of high culture available to a broad public. The Book-of-the-Month Club, 'Great Books' discussion groups and university degrees such as that offered at Nabokov's own St John's College, the growth of correspondence courses, night schools and public lectures, all these were symptoms of the new trend (Rubin, 1992, pp. xi–xii and p. 1). In an increasingly literate society, and one which – at least from the 1940s – offered unprecedented security and disposable income to the middle and lower classes, such ventures fed a widespread hunger for improvement. Rubin's focus is primarily literary, but the phenomenon she describes also embraced music: consider the vogue for 'music appreciation' classes, the spread of classical music on the radio, and the fusion of the two in Walter Damrosch's *NBC Music Appreciation Hour*. If the increasingly ubiquitous gramophone and the growing market for classical recordings formed the foundation of these developments, its driving force came from a general desire for education and cultural self-advancement (Horowitz, 1987, pp. 226–35).

As for the term 'middlebrow' itself, 'highbrow' (with its origins in phrenology) had already been established by the 1880s and, by the turn of the century, it had been joined by 'lowbrow'. Around the First World War, Van Wyck Brooks, bemoaning what he saw as the highbrow/lowbrow division in American life, hoped instead for a 'genial middle ground'. Then in 1933 Margaret Widdemer published an article called 'Message and Middlebrow'. In Widdemer's hands, the term seems to have been used neutrally, to describe the average, reasonably intelligent reader but, as Rubin shows, the term quickly became ever more loaded and negative. In particular Virginia Woolf, in an essay of 1942, sets both the (contemptuous) tone and the agenda for much of what follows, establishing two important themes. First, the middlebrow is judged guilty of crimes against art – someone by whom and in whose name good taste has been corrupted by commerce. Second, she suggests that both highbrows and lowbrows formed a natural alliance against 'the pernicious pest who comes in between' (Rubin, 1992, p. xii). Writer and ACCF member Leslie Fiedler would later distil this idea memorably into the title of an essay for *Encounter* – 'The Middle Against Both Ends' (1955). Both themes resonate in the writings of Clement Greenberg and Dwight Macdonald.

Middlebrow culture, as defined by these commentators, was a hybrid. It used the *means* of mass culture (the mass media) in pursuit of the same goal (sales and profit) but drew on the *materials* of high culture – the 'classics' of music, painting and literature; in short, it involved the appropriation and use of high culture by the culture industries. This would necessarily entail some selection: which paintings, books or symphonies were potentially acceptable to a mass audience? Some changes might have to be made in the process – musical arrangements, editing or abridging – along, typically, with an attempt to *explain*. New works could also be drawn into this process, but only if they used those aspects of high cultural tradition which could be easily assimilated.

ACCF intellectuals found all this highly alarming. Greenberg had touched on the idea of middlebrow culture in his concept of 'kitsch' – a type of debased, academicised high art, in which the original models are drained of all vitality. Kitsch – pre-digested, manipulative, essentially *coercive* of its audience – had to be opposed. Macdonald's cultural model, begun in his 1944 'A Theory of Mass Culture' as a tripartite system of high, mass and folk cultures was developed through the 1950s and finally consolidated in 'Mass Cult and Mid Cult' of 1960. Here Macdonald – mocking Soviet language (as Orwell had done in *1984*, for example with 'EngSoc') – adds a fourth category: middlebrow culture, or 'midcult'. This, he argues, is a far more worrying development than the advent of mass culture:

> The danger to High Culture is not so much from mass cult as from a peculiar hybrid bred from the latter's unnatural intercourse with the former. A whole middle culture has come into existence and it threatens to absorb both its parents. This intermediate form – let us call it Mid cult – has the essential qualities of mass cult – the formula, the built-in reaction, the lack of any standard except popularity – but it decently covers them with a cultural figleaf. (Quoted in Brookeman, 1984, p. 51)

Middlebrow culture, then, was seen as an outgrowth of mass culture and, as such, it inherited all the traits of mass culture which so exercised the coterie around *Partisan Review*. It broke down boundaries and blurred distinctions of quality in cultural life. It was fundamentally bland, undemanding and *easy*. Exploiting the emotional response, it was typically sentimental in tone. However, where it differed, crucially, from mass culture, was in its parasitic relationship to high culture, a relationship which threatened to fatally weaken the host. This fear was expressed succinctly by the author of *The Origins of Totalitarianism*, Hannah Arendt, another of the Frankfurt School exiles who exercised much influence over the *PR*/ACCF group. At a 1959 conference which also featured prominent Congress 'names' Irving Kristol, Sidney Hook, Daniel Bell, Arthur Schlesinger Jr and Edward Shils, she expressed this fear in a paper entitled 'Society and Culture'. Although written a few years after the period which is the main focus of this study, the argument is very characteristic of that deployed by ACCF intellectuals in the early 1950s. Arendt points out that the consumption process is just that – one in which products are *consumed*, which is to say destroyed – and that when the scale of the appetites faced by the producers of entertainment is also recognised, the net result must be a constant search for new products.

> In this predicament those who produce for the mass media ransack the entire range of past and present culture in the hope of finding suitable material. This material, however, cannot be offered as it is; it must be prepared and altered in order to become entertaining; it cannot be consumed as it is. (Arendt, 1964, p. 48)[1]

The problem, then, is not the mass distribution of cultural objects: what is at issue for Arendt is the reprocessing (into kitsch) which is, she argues, the *precondition* of mass distribution. Art objects are not for *use*. Once art is made to fulfil functions, such as entertainment, once it is taken up and used, it disappears. We should not, then, speak of mass culture, but rather

> ... the decay of culture in mass society ... . [Those responsible are] not the Tin Pan Alley composers [but] a special kind of intellectual, often well-read and well-informed, whose sole function is to organise, disseminate and change cultural objects in order to make them palatable to those who want to be entertained or – and this is worse – to be 'educated', that is, to acquire as cheaply as possible some kind of cultural knowledge to improve their social status. (Arendt, 1964, p. 49)

Although the term 'middlebrow' is not used, the whole focus – on the corrosion of art when (mis)used by commerce, whether for entertainment or 'education' – suggests a development that can be distinguished from the basic mass culture idea. The pointed reference to 'the decay of culture [which we may take to mean *high* culture] in mass society' makes this clear. In what may be a revealing comment, Arendt adds that the current malaise among intellectuals is due to the activities of the group she identifies: her concern is with the health of art, but also that of the intellectual community.

In these fears over middlebrow culture intellectuals gave their community (that is, intellectuals *proper*, as opposed to the midcult technicians referred to by Arendt) the vital role of preserving high culture. They also developed an analysis suggesting that even more was at stake than the 'Survival Of Art'; this analysis presented middlebrow culture as a symptom of larger forces and neatly fused their cultural and political concerns. In short, a number of these writers began to associate middlebrow culture with Stalinism. The Popular Front policy of the 1930s had been seen by *PR* writers as leading to a cultural dilution of the Left, in its promotion of accessibility and Americanism. Recall also Irving Howe's comment about the poets having been replaced by journalists – again, an intellectual and social dilution caused by middle-class influence within the communist movement. In the relationship between middlebrow culture and Stalinism, cause and effect could flow either way, so that, on the one hand, Phillip Rahv could argue that American Stalinists had taken on the 'genteel and chauvinistic norms of the liberal middle classes', whilst on the other, Lionel Trilling suggested that this culture *generated* Stalinism, which becomes

---

1   The original seminar was held in June 1959. Jacobs served as Executive Director of the ACCF from 1956, having previously worked for Voice of America.

'endemic in the American middle class as soon as that class begins to think; it is a cultural Stalinism, independent of any political belief' (Wilford, 1995, p. 63). But whether the Stalinists were becoming middle-class or the middle class was becoming Stalinist, the net result was the same.

Andrew Ross uses another Leslie Fiedler article, 'Reading the Rosenberg Letters' (published in the first *Encounter*, along with Nabokov's 'No Cantatas for Stalin') to draw out aspects of this theme. For Fiedler, Julius and Ethel Rosenberg's published collection of prison letters illustrate a particularly petit-bourgeois strain of sentimental egalitarianism which threatens to destroy high art and level the class distinctions that sustain it. The Rosenbergs' communism and their middlebrow tastes meet in that both projects require 'rigid standardisation and homogeneity' (Ross, 1989, p. 15). Their mode of expression reveals the sad results of misguided attempts at 'improvement', so that Ethel's writing is condemned as 'the language of ordinary people writing for literary effect', whilst their tastes are the middlebrow's typical boundary-blurring *mélange*: Julius would sing 'mostly folk music, worker's songs, people's songs, popular tunes plus excerpts from operas and symphonies [such as Beethoven's Ninth]', Ethel's choice would place snatches of *Madame Butterfly* alongside Sinatra (Ross, 1989, pp. 24–7). Fiedler's use of the musical example allows him to illustrate two key points in the attack on middlebrow taste. The Rosenbergs' fasten on nineteenth-century classical music, but reduce it to 'the tunes': apparently undiscriminating, they serve up this filleted material alongside the pop hits of the day, so that the richness and complexity of Beethoven is first reduced to the *Ode to Joy*, then segued into *Fly Me to the Moon*. The middlebrow's double crime – the trivialisation of high culture and the erosion of aesthetic distinctions – is clear.

Ross also draws attention to Fiedler's use of the term 'secondhand' which is, he argues, also important. The middlebrow has no culture of his or her own: all is false, imitation, *ersatz*, and it is here that one can begin to grasp the argument connecting middlebrow culture and Stalinism. There is nothing *authentic* about the Rosenbergs who have, in effect, been formed by a double manipulation. They are, first, creatures of communism, which by its very nature manipulates and controls – exploiting and directing its followers, Equally, however, they have given themselves up to the culture industry which coerces its audience, creating a 'prefabricated public'. Both of these control mechanisms aim to deny the masses the capacity for critical, independent thought: both communism *and* the culture industry, then, are totalitarian forces.[2]

---

2   According to Janice Radway, that archetypal manifestation of the middlebrow, the Book of the Month Club, was already being linked to 'Bolshevism' in the mid-1920s. In common with themes emerging in the present study, she concludes that the heat generated by the BOTMC in literary circles derived from a fear of rival cultural authorities. See Radway, (1990, pp. 704–8).

Nabokov on 'middlebrow culture'

And so we return to Nicolas Nabokov. This examination of mass cultural ideas, and the concept of 'middlebrow' culture which grew from them, may seem to have been a rather lengthy diversion from our central concerns. It is important, however, to understand both the theory itself – at least, in its fundamentals – and its currency within the CCF, since a close reading of Nabokov's writings shows them to be thoroughly permeated by the language and assumptions of mass culture theory, and above all its fear of the middlebrow.

To begin with, recall some of the terms he uses to describe Shostakovich's music – the 'banal' and 'trite' *Fifth Symphony*, the 'dated formulae' and 'commonplace patterns' of *Lady Macbeth*. The jibes which compare the Russian composer to a nineteenth-century Conservatory student (whilst faintly praising his 'excellent' craftsmanship) now also take on more meaning: guilty of a pallid and exhausted academicism, Shostakovich is almost becoming a producer of Greenbergian kitsch. And, like the New York Intellectuals surveying the domestic cultural landscape, Nabokov could not help but read this as a warning:

> I ... remained worried over this music, and the reason for my worry was something outside of Shostakovich himself. It seemed to me ... that Shostakovich might be a symptom of a new era approaching in art ... . This synthetic and retrospective score ... was perhaps the true expression of a new period in which the aim was to establish easily comprehensible, utilitarian, and at the same time contemporaneous art. Perhaps some of the principles which had been the cornerstones of the artistic philosophy of the past two generations would be put aside by the composers of this approaching era; perhaps our demand that music be primarily good in quality, new in spirit and technique, original in outlook would be subordinated to such principles as absolute and immediate comprehensibility to large masses of people and fulfilment of an educational mission, political and social. (Nabokov, 1951d, p. 192)[3]

This is an important passage, since what 'worries' Nabokov is not so much communism, or even communist control of art, but what seems to him an alternative set of values by which art should be judged, values which – if they should prevail – would place the whole modernist enterprise in jeopardy. This value system constitutes a danger independent of communism, so that the 'new era' hinted at by Shostakovich is very much a threat to 'our' music and 'our' principles (that is, in the West). The problematic ideas of artistic accessibility, education and utility might not be confined by Churchill's Iron Curtain. Indeed, they seemed to threaten the modernist project which Nabokov, in his Paris festival, would later set out to celebrate – and defend.

He believed, as we have seen, that the roots of what he called 'middle-brow' Soviet culture must be sought in *pre*-revolutionary Russia, in the late nineteenth-century emergence of the 'petite bourgeoisie'. The 1917 Revolution merely began a process which would bring this class to power and institutionalise its tastes, the reciprocal of which was, of course, the destruction of the old intelligentsia with its Western-oriented modernism. In other words, the Soviet Union demonstrated the victory of the

---

3   Nabokov is recalling his encounter with the First Symphony, some time in the late 1920s.

provincial over the cosmopolitan – again, forces which operated independently of communism. Nabokov hoped that his readers would draw the conclusion that the elite – as guardians of cultural value and progress – should be defended (a central aim of mass culture theorists). The culture of the West could still be defended; Nabokov aimed, by pointing to what had happened in Russia, to show the high price of failure.

The idea of middlebrow culture identifies a mass response to art which marries a shallow interest in cultural elevation, to a desire for emotional release which precludes any effort, any engagement with 'difficult' material. It is a mode of reception which, superficial and above all sentimental, halts artistic advance, and what Nabokov tells us about his own experience of the Soviet musical public perfectly fits such an analysis. The 1951 essay 'Music under the Generals' gives a detailed description of a Russian military concert attended whilst the writer served with the US army in occupied Berlin. This was, he tells us, 'fascinating to see' since it reflected 'average Russian tastes'. The passage dealing with the performance of the tenor Kozlovsky (who sang arias from *Eugene Onegin* and *Sadko* along with songs by Tchaikovsky, Glinka, Arensky and Rachmaninov), is significant. The singer gave a performance which Nabokov considered technically accomplished (another 'good craftsman') but which appalled him as an artist:

> His breath was controlled and completely inaudible. His dynamics were smooth and his intonation perfect; but ... but ... his interpretation! The awful provincial taste in delivery, its greasy outmoded sentimentality reminiscent of the worst habits of the American radio crooner.

But what of the audience? How was this travesty received?

> After each of his numbers the audience clapped and cheered furiously. Their faces got red and their eyes wet. The stocky pomaded little colonels and their round middle-class wives dressed in pre-war evening gowns, a plump brooch keeping the V-shaped neckline from bursting out under the heavy milk-farm equipment, jumped to their feet and bellowed .... (Nabokov, 1951a, p. 51)

In recounting the tale Nabokov associates Kozlovsky with that archetypal mass cultural figure, the 'American radio crooner': his sentimental performance evidently meets the needs of the 'middle-class' listeners who respond appropriately, with tears. Nabokov's contempt for this audience – mocked for their physical appearance, dress sense and lack of decorum – is self-evident (and not unimportant if, as it begins to appear, his cultural–political project overlaps with the anti-middlebrow crusade of the *PR* group), but the key point here is their response to the music. The red faces, the furious cheering, the damp eyes and the bellowing – nothing but emotion. This is a double affront: it suggests an ignorance of genteel concertgoing norms but also, and more importantly, it offends against the modernist privileging of the intellectual response over any other. The sense of the passage is that here is an audience – from 'the new uneducated middle strata of Soviet society' – which *does not know how to receive classical music*: in short, its reactions are *wrong*.

Later, talking to some of the performers and the audience, he learns that they are uncomfortable with even contemporary *Soviet* music. When they tell him that 'It's strange to us ... its language is unfamiliar ... and not enough *melodichna*' (Nabokov, 1951a, p. 52), then the largely nineteenth-century nature of the programme and, on a broader scale, the reason for 'the iron curtain which ... limit[s] the Soviet repertoire' becomes apparent (Nabokov, 1953, p. 52). In his account of this concert Nabokov has, in effect, outlined the case against the middlebrow 'music-lover'. Seeking only the easy, the familiar, the tuneful, ever-willing to weep on cue, to submit, in Adorno's words, to 'a catharsis which keeps them all the more firmly in line' (Adorno, 1994, pp. 212–13), these officers and their wives are helping to create a petrified canon which threatens forever to exclude the music of their own time.

There is also some suggestion that the danger is one which spans the Iron Curtain, that levelling down is levelling down wherever it occurs, and whether in the service of socialism or stockholders. When Nabokov wants to convey the 'oppressive uniformity' of Soviet music, he remarks that 'The musical products of different parts of the Socialist Fatherland all sound as though they had been turned out by Ford or General Motors' (Nabokov, 1953, p. 51). In the same vein, Shostakovich's *First Symphony* is

> ... like a good suit of ready-made clothes, which reminds you longingly of a good London tailor, or like one of those tidy modern cubicles in a Dutch or German workers' settlement – all perfectly built, according to the best-known techniques, very proper and neat yet infinitely impersonal and, in the long run, extremely dull. (Nabokov, 1943, p. 423)

Nabokov finds another link between Shostakovich and mass culture: he attributes the latter's Western success to the machinations of the culture industry. The original (1943) version of 'The Case of Dmitri Shostakovich' concludes by accounting for the disparity between the composer's celebrity and the intrinsic worth of his music. 'There are', he writes, 'many composers who both write better and have more to say than Shostakovich', so why are their works not found in concert programmes all across America? He supplies the answer:

> ... because our maestros and their managers ordain otherwise. It is these maestros and managers who are chiefly responsible for all the uproar in this country over one or two composers for one or two seasons. They have learned too well how to exploit a propitious political situation (what has become now of the 'beloved' Finn, Sibelius?) and create a bubble reputation to relieve the stagnation of the concert repertory. ... (Nabokov, 1943, pp. 430–1)[4]

---

4   An earlier section covers the same ground: 'Shostakovich is the undisputed idol of all the "maestros", blond, bald or grey, who in homage to Russia serve his seven symphonies at regular intervals ... he is referred to as "the new Beethoven", or "the new Berlioz" etc.' The reference to Sibelius, that he has been much played 'until recently' (Nabokov, 1943, p. 424) is interesting. This presumably implies that, 'exploiting a propitious political situation', Sibelius was taken up after the Soviet invasion of Finland, only to be dropped 'in homage to Russia' after the Nazi invasion and America's entry into the war on the Allied side. Later, as the maestro-manager organising the 1952 festival in Paris, Nabokov would himself seek to exploit the political resonance of Sibelius. Discussing a possible programme with Stokowski, who he hoped would appear at the festival, he wrote: 'I would urge you very much to include *Finlandia* by Sibelius in your program ... The paramount [reason] ... is that we should pay tribute to

It is, perhaps, a slight reference. However, consider it in the light of the musical critique which the essay has also provided. This concludes that the music is 'retrospective' and 'synthetic' which, in mass culture terms, translates as 'standardised' and 'secondhand' (or perhaps 'composed of various secondhand elements'). The managers (as part of the culture industry) and maestros (as part of its 'star' system) need to relieve the stagnation of the repertory (which, Nabokov might easily have added, their own provincialism has created). According to Adorno, this industry needs to reconcile the need to stimulate the mass audience's jaded palates with the equal requirement for musical security and familiarity. The whole thrust of Nabokov's argument is that Shostakovich's music is essentially orthodox, its apparent newness mere novelty due to multiple borrowings from disparate sources. It is therefore ideal for the purposes of the culture industry. Much later, a booklet outlining the aims of the CCF would offer as the 'dangers faced by art' both 'oppression' *and* 'commercialised patronage':[5] the case of Shostakovich, as presented here, illustrates both forces in action – the one accounting for the nature of the music, the other for its unmerited success.

And just as standardisation can be found both East and West – in a symphony or an off-the-peg suit – so can ill-educated, philistine audiences. The same 'Music Under the Generals' which offers its account of the Red Army concert also contains a section on its author's evening at a Berlin performance of *Madame Butterfly* in the company of two Americans: 'General X' and 'Colonel W'. General X, who appears to know little of classical music, explains to his companion that 'Nick here ... is hep on music and shows the Krauts how to go about it. He'll tell us what this g.d thing is about'. When 'Nick' tries to do that, however, the General becomes outraged at the opera's portrayal of an American officer as a liar and a bigamist (this offence compounded by the fact that the performers were *German* and the performance in the *Russian* sector). After the three have sat through the opera (with its 'oily tunes') in 'awkward, frozen silence', Nabokov tries to pacify the General, telling him that this is, after all, a famous piece – a classic – often heard at the New York 'Met' and indeed all over the USA. The General retorts that, of course, he knows that, adding 'I've heard that g.d music played by our band in Fort Worth, and better than those Germans, too' (Nabokov, 1951a, p. 50). 'Music Under the Generals' is a light piece – Nabokov as raconteur, as entertainer – but the effect of yoking together these two concert experiences, linked by their amused but disdainful view of officers' tastes is clear: it leaves the impression that a misunderstanding of, and disregard for, culture among the middle classes is no respecter of political boundaries.

In mass culture theory, the arrival of the middlebrow variant is held to be particularly ominous on account of its alleged tendency to blur the boundaries between categories – between high art and popular culture, and ultimately between good and bad. The middlebrow takes on the easily digested parts of the classical repertory as

---

Sibelius ... Secondly Finland has become in the minds of the free world a symbol of courage and resistance' (letter, Nabokov to Stokowski, 25 January 1952).

    5   *The Congress for Cultural Freedom* (Paris: CCF 1963). This is an unattributed brochure outlining the Congress, its aims and work. The quotations are from a section titled 'In the World of the Arts' and appear next to a photograph of Nabokov.

part of an undiscriminating cultural diet. Responding 'wrongly', 'uneducated' and therefore quite unable to genuinely understand high art, his unthinking consumption threatens to erode the distinctions necessary for its survival. Nabokov's account of what he saw as the late nineteenth-century origins of Soviet middlebrow culture argued that this sort of aesthetic transgression was an important part of the process, the foundations of this 'petit bourgeois taste' comprising equal measures of pan-European popular song and light classical music ('Russian sentimental romance ... Viennese operetta, cozy Tchaikovskiana ... French importations of the Chaminade variety'). This is faithfully reflected in the taste of the leadership, he continues, so that Stalin's ideal musical evening places Beethoven alongside Red Army songs, the *Merry Widow* and 'fake night-club Caucasiana' (Nabokov, nd 4, unpublished, p. 5).[6]

The military concert in Berlin followed the same pattern. Nabokov reports that Kozlovsky was followed by the Beethoven String Quartet of Moscow with Borodin's *Second Quartet* and the 'oozy' *Andante Cantabile* of Tchaikovsky ('the audience sat in respectful though fidgety silence'), then some piano – Liszt, Chopin ('hackneyed') and Rachmaninov ('[p]ainfully boring'). Equal weight on the programme, however, was given to popular song and 'folk' music, for at that point 'a troupe of Ukrainian singers and dancers appeared and did what Ukrainian singers and dancers are supposed to do and have been doing whenever and wherever they are on the stage of a theater, a concert hall or a cabaret' (Nabokov, 1951a, p. 51).[7] Finally came the Red Army Chorus, beginning with 'Russian sentimentalia (akin in spirit, period, and quality to American barbershopiana)' and moving on to patriotic songs – some old, some dating from the recent war. High and low culture are casually, transgressively, thrown together in the service of 'average Russian taste'.

Nabokov's weary description of the Ukranian troupe's performance leads to an issue which was to become of increasing importance to him, and which suggests another area of overlap between the practice of his cultural policy and the idea of the middlebrow. In that theory, middlebrow culture is frequently held to be a threat to high culture, but equally – because of its voracious appetite and the need to *remake* cultural materials described by Arendt – to surviving folk and non-European cultures. It is in this sense that Virginia Woolf wrote of 'the pernicious pest that comes in between', and Leslie Fiedler of 'The Middle Against Both Ends'. According to this way of thinking, from the boundary-blurring melting pot of lower middle-class taste neither high culture or low, neither the art songs of St Petersburg or the folksongs of the Ukraine could emerge unscathed.

Already in the early 1950s some of Nabokov's remarks show a concern for the effects of official Soviet culture on folk music: the music of the Russian peasantry, 'modal in texture, ritualistic and reflective in character, often permeated with a

---

6   The full quotation is to be found in Chapter 3. Note that Stalin allegedly likes to hear only the *slow* movements (sentimental ?) of Beethoven quartets. He also has them played by three quartets at once, presumably demonstrating, for Nabokov, his lack of education and sensibility. Only a middlebrow would mistake bigger for better.

7   Namely: 'the male dancers kicked about on the floor in crouched positions, surrounded by a flock of bouncing girls who zigzagged between them waiving colored kerchiefs. The chorus, in a semicircle behind them, bellowed and clapped to the strumming of three pandura players.'

profound religious spirit' gave way before the advance of the petit-bourgeois taste –
'the loss of an ancient and infinitely rich tradition' (Nabokov, nd 4, unpublished, p. 6).
But folk music is not merely displaced – purged away to some musical gulag – but
adapted and deformed by Soviet composers:

> In general, the dividing line between musical ethnography and composition proper – always
> imprecise in Russian musical life – has now completely disappeared. The new Soviet works
> have been invaded by an entirely conventional musical ethnography, often foreign to the real
> nature of Russian music or the music of the country it derives from.[8]

Whilst Armenian, Georgian and Korean composers all use themes drawn from folk
music, this is carried out 'in their first-year conservatory student's language, and ...
produces a certain falsification of the authentic music, in a frightful system which
may be good for schoolchildren, but not for men of talent and free invention'. It
follows naturally from these remarks that the *preservation* of musics would later
become important to Nabokov, along with the idea of designing festivals which could
present both Western and non-Western musics. The CCF's last musical event was
the Tokyo 'East–West Music Encounter' of 1961, whose programme, as the title
suggests, included both Western and Oriental music.[9] Out of this festival also
emerged plans which would come to fruition in the founding of the International
Institute of Comparative Music Studies in Berlin. A plan for what Nabokov called
a 'rencontre noir' in Rio de Janeiro, featuring the music of Brazil, North America
and Africa came to nothing (letter to Hunt, 13 November 1961)[10] but, as the newly
appointed director of the Berlin Festival in 1963, he was able to open his account with
a festival on the theme of 'Black and White' for 1964.[11]

---

8   Nabokov, Nicolas, 'La Musique en Russie Sovietique et dans les Pays
Limotrophes', unpublished manuscript in NN, p. 7 (my translation). Nabokov also takes Soviet
scholarship to task: whilst in China they are using notation after the Bartók model, as well as
recording on disc and now tape, in the USSR 'there is a bad practice ... which is that when [the
music] is transcribed, this is done more or less according to the orthodoxies prescribed by
socialist ideology ...' (p. 14).
9   The EWME may have had a long gestation period. In 1952, the executive director
of the ACCF, Irving Kristol, relayed the opinions of one Theodore Cohen to Nabokov. Cohen
represented American business in Japan and had helped found the Japanese affiliate of the CCF.
Kristol wrote that Cohen 'is strongly of the opinion that the best cultural means of establishing
contact with the Japanese is in the field of music. For one thing, Japanese music is Westernising
itself, and practically every Western performance plays to packed houses. Now I don't know
what we can do, if anything ... perhaps you will have some specific idea ...' (letter, Kristol to
Nabokov, 30 October 1952).
10   In fact, the plan here was originally to include Western classical music, but
this was dropped since Nabokov felt it would lay Congress open to charges of 'no Soviet
involvement'. Nonetheless he expected opposition: 'we will have to face the same attempts at
sabotage, intellectual opposition etc. as in Tokyo. Except that here it will probably be more
vociferous and violent. ...'
11   Nabokov took over the direction of the Berliner Festwochen following the death,
in February 1963, of Gustav von Westermann, its founder, and director since 1950.

Although his remarks about 'other' musics contain contradictory elements, an illuminating account of his views has been found in a letter of 1972 written to Ulli Beier, the German-born specialist on African literature and another member of the Congress diaspora, who had, in 1956, founded *Black Orpheus*, an African literary magazine published in Ibadan, Nigeria, which would later receive CCF support (Coleman, 1989, pp. 203–5).[12] Although written later in his life when Nabokov had returned to composition – and therefore raising the possibility that his views had by then changed – as evidence, it has the merit of being a private communication, free from the need for public relations tact and gloss. Responding to an unspecified invitation from Beier, by then based at the University of Ife, Nabokov is moved to launch a denunciation of 'cross-fertilisation' in music. What Beier had in mind – presumably some conference or seminar dealing with multiculturalism – is not known, but Nabokov's reply, which makes very clear his views on the relationships between different types of music, is extremely useful for our current purposes, and worth quoting at length. He writes:

As time goes I become more and more persuaded that this so-called 'cross-fertilisation' is nothing but humbug. It has only lead [*sic*] to second rate imitations of worn-out models in the very recent past. Even during all of my 'Congress for Cultural Freedom' career and later in Berlin, I was more concerned with the <u>preservation</u> of pure, as yet untarnished (i.e. uncrossbred) non-European music, than with its <u>propagation</u> in the West. This is why I have so greatly admired the work of Professor A. Danielou and of his colleagues at the Institute of Comparative Music Studies in Berlin. As you perhaps know I was largely responsible for its establishment there. It is for the same reason that I have deplored the 'potpourri' of inherent musical nonsense produced by Yehudi Menuhin and Ravi Shankar, both of whom independently I admire as excellent performers, but only wish they would exercise their art separately and not serenade each other in joint 'jumbo-mumbo' activities. Nothing is worse than <u>mish-mash</u>, yet, I'm afraid that this is what has been taking place in the formerly colonial worlds of which Africa is, I suppose, the saddest victim. (Letter to Beier, 26 February 1972, original emphasis)

The thrust of this extract – a concern with maintaining divisions and policing boundaries between musics – is certainly very characteristic of the mass culture theorists' prescriptions, and the notion of 'uncrossbred' music calls to mind Dwight Macdonald's description of middlebrow culture as the product of the 'unnatural intercourse' of high and mass culture. What, however, can we make of his example of the Shankar–Menuhin collaboration? On the face of it, it seems difficult to tie this into the mass culture scheme. However, the 'star' status of both performers and the novelty value of the project could both be seen as congenial to a culture industry hungry for media-friendly 'events' to lubricate their marketing strategies and stimulate consumption.

---

12 Apparently, Josselson wrote to Beier in 1960 looking for ways to celebrate Nigerian independence in October 1960. Josselson and Beier, with a common background in Weimar Berlin, struck up a friendship and devised a drama competition to be run by *Encounter* and judged by Beier, Ezekiel Mphahlele and Stephen Spender. This was won by Wole Soyinka, with *A Dance of the Forest*.

Nabokov is clear that both Western and other music can only lose by their involvement with one another:

> I do not believe in the 'co-equality' in value and meaning of so-called 'Western' music as related to the different musics that have had an admirable, ancient, but solely ritualistic and craftsmanlike development. Nor do I believe they should be taken out of their ethnic context. Furthermore, I do not believe they can be '<u>befruchtend</u>' to the art of music as I know it, except as a passing fad or as an exotic stimulant. You see, I am totally un-Unesco-ish about all this …
> … No, dear Ulli, I do not want to be <u>at</u> or have any part <u>in</u> your projected festival, unless you would want to have among you and [*sic*] acid and uninhibited critic. If, on the contrary, you were to deal with the <u>authentic</u> traditions of African music unpolluted by their low-level contacts with the only art of music I recognise and belong to, then of course I would be glad to participate. … (Ibid., original emphasis)

Some elements here – particularly the clear assertion of Western music's superiority, and the uselessness of other music in comparison to it – that, on the face of it, seem contradictory when set against the stated rationale for such festivals as the 'East–West Music Encounter' and the 'Black and White' Festwochen of 1964.[13] The mention of Daniélou is, however, interesting and helps clarify these views. Daniélou, a specialist in Indian music, had delivered a paper to a 1958 CCF festival and conference in Venice ('Tradition and Change in Music') which described a crisis of 'modernisation' facing Asian music:

> Age-old civilisations that have developed learned and intricate musical systems and evolved musical languages suited to the expression of subtle and deep emotions, find themselves unable to keep alive their traditions before the impact of Western musical experiments and popular music forms. … I do not know whether the cataclysm that threatens to sweep away some very important sections of the world's cultural heritage can be averted. (Daniélou, nd, unpublished, p. 1)

Daniélou argues that, as a matter of urgency, the 'great traditions' should be identified, supported and preserved, arriving at three practical proposals: first, a few centres for the study of comparative musicology which would devote themselves not only to recording musics but to the theoretical investigation of their concepts and systems; second, any means by which the best exponents of the great traditions – East and West – can meet; and, third, an effort by national governments to 'strictly maintain the old methods of teaching, [and] the purity of style'. Since Nabokov and

---

13   Indeed, it would seem to be intriguingly at odds with both. A press release about the proposed Berlin Institute, released by the Executive Office of the *EWME* (unattributed but almost certainly by Nabokov), speaks not of Western superiority, but of 'the various systems of learned music which represent the fruit of centuries of refined culture' ('An International Institute for Comparative Music Studies', IACF papers). As for the 'Black and White' Festival in Berlin, he wrote that it was 'dedicated to one of the most important events of the twentieth century [!], which has been the influence of <u>art nègre,</u> and in general of the indigenous non-European arts upon painting, sculpture and music of our time' (Nicolas Nabokov to Mrs Albert Lasker, dated 12 June 1964. IACF). Not '<u>befruchtend</u>'?

Daniélou were to be jointly involved in undertakings – the 1961 'East–West Music Encounter', and the setting-up of the Berlin Institute – which mirror the first two of these, and given the comment in the letter to Beier, it seems reasonable to assume that this paper is close to Nabokov's own thinking.

The root of the problem, Daniélou argues, is that the West's representatives all too often lack real understanding both of the cultures into which they intrude, and of the heights of their *own* culture. On the one hand, they denigrate local culture and casually compare it to that of the West, (it is always, of course, found wanting). Since they rely unthinkingly on inappropriate conventions of Western musical life, much damage is done: faced with repeated Unesco questionnaires asking for details of 'orchestras, conductors, composers, modern works, concert halls etc. and nothing else', it is hardly surprising that Iranians or Indians 'try to reform, to develop, to Borodinize, to Stokowskize their music … in the hope that it may, at least nominally, be compared to that music which has been made a symbol of Western power'. This effect is compounded by the quality of these emissaries themselves, and therefore of the cultural influence they bring to bear:

> Europe does not easily export the ferment of its intellectual life towards which public institutions remain diffident. Art must become outmoded to become official. The image the East gets of the West is mainly based on the ideas minor French or English civil servants have of the national culture. We find everywhere in the East a picture, painted with meticulous care … that is really the opposite of what we are. (Daniélou, nd, unpublished, p. 1)

And so it is that:

> … the Chinese, the Coreans [*sic*], the Japanese are trying to alter their vocal technique … to imitate the crooners of New York's and Paris's night clubs … to imitate not the difficult art of our great performers, but the easier styles of Italian, French, American popular songs of which the recordings are too often the only ones that the most noisy representatives of the West bring with their gramophone on their civilising missions. (Ibid., p. 3)

The congruence with mass culture ideas is clear: the invasive, corrosive nature of this 'overflow of mediocrity'; the perilous situation of high culture(s) and the absolute urgency of redress; the malign influence of bureaucracy and especially its ill-educated petit-bourgeois functionaries with their misguided ideas of 'improvement'. In a further echo of Greenberg and Macdonald, not to mention Nabokov's letter to Ulli Beier, he adds that 'what must be opposed at all costs are the hybrids', recalling again that preoccupation with the loss of categories, distinctions and boundaries so characteristic of the concerns about middlebrow culture. As an aside, Daniélou adds that Western scholarship is not exempt from this process of erosion:

> I should like to mention here a weapon of psychological destruction particularly pernicious which is today called ethno-musicology and which deals in the same breath with learned systems of music considered exotic and with the lowest forms of popular or primitive music. Too often these friends of all that is picturesque, who travel extensively, record haphazardly … collect in one record the great music codified by Avicenna and Farabi and a little song of a Kermanshah shoe maker. They create collections where you find, side by side, the

brilliant technique of an Indian classical performance and the cries of pigmy ladies going to market … . (Ibid., p. 3)

This analysis, then, is not quite 'the middle against both ends' as proposed by Fiedler and Macdonald, among others: in *that* account both high and low culture (which, being vigorous and authentic, has *something* to offer) are endangered by, and should unite against, the 'pernicious pest that comes in between'. Daniélou, by contrast, believes firmly in sorting the art music sheep from the folk music goats, but the apocalyptic tone and the warnings of cultural extinction are familiar. His particular contribution – and it is this that seems to have struck Nabokov[14] – was to insist that there is more than one 'great tradition', more than one culture that deserves to be considered 'high', and that *all* face the same threat. It remains an analysis shot through with the assumptions and concerns of the mass culture theorists – an analysis that, like the Nabokov 'East–West Music Encounter' which it helped to inspire, is thoroughly permeated by the 'Great Fear of the Middlebrow'.[15]

Both Nabokov's writings and the musical events he organised for the CCF carry the marks of mass culture theory, and especially the 'midcult' variant of it which so exercised the intellectuals grouped around the American Congress for Cultural Freedom. The Congress's cultural strategy, its high-profile musical events, might now begin to seem less a matter of narrow anti-communism and more part of a wider crusade against the cultural influence of the middle classes on both sides of the Iron Curtain. To argue this, however, is not to suggest that the secretary-general simply used his position in the CCF for the greater glory of Nicolas Nabokov, that the festivals were no more than self-indulgence masked by a flimsy political screen. Although, as we have seen, this is the implication of retrospective comments by

---

14   Further evidence of the closeness of Nabokov and Daniélou's thinking is provided in an outline of the 'East–West Music Encounter', written for the CCF. The document is undated, but proposes that the festival should be held in 1957 in Tokyo: clearly, this project had a long gestation period. Nabokov writes:

It should not aim at too broad a view of worldwide musical culture (i.e. it should not degenerate into a kind of senseless 'musical circus'), but should rather limit itself to the most valuable, the most exquisite, the most perfect examples thereof. As sharp a distinction as possible should be drawn between purely folk-loristic and traditionally artistic elements – which at times is a hard line to draw but should always be attempted; (only those examples of musical culture which in their own right can be termed works of art should be presented). (Nabokov, nd 1, unpublished, p. 8)

15   Kathleen McCarthy's study of the Ford Foundation suggests that cultural 'conservation' of the Daniélou type was used elsewhere by the USA in the cultural Cold War. The Ford Foundation's aims overlapped to a considerable degree with those of the CCF, and indeed it supported both the Congress itself (from 1957), and individual projects with which it was associated (such as the Philharmonia Hungarica – see Chapter 8). According to McCarthy, strengthening local cultures was seen by the Foundation as a means of restraining the influence of communism. This suggests that the interests suggested by the EWME, the involvement with Daniélou and the plans for the Institute in Berlin were more than merely Nabokovian caprice. See McCarthy (1987).

William Phillips and Sidney Hook, Nabokov's political motivation should be considered as bona fide. It might perhaps be naive and misguided, but the cultural strategy was not a mere sham.

The strategy was, however, more than merely political, as this chapter has shown. In fact, its deeper concerns can be seen to mesh neatly with those of the *PR* coterie. Whilst Secretary-General Nabokov certainly advanced his own career through the CCF, becoming, in the words of his friend Isaiah Berlin, 'the best organiser of music festivals in his day', he led it on a path that linked anti-Stalinism with broader cultural concerns. Well-exposed to the ideas of the mass culture theorists, and with particular links to the important figure of Dwight Macdonald, Nabokov attacked Soviet culture as the triumph of the middlebrow, drawing on the key issues in the critique of middlebrow culture. The creation of this communist/middlebrow linkage, he may have supposed, would assist the attack against both enemies, so that the identification of Soviet music as 'middle class' would confirm it as bad, whilst the Western middlebrows would receive the taint of communism. The strategy was at once anti-communist *and* part of an attempt to buttress high culture – in particular, musical modernism – everywhere.

As such, it appears as a particular example of the more general case represented – as some have suggested – by the ACCF intellectuals, who are held to have used the Cold War to advance the interests of intellectuals as a class, seeking to maintain a privileged sphere of culture, and their own authority within it (Pells, 1985, p. 122; Lasch, 1968, esp. pp. 342–8). Despite the split that opened up between them over Congress policy, the Cold War enterprise of both Nabokov *and* the ACCF intellectuals can be seen as a compound of politics, culture and self-interest: in it, the horror of the purge and the gulag meets the horror of Rachmaninov and the Book of the Month club, the defence of the Free World from the Red Menace meets the defence of art from the invading mass audience. Both Paris and New York offered the communist threat and need to defend cultural freedom as the mainspring of their actions. This, however, was only part of the story.

Chapter 8

Authority and Exclusion:
The Cold War and 'Difficult' Music

Looking back on Nabokov's project

The festivals that Nicolas Nabokov organised for the Congress for Cultural Freedom formed only a small part of the overall operation. A number of parties – Tom Braden and the CIA, 'Junkie' Fleischmann and the bogus Farfield Foundation, Michael Josselson, Nabokov himself – were engaged in pursuit of a common end: a decisive shift in the political allegiance of intellectuals. And this was straightforwardly a conspiracy; it cannot be seen as merely a 'British Council' type of operation, the secrecy of which was incidental.[1] For one thing, the stakes – at the height of the Cold War – were perceived on all sides to be *immeasurably higher* than those involved in the promotion of trade, influence and goodwill via culture. For partisans, both left-wing and right-wing politics seemed utterly polarised, the choices stark, the ambition and global appetites of the other side limitless. Ultimately, there was in the spiralling arms race – driven, of course, by the ruthless, megalomaniac 'other side' – the prospect of apocalypse. In this context, intellectuals and opinion-formers were seen, by all sides, as strategic assets – hence the conviction of those directing and financing the CCF that it constituted, potentially at least, a vital weapon in the Western armoury. Secrecy was an integral part of the operation; far more than just a means of sidestepping an inconvenient American legislature, for it was seen by all concerned that its aims could not be achieved openly. All of which suggests that Nabokov's CCF work should be seen as something quite distinct from the routine of government-sponsored cultural exchanges.

And yet, in the long term, we seem to be left with only two legacies of substance. One is the International Institute for Comparative Music Studies in Berlin, founded in 1963 by the Oriental music specialist and CCF supporter Alain Daniélou with Nabokov's support, and based on a proposal that emerged from his 'East–West Music Encounter'. The second is the Philharmonia Hungarica, an orchestra initially comprised of refugee musicians who fled Hungary after the Soviet invasion of 1956. Nabokov became committed, along with his International Music Council colleague,

---

1   Nabokov, of course, claimed not to have known of the CIA connection, although his friend Isaiah Berlin suspected that he did, pointing out how close he had been to both Josselson and Melvin Lasky, the editor of *Encounter* (Sir Isaiah Berlin, interviewed by the author, 11 June 1997).

Yehudi Menuhin, and the conductor Antal Dorati, to the idea of forming an orchestra out of refugees in Germany. The process was fraught with problems, particularly concerning the political past of some of those involved[2] and doubts over the musical quality of the emerging ensemble.[3] Nevertheless Nabokov managed to secure interim grants from the Ford and Rockefeller Foundations, and these were followed by direct CCF support, thereby ensuring the orchestra's survival until a long-term solution could be found. This was to come in the form of the orchestra's adoption by the German city of Marl, where it is still based today.[4] It may be worth mentioning in passing that Nabokov also helped the Polish composer Andrzej Panufnik on his defection to the West in 1954, arranging for at least one grant from the Farfield Foundation – $2000 dollars agreed in September 1954 (letter, Farfield Foundation to Nabokov, 30 September 1954)[5] and using his good offices with Samuel Barber towards a possible residency at Tanglewood (letter to Panufnik, 3 November 1954), the Rockefeller Foundation and Radio Free Europe (letter to Panufnik, 19 January 1955). The assistance given to the composer by Nabokov and the Farfield, of which

---

2   After Dorati had conducted a concert of the Philharmonia to mark the first anniversary of the Hungarian uprising (25 October 1957, in Geneva), Nabokov wrote with concerns about the orchestra's manager, one Fussl, previously a Party member and music critic for a CP paper. Dorati, meanwhile, wrote to Georg Fuerstenberg ('Chairman of the PH Trustees Committee') in somewhat contradictory terms: on the one hand 'the PH, which is a most exposed non-Communist organisation, should not line itself up publicly with an ex-Communist journalist in its ranks', on the other 'it would be a flagrant "unwestern" attitude to deny any person his future because of his past' (letters, Nabokov to Dorati, 18 November 1957 and Dorati to Fuerstenberg, 18 November 1957).

3   In April of 1957 Menuhin wrote to Nabokov after hearing the orchestra in Baden. It is good, he says, but not good enough, and he worries that should the orchestra fail – through its inability to compete in terms of quality – this could provide a propaganda victory for the other side: 'When eventually the … subsidy is withdrawn and the orchestra is left to its own devices – and as far as I can see it will not survive – the world will merely say the Americans have abandoned the Hungarian orchestra … [and] let it go down the drain.' Nabokov subsequently delivered what amounted to an ultimatum to the Philharmonia's conductor, Zoltan Rosznyay: reminding him that the orchestra has 'not only an artistic role to play … but a cultural-political task to accomplish'; he insists that the problem of poor musicians *must* be resolved, or funding will cease in two weeks' time (letters, Menuhin to Nabokov, 29 April 1957 and Nabokov to Rosznyay, 13 August 1957).

4   Even as late as mid-1959 the future of the orchestra was not secure, with Nabokov sending a desperate 'round robin' letter to wealthy and well-connected friends, appealing for funds to keep it afloat until the next year, when the subsidy from Marl was due to start (Nicolas Nabokov to Arthur Schlesinger Jr, 5 August 1959, NN). Looking back, he seems to have been proud of his involvement: in 1975 he wrote to Josselson that 'at least one of the things we started goes on and according to friends is a very orchestra indeed [*sic*]. Rather amusing to have them perform with the Bulgarian Chorus! … Les temps changent!' (Nicolas Nabokov to Michael Josselson, 24 August 1975, NN).

5   Nabokov wrote to Panufnik on 14 November confirming the grant (also IACF papers). The Farfield letter speaks of the grant as 'for the purpose of assisting in *securing the services* of Mr Andre [*sic*] Panufnik' (my italics). The wording is intriguing, but well may have no special significance. Nabokov, in his letter, merely says that he hopes Panufnik will 'remain a friend' of the CCF and 'assist it'.

Panufnik's wife seems to have been unaware, goes unmentioned in his memoir of 1987.[6]

If this is all that Nabokov's project has left us – and it is hard to argue for much real influence over the course of postwar music – it may seem less than irresistible to the music historian. From the perspective of the relationship between music and politics, however, it deserves attention for its very uniqueness – in terms of its aims, its ambitions and its cloak of secrecy – and because it has remained routinely absent from accounts of both the history and politics of postwar music.[7] And what is surely fascinating is the fleeting conjunction, during the early Cold War period, of the American secret service and the world of contemporary art music. Now troubled, embattled, discredited even, these two apparently disparate worlds were perhaps then at the peak of their confidence, secure and settled in their belief that the future was theirs: a future, they believed, which could be made safe for democracy – and modernism. That era has long passed. The CIA became tarnished in the 1960s by its associations with coups, 'counter-insurgency' and a constellation of US-sponsored Third World despots, not to mention the disclosures of 1966 and 1967 (concerning the CCF and other fronts) which revealed an organisation systematically deceiving the American public. For its part, the mainstream of musical modernism came under attack on two fronts: from within, a new generation of experimentally-inclined composers began to experience it as a suffocating orthodoxy,[8] whilst, externally, the new rock music of the 1960s – dynamic, oppositional and powerfully allied to radical youth – seemed to render the cerebral academicism of the previous generation irrelevant. All this, however, came later: in the early 1950s the elites of modernism and the CIA could still feel optimistic and, even if Nabokov's project was the only evidence available (although, of course, it is far from that), one would have to conclude from it that *some* parties in each camp envisaged a fruitful relationship.

Frances Stonor Saunders' *Who Paid the Piper?* has surely established the general links between modernism and the CIA beyond reasonable doubt. The idea itself, however, was not new. In 1973 Max Kozloff argued that if the way in which abstract expressionists tended to present their work was seen in the light of American Cold War rhetoric, significant correspondences emerged (see Kozloff, 1985). The following year Eva Cockcroft went further. Unlike Kozloff, who argued for connections only at the level of imagery and abstract values, Cockcroft suggested that the links were *real* – 'consciously forged at the time by some of the most influential figures controlling museum politics and advocating enlightened cold war tactics designed to woo European intellectuals' (Cockcroft, 1992, p. 83). In particular, the

---

6   'I remember my husband mentioning Nicolas Nabokov, though as a friend rather than in any context of active help ... I am not aware of any American grants other than the Kosciuszko Foundation ... in 1966' (letter, Lady Panufnik to Wellens, 18 July 1997). The memoir is Panufnik (1987).

7   Case in point: the 1998 'Proms' featured a 'music and politics' strand. In the Proms guide, Vernon Bogdanor's introduction ran absolutely true to form, with a roll call of the usual suspects – Beethoven, Verdi and Shostakovich, naturally. See Bogdanor (1998).

8   See, for example, Smith and Smith (1994). A major theme of the conversations in this book – with 'downtown' or 'experimental' composers – is their reaction against the high modernism of the previous generation.

international programmes of New York's Museum of Modern Art (Tom Braden had been its executive secretary from 1948–49) became a means of promoting abstract expressionism – avant-garde, original, above all *apolitical* – which, after the 'end of ideology', could be made to dovetail neatly with the needs of the state. Annette Cox has described the way in which the art critics Harold Rosenberg and Clement Greenberg (both ACCF members) interpreted the same group as political by virtue of their insistence on freedom and independence (Rosenberg) and as evidence that America, unique and exceptional in the world, was producing correspondingly remarkable art (Greenberg) (Cox, 1977, chapters 7 and 8). Similarly, Serge Guilbaut has found that the artistic avant-garde in the Cold War era formed an alliance with anti-communist liberalism in terms of the ideas of individuality, risk and the 'new frontier', specifically as these were expressed in Schlesinger's *The Vital Center* of 1949. Modern art was internationalist, cherished risk and honoured the bold, like the USA; its controversial works were evidence of American freedom. Ultimately, Guilbaut argues that the action painters' refusal of the image, the message and the statement, what he calls their 'morbid fear of expression' – in itself a rejection of traditional American and Popular Front aesthetics – was the foundation of their international success, but also allowed them 'to topple into the once disgraced arms of the mother country' (Guilbaut, 1992, p. 249).

In literature, Alan Sinfield has written of 'what modernism was *made to be* in the United States during the Cold War' (his emphasis), and of how it was reinvigorated partly because it could be interpreted in a manner congenial to American political needs. He finds four major characteristics of modernism which offer 'hospitality to NATO ideology'. First is its internationalism: for Sinfield, the disparagement and dissolution of the local and the national fits neatly with the actual global power of the USA and its political and economic ambitions, and he quotes John Cage on European music:

> 'It will not be easy ... for Europe to give up being Europe. It will, however, and it must: for the world is one world now.' Cage's 'one world' is, in actuality, a world dominated by the United States; and US modernism, thus understood, merges internationalist and chauvinist criteria, folding the two together so that world culture *is* US culture. (Sinfield, 1987, p. 111, original emphasis)

Second, the ideal of the autonomous artwork held that art – entire unto itself – should not be considered in social or political terms: it could not therefore be interpreted as critical of existing structures. Third, the idea of the 'modern condition' made manifest by modernism is, Sinfield believes, a sleight of hand, since 'the concept of the artist alienated by the special intensity of his (usually his) vision of the modern condition' is merely a local construct of some Western intellectuals, universalised. Romantic and extreme, it reinforces the idea of 'autonomy' in discouraging attention to the realities of power and the real choices open to people. Finally, he argues for a relationship between avant-gardism and consumer capitalism, in terms of the reliance of both on a relentless cycle of innovations (or novelties) which condemn earlier models to obsolescence.

Martin Brody has put the case for a link between the Cold War and musical modernism in relation to Milton Babbitt. In his essay 'Music for the Masses: Milton

Babbitt's Cold War Music Theory' he argues that Babbitt's development, and especially his insistence that composers should be able to justify their practice in 'scientific language', has been decisively influenced by political factors. In particular, he cites the dissolution of the American Left touched on in Chapter 6 of this study. The composer's early studies in New York had set him very much in the orbit of the New York Intellectuals and, indeed, he was published in Dwight Macdonald's *Politics* in 1945 (Brody, 1993, p. 173).[9] For Brody, the Left's evolution from outright revolutionism to defenders of high culture, the Greenberg–Macdonald analysis of mass culture, the totalitarian quality of 'kitsch' all feeds into Babbitt's attempt to secure a space – the university – for a rarified musical practice defined in terms of the scientific language and methods it employs.

All of this work finds echoes in the present study. Where Kozloff, Guilbaut and Sinfield point out that aspects of modernism made it appropriate for political use in the Cold War, we have seen that Nicolas Nabokov capitalised on exactly that: his writings (and the rationale for the Paris festival) argued that the great musical revolution of the early twentieth century should be seen as the fruits of political freedom, whereas in the Soviet Union such artistic advance had been stifled at birth. Where Cockcroft argues that abstract expressionism was promoted by institutions with a conscious political agenda, we have established that the CIA, through the Congress for Cultural Freedom, was similarly involved (only more directly) in the legitimation and support of contemporary art music. Where Brody suggests that the milieu of the New York Intellectuals, and the link they forged between mass culture and totalitarianism, is important in understanding Babbitt's practice, this study has shown how traces of such ideas can also be found in Nabokov's Cold War polemics (as well as pointing out the very real links between Nabokov and the New Yorkers).

The CIA as patron of the New Music?

This Cold War co-option of contemporary music happened just at the point when a New Music was being incubated at Darmstadt and Donauschingen – a music in which existing tendencies towards exclusivity, 'difficulty' and the cerebral were powerfully reinforced, and a practice whose seizure of legitimacy and authority would ensure dominance in the world of academic music for several decades. Given the coincidence in timing – this happened at the height of the Cold War – and the existence of arguments such as those above, it is a short step to surmise that the CIA might have been directly involved in this process, that the Agency somehow backed these departures, encouraged and underwrote this new ferment within the overall modernist project. There is undoubtedly a sense, in some historical accounts, that the emergence of the New Music was *somehow* connected to the Cold War context, and occasionally even some substance for such ideas, such as when links between Pierre Boulez's IRCAM and the arms industry are revealed (Lebrecht, 1985, p. 48; Born, 1995,

---

9   The piece in question was a short poem, 'Battle Cry', published in the November issue.

pp. 110, 159–63).[10] More often the claims, though plausible, remain unsubstantiated. Thus, for example, William Brooks on the new electronic music studios:

> Their development reached a peak between 1958 and 1965, partly … because of the surge of anxiety created when Sputnik was launched in 1957. Suddenly the USA was convinced that it had 'fallen behind' the Russians and resources were devoted to technological and scientific areas. … (Brooks, 1993, p. 319)

This may well be right, but the fact is that Brooks's assertion is unsupported by any evidence. Later, in his discussion of Babbitt, he observes that, in its emphasis on music as *research*, the composer's position was 'in a sense an extension of the corporate, scientific ideology of the early cold war years', adding that the musical polarisation of this period (of which Babbitt and his Columbia–Princeton Electronic Music Center represent one extreme) is merely a reflection of a more general polarisation. This idea of the New Music as some sort of expression of a Cold War *zeitgeist*, appears elsewhere: recalling the radical departures of the early postwar period, Reginald Smith Brindle ties these to the nature of life in the mid- and late twentieth century, with its rate of change, its apparently endemic conflicts and the atomic bomb, insisting:

> The truth was that the intellectual climate of the atomic age *demanded* to be expressed through sounds completely different in nature. And these sounds were characterised by the omission of traditional elements … rather than by their inclusion. (Brindle, 1987, p. 5, my italics)

The language of inevitability – of necessity – is a familiar part of the modernists' polemical armoury (as it had been for the Romantics before). Here, however, the impossibility of going on as before is tied in with the Cold War, so that a world which stands on the brink of the nuclear abyss calls forth a music equal to the extremity of the times: these developments simply *had* to happen. Now, clearly, one can call on the Cold War to defend and account for the New Music, as Brindle is doing, or in order to apportion blame (as Brooks almost seems to do[11]). Is it possible, however,

---

10   Born reports that IRCAM technology was sold to Sogitech (later part of Dassault) for use in a flight simulator; Lebrecht adds that the 4X computer's designer Jean-Pierre Armand has 'conceived a pattern of underwater noises so realistic that it has been protected as classified defence information and prompted the French Navy to order its own 4X. Even if it fails to make great music, IRCAM may yet win the next world war.' These connections are fascinating, and undoubtedly provide good material for Boulez's opponents. However, in neither case is the author able to argue from these facts to a *general* relationship between high-tech music and the arms industry or the Cold War.

11   Brooks's essay is not explicitly anti-New Music. He is, however, hard on what he sees as the elitism of postwar art music: 'Its inherent self-preoccupation was only furthered by the development of academic sanctuaries … like most intellectuals during the postwar years, composers essentially abrogated their responsibilities as citizens in the name of their art' (Brooks, 1993, p. 311). Later he writes of 'pedagogues whose purpose is to promote the system which justifies their employment … an outdated ruling class and [its] educational model' (p. 314).

to go *beyond* such ideas of vague homology – beyond the idea that music in some unspecified way 'reflects' the times – and demonstrate that some part of the American military–political establishment actively supported the new radicalism? Did the CIA back the New Music?

Stonor Saunders believes it did. On Nabokov's 1954 festival in Rome – 'Music of the XXth Century' – she writes:

> With a heavy concentration on atonal, dodecaphonic composition, the aesthetic direction of the event pointed very much to the progressive avant-garde of Alban Berg, Elliott Carter, Luigi Dallapiccola and Luigi Nono. Amongst the 'new' composers were Peter Racine Fricker, Lou Harrison and Mario Peragallo, whose work was influenced in varying degrees by twelve-tone composition. ... A recent convert to twelve-tone music was Stravinsky, whose prescence in Rome signalled a major moment in the convergence of modernist tributaries in the 'serialist orthodoxy'. ... (Stonor Saunders, 1999, p. 223).

A heavy concentration? In fact non-serial composers represented in Rome outnumbered thoroughgoing serialists by more than two to one.[12] Certainly, the programme included all three of the Second Viennese School, along with younger disciples such as Nono, Dallapiccola, Blacher and Petrassi. As in Paris, however, the breadth of twentieth-century music was also well represented (Satie, Messiaen, Martin, Thomson), including many names that were anathema to the 'progressive avant-garde': Auric, Britten, Shostakovich, Milhaud, Barber, Poulenc, Vaughan Williams, Prokofiev and others. Indeed, a 'heavy concentration' of dodecaphonic works would have been surprising, given the composition of the festival's 'Music Council': Barber, Blacher, Britten, Chavez, Dallapiccola, Honegger, G.F. Malapiero, Martin, Milhaud, Stravinsky, Thomson and Villa Lobos (a 'broad church' if ever there was one). Whilst serialist trends are represented – and one would expect serialism to make a good showing at *any* festival of contemporary music in the mid-1950s – they did not dominate as Stonor Saunders suggests. Admittedly, serial composers were more heavily represented among the 12 entrants to the competition attached to the festival, but the winner – Lou Harrison – is better known for his use of non-Western

---

12   A division into 'serial' and 'non-serial' cannot of course be achieved definitively, given the composers who experimented with the technique without becoming committed, or moved in and out of it in the course of a career. The following categorisation is, no doubt, open to much criticism, but at the very least does present a picture less clear cut than Stonor Saunders suggests. Stravinsky was in his serial period at this time.

Serial: R. Malipiero; Berg; Blacher; Boulez; Stravinsky; Schoenberg; Nono; Dallapiccola; Webern; Petrassi.

Non-serial: G.F. Malapiero; Martin; Roussel; Milhaud; Satie; Britten; Janacek; Messiaen; Honegger; Thomson; Kodaly; Prokofiev; Rieti; von Einem; Hindemith; Auric; Barber; Copland; Shostakovich; Pizzetti; Poulenc; Casella; Vaughan Williams; Varese; Rawsthorne; Koechlin; Sauguet.

Also included were K.A. Hartmann, Turchi, Valen, and Fartein, who I have found particularly difficult to place: all used serial techniques to some extent but not, it seems, systematically. Source for these details: *Music in the XXth Century* brochure, IACF.

sources (adding a further twist to issues discussed in the previous chapter). As for Stravinsky, far from being 'a recent convert to twelve-tone music', 1954 found him in a transitional phase. *Agon* was under way, but incomplete until 1957, and it was to be still another year before the completion of the first fully serial piece (*Threni*, 1958). Furthermore, we can be quite sure that Stravinsky's presence was wholly due to Nabokov's personal devotion to his friend, and despite of any serial leanings rather than because of them. Speaking of their friendship in this period, he wrote:

> ... we rarely discussed his new music, nor did he show me, as he used to before, his 'work in progress' ... I listened to most of his new music at rehearsals, but he never asked my opinion of it. It was as if we had tacitly agreed to avoid some corpse in a closet. I did not, I could not, at least not fast enough, and not as wholeheartedly as I would have wished to, learn to love any of Stravinsky's new 'serial' compositions ... with a few exceptions these latest works of his seemed remote and forbidding to me. I remained, and I'm afraid will always remain, deeply rooted in the 'tonal' tradition of Russian music .... (Nabokov, 1975, pp. 178–9)

We must also deal with another claim made by Stonor Saunders. Following on from her characterisation of the Rome festival, she argues that 'for Nabokov, there was a clear political message to be imparted by promoting music which announced itself as doing away with natural hierarchies, as a liberation from previous laws about music's inner logic' (Stonor Saunders, 1999, p. 223). As we shall see, the association of the New Music and its techniques with an emancipatory strain in postwar politics is a commonplace, though a highly questionable one – even at the time, avant-garde music was something of a political football, claimed as 'progressive' by some and denounced as 'fascist' by others. There is, however, no record of Nabokov taking a position in what now seems a rather fatuous debate nor any evidence that – despite his own leanings – he could see some sort of political advantage in promoting serialism. This is an important point. Stonor Saunders' general thesis is that the CIA promoted 'cutting edge' modernism, and that this can be seen in painting, in literature and in music. A close study of Nabokov, his writings and his CCF work simply does not support that.

To underline the point, consider this evidence. What were his views on the Young Turks of the New Music scene? In 1948 he wrote a piece for *Partisan Review* entitled 'The Atonal Trail: A Communication', as a response to an earlier essay by René Leibowitz, the influential Paris-based composer and teacher, which had unfavourably compared Stravinsky to Schoenberg: Nabokov weighed in on the side of his friend, not missing the opportunity to issue a number of side-swipes at serialism and its adherents:

> Atonality or Dodecatonalism [*sic*] as a system of musical composition is, as everyone knows, a product of Central Europe. As such it had from the outset all the earmarks of a Messianic cult and a determinist religion. Like the Bauhaus, Gestalt philosophy, Antroposophy [*sic*] and many other Central European 'currents' of the teens and twenties, it had its God and Master, its prophets and disciples, its interpretation of history, its fervent adepts and converts and its no less fervent financial backers. (Nabokov, 1948b, p. 580).[13]

He goes on to sketch the emergence of the twelve-tone system out of atonality, and the debates of the 1920s which pitched its followers against those advocating some form of adapted tonality or modality. But the 'adepts and converts' were a fringe group, he argues – and deservedly so, since 'they created a strange kind of fetish, a hermetic cult, mechanistic in its technique and depressingly dull to the uninitiated listener'. Leibowitz's argument is stale, a throwback to the 1920s: 'a superficial piece, [it is] politely vicious and presumptuous and at the same time full of weak and untenable arguments'. Finally, he argues for the greater importance of Stravinsky, whose *Le Sacre* represented the real 'caesura in modern harmony' (that is, as opposed to Schoenberg's earlier pieces) and which, moreover, announced a new era in which rhythm was to be the cornerstone. Schoenberg, by contrast, represents the end of an era: the end of the 'harmonic era' (and note that this view of musical history is the one expressed in his 'Introduction' to the 1952 Paris festival).

These views are reflected in the programme for the Paris festival in which Stravinsky is represented by nine pieces: *The Rite of Spring, Concerto in D, The Firebird, Orpheus, Scenes du Ballet, Oedipus Rex, Symphony in C, Capriccio for Piano* and the *Symphony in Three Movements*. This contrasts with two each for Schoenberg and Webern (respectively, *Erwartung* and the *Second String Quartet*, and *Five Pieces for String Quartet* and an unaccompanied choral work), and Berg's one (*Wozzeck*). As for his attitude to the central figures of the younger generation, I have found no reference whatever to Cage in the archives, whilst Stockhausen features once only, and then dismissively. In 1958, while preparing his seminar and mini-festival 'Tradition and Change in Music' (held in Venice), he wrote to Robert Craft: 'As for Stockhausen, I personally could not care whether his music is represented at the Festival or not', adding that 'in a way, I must say it is a little refreshing not always to have the staples in festivals – i.e. the advanced 12-tone school and their conductors .... it is a pity that neither Webern or Schoenberg are on the programme, but we cannot have everything' (letter to Craft, 24 March 1958). This comment, assuming it to be sincere (and we cannot be entirely sure) is not necessarily contradictory. The point is that he was less an outright opponent of the serialists, and more someone who remained sceptical about the value of their methods, whilst grudgingly accepting their present ascendancy.

Nabokov's relationship to Boulez was ambiguous: *Structures*, Book One, had its premiere at the Paris festival, performed by the composer and Messiaen. Later, Nabokov seems to have wanted Boulez to direct *Le Marteau sans Maitre* for the 1958 Venice event (although there were worries about the size of the French composer's fee)[14] but, as it turned out, a conflict with Boulez's Donauschingen commitments made it impossible. In his autobiography, *Bagàzh*, Nabokov tells of lunch with Boulez and Stravinsky in Paris (in the early 1950s?); later, the three repair to Boulez's flat where their host plays a Stockhausen piece 'with extraordinary skill and dexterity ...

---

13   The Leibowitz piece – 'Two Composers: A Letter from Hollywood' – had been published in March.

14   'Apparently Boulez wants nearly F11,000 for the performance in Venice of his "Marteau sans Maitre". This is, I agree, relatively speaking, too high a figure. Don't you think so?' (letter to Craft, 13 February 1958).

while he played, he continued to explain with didactic precision how the piece had been worked out' (Nabokov, 1975, pp. 175–6). Stravinsky, apparently, was fascinated. However, in the IACF papers, there is an extraordinary exchange of letters between Nabokov and Boulez from 1954. Apparently, Boulez had been invited to the 1954 festival in Rome. This event was the one aimed 'against provincialism of all kinds', and which featured a competition (won, in the event, by Lou Harrison). It is not known whether Boulez was invited as potential competitor, judge or organising committee member. Whatever, his response was contemptuous:

> The worst thing is that you seem to think that the situation [composer's isolation from one another] can be improved by these congresses. What stupidity! What do you think is resolved through muddy waffling, by gathering a few puppets together in a well staked-out cesspit. They may be able to enjoy the quality of each others sweat; nothing more fruitful. Have you really not understood that achievement belongs to individuals: a thousand congresses will never do more than skim the surface. (Letter, Boulez to Nabokov, translated)

And so it goes on. The whole thing is fatuous and unnecessary, serving only, Boulez implies, Nabokov's own needs: 'Bureaucracy has at last made its thunderous entrance into a world it should have had the tact to keep away from. But then, of course, some of us have to make our living from bureaucracy, don't we?' To take part in the competition would be an act of humiliation ('The composers who take part ... have condemned themselves before any jury ... has been elected') and as for the 'illustrious' organising committee: 'One may venture to question the "illustrious" quality of the members of this Music Council – or even the quality, full stop.' The letter finishes:

> Feel free to organise your puny calf's corrida, and enjoy it as best you can, but don't insult me by sending me an official invitation. I would be left speechless .... I find these desperate markets, where prefabricated contests are organised, and committees sit in judgement on creativity, to be vile and disgusting. Do, please, send my invitation to a lover of carnivals. Next time I suggest you organise a congress on the issue of the condom in the twentieth century: it would be in equally good taste. (Ibid.)

Nabokov's reply was curt. Returning the letter, he hopes that:

> ... in a few years time, when you have grown up a little, you will be glad it is not lying somewhere in a drawer or a file, as it does not do justice to your intelligence or your judgement. In fact it demonstrates how far you are prepared to mis-represent the views of others so that you can play the 'puritan individualist'. It also demonstrates a sectarian spirit, pretentious and out of date, characteristics one would hope not to have found in a man of your generation. Since I have no taste for tedium and no time for such correspondence, I would be grateful if you would not contact me again. (Letter to Boulez, 14 September 1954)[15]

Nabokov's relationship with Boulez, which evidently recovered enough for discussions about *Le Marteau* to take place four years later, is, in terms of our present

---

15 Despite what Nabokov says, clearly a copy *was* kept.

purposes, a diversion, although an undeniably entertaining one. Its relevance is chiefly that it shows Nabokov to have been distanced from the world of New Music, and this *is* important. If a relatively conservative modernist was maintained as secretary-general of the CCF for 13 years, arguably the CIA was *not* aiming to encourage the musical 'cutting edge'. From his Paris office, Nabokov aimed to consolidate the gains of an earlier revolution, not to inaugurate a new one. As far as the New Music is concerned, there is no evidence to suggest that a 'hidden hand' was at work.

The insecurity of High Culture

So the New Music was no CIA plot. It would be hasty to conclude, however, that the Nabokov story has nothing to tell us about the politics of Western art music. In considering what implications there may be, one is struck first of all by its necessary modification – if not contradiction – of one of the staples of musical scholarship. There is a conventional wisdom in music history which sees postwar modernism as a reaction to Nazism. So, for example, Eliott Schwarz and Daniel Godfrey (1993, p. 44) speak of 'a longing to wipe the slate clean', whilst Andrew Clements (1993, p. 261) describes composers pledging 'allegiance to the very music banned by the Nazis'. 'An unexpected link was forged between serialism and progressive politics', writes Leon Botstein, in that 'radical modernism became the morally superior language, the voice of rebellion against fascism' (Botstein, 1995, p. 229), whilst Christopher Small explains the appeal of Webern in the early Darmstadt years in terms of the need to throw off a traditional language left tainted after the Nazi years: it was, he says, 'a necessary purification of style' (Small, 1977, pp. 119–21).[16]

The use of the terms 'radical' or 'progressive' to describe trends in both music and politics has certainly assisted the idea of an link between the two, and from the perspective of an art music world dogged by accusations of elitism, such a linkage was undoubtedly to be desired throughout that long period in which the Left dominated intellectual life. Probably, however, the political radicalism of contemporary music was always more a matter of style than substance (the sincerity of some individuals notwithstanding), and perhaps the existence of a project which enlisted contemporary music not to purge the system of the traces of fascism, but to attack Stalinism, underlines the point. The Congress's festivals – with their well-known anti-communist, pro-USA subtext – were, after all, well supported, and whilst a concept of anti-totalitarianism could embrace both the anti-communism of the Paris festival *and* the anti-fascism proposed by Botstein, Small and the others, the polarising politics of the era tended, in practice, to create an orientation against *either* regimes of the Left *or* the Right. In other words, a composer of thoroughgoing left-wing convictions would

---

16   At the time there was clearly, also, the occasional suggestion that aspects of the New Music corresponded to authoritarian politics. 'At present', wrote Herbert Eimert, 'it is the fashion for empty-headed critics to make out that the systematic "management" of musical material is identical with the terrorist rule of force in totalitarian political systems.' He goes on to devote the rest of a lengthy footnote to refuting this 'witless' argument. Significantly, he casts the accusation back on the accusers. See Eimert, (1959, p. 9).

probably have had real difficulty accepting the political subtext of a festival sponsored by the CCF. There is, however, no evidence of any political boycott.

Ultimately Nabokov's project was probably too peripheral within the contemporary music world to force a wholesale revision of music history. Perhaps, however, one implication of this study is that the politics of modernism were less simple than some writers seem to suggest: we have, after all, seen that the anti-Soviet politics of the 1952 festival were clearly set out, and that the CCF was widely perceived (rightly, of course) to be some sort of American front organisation. If radical music and progressive, left-wing politics were indeed in alliance, as Botstein argues, it is surprising that composers and musicians seem to have had little objection to his festivals (which did, certainly at Paris, Rome and Tokyo, attract political opposition from the Left): Boulez objected to the Rome event as a pompous irrelevance, not as a political affront.[17] It is probably nearer to the truth to see postwar modernism not as a political statement, but as a withdrawal from conventional politics, and one which – just as Guilbaut observed in the case of the abstract expressionists – laid it open to appropriation.

The political implications of this study do not, however, require the rebranding of postwar Western art as 'anti-communist'. Rather, they emerge from what the previous chapter has argued should be seen as subtexts of Nabokov's CCF enterprise: the fear of a developing 'middlebrow' culture; the contempt for the new middle-class audience, its aesthetics and aspirations; and the concern over the prospects for 'serious' music in the age of the gramophone and the wireless. As we have seen, such fears – simultaneously accounted for and enlarged by mass culture theory – were widespread in the postwar period. Our close reading of Nabokov reveals that – ironically, given the CCF's focus on the *external* Soviet threat – his project was also directed politically inwards; it was, indeed, a symptom of the insecurities of what Daniel Bell has called the 'cultural class' (Bell, 1979, p. 41), part of an attempt to maintain cultural authority and power in the face of new media and widened access to education. Nabokov and the Congress were most certainly engaged in a contest with communism, but his writings contain traces of a whole set of background assumptions – assumptions which our diversion into mass culture theory should have helped bring into focus.

It must, however, be admitted that an explicit engagement with theory – even musical theory – was not in the Nabokov style. Composer, impresario, communicator, showman, a teller of stories and oiler of wheels, a flatterer, charmer and self-mythologiser; Nicolas Nabokov was all of these. Theory, however, he left to others. It follows that much of what he believed, about music and about culture, is buried – a set of values which only surface piecemeal, and in his casual, but telling, use of the terms 'provincial' and 'cosmopolitan', whose meaning is taken for granted. This study has attempted to unearth these hidden values, to reassemble and assess them, and what emerges is two levels of political engagement, a double-headed struggle against both communism and 'middlebrow' culture. As such, it was part of a contest for political power in the first instance, and cultural power in the second. The connection

---

17   If, of course, the view of Peter Coleman is adopted – that the CCF *was* progressive ('on the Left and of the Left') – then the present study leaves Botstein's view intact.

between the two is suggested by Spender's view – expressed in defence of the Nabokov–Josselson strategy against the ACCF criticism – of how the Congress should proceed. Spender argued that 'our politics should be the implications of our interest in culture' (Wilford, 1994, p. 317). Nabokov's 'interest in culture' led him to conclude that the backward tastes of the rising middle class had, in the Soviet Union, been institutionalised, adding significantly to the visibility and impetus of middlebrow culture everywhere. For all those concerned with the health of the Western tradition, the implications for 'our politics' were clear: *to save music and culture one must fight communism*.

To repeat a point already made, this is not to suggest that Nabokov merely used the anti-communist struggle as a vehicle for his own concerns; indeed, there is every reason to suppose that his politics were sincere. Rather, he attempted to fuse the musical (which was, after all, his overriding 'interest in culture') and the political. In terms of lasting influence, this may fairly be considered a notably unsuccessful attempt, due in no small part to its leader's failure to promote the avant-garde trends which would later be judged most significant. However, whilst it can easily be viewed with hindsight as a bizarre anomaly, it *is* possible to identify some correspondences between the guiding myths of the contemporary music world on the one hand, and Cold War culture on the other – points of contact which provided something of a foundation for the undertaking.

The Cold War world was a polarised one, and it is easy to see that polarisation reflected in the music of the time, as William Brooks (1993, p. 331) suggested.[18] For Nabokov's purposes, a world which seemed to present a stark and simple choice between the USSR and the USA, communist and capitalist, slavery and freedom, found a parallel in the conventional modernist opposition of provincial/cosmopolitan, national/universal, nineteenth century/twentieth century.[19] In his writings he folded these two systems of opposites together: communist music was therefore provincial, nationalist and nineteenth-century; Western music was cosmopolitan, universal and contemporary. Within such a system of opposites it was necessary to deny the existence of any 'shades of grey' (and so Shostakovich's works *had* to be backward). There was only the choice: either freedom and 'the great Renaissance of Western music' or totalitarianism and 'pseudo-art, sad, grey, academic … outmoded [and] provincial' (Nabokov, nd 5, unpublished, p. 2). Neutrality – in music no less than in politics – was unthinkable.

This language of extremes was bound up with fears of extinction. It must be one or the other; one had to take sides, because nothing less than survival was at stake. Both in mass culture theory and in the rhetoric of the Cold War, failure meant extinction. A sense of the nation under permanent threat has particularly deep roots in American culture, according to Robert B. Reich, who has argued that the idea of the 'mob at

---

18 Brooks is actually talking about what he terms a 'dialectic of control' *within the avant-garde*, symbolised by the polar figures of Babbitt and Cage; ours is a polarisation at a higher structural level.

19 In his essay 'Aimez-vous Brahms: On Polarities in Modernism', Peter Gay has called attention to the use of binary oppositions as conventions within modernism: among those he cites are 'difficult' / popular, cerebral / sentimental, traditional / innovative, alienated / conformist. See Gay (1978, pp. 253–5).

the gates' is one of its guiding myths. The USA is 'a beacon light of virtue in a world of darkness, a small island of freedom and democracy in a perilous sea'. And the corresponding fear? 'We must beware, lest the forces of darkness overwhelm us – our liberties are fragile … vulnerable to exploitation or infection from beyond' (Reich, 1987, pp. 8–9).[20] In the Cold War, of course, this myth of exceptionalism expanded so that the USA became responsible not only for its own citizens but for the whole beleaguered 'Free World'. Now the 'mob at the gates' was more powerful than ever (and, according to McCarthy, of course, the gates were down and the mob was inside). The important point is that in Cold War America a part of the existing national myth seemed to be reinforced and amplified by events. Reich's choice of the word 'infection' is interesting, since Andrew Ross has argued that such metaphors of disease were common both in the USA's foreign policy of 'containment' (of the Soviet Union) and in the mass culture polemics of the time (Ross, 1989, pp. 42–5).[21] Nation, democracy, art – all stood on the brink of extinction, and music was no more secure: informed by the assumptions of mass culture theory, the art music world tended to employ the same rhetorical devices. Surveying a number of polemics on behalf of the musical avant-garde, Susan McClary has observed that:

> … the rhetoric of survival – the survival not of serial or electronic music, but of music *tout court* – runs through virtually all [of them] … . We are back to the Fall of Rome with the barbarians at the gates; we are encouraged to perceive the serious composer as an endangered species. … (McClary, 1989, pp. 62–3)

When, therefore, Nabokov worried that Shostakovich might be a symptom of a 'new era' in which new values would displace 'the principles which had been the cornerstones of the artistic philosophy of the previous two generations' (Nabokov, 1943, p. 423), and when he later worked towards the 'preservation of pure, as yet untarnished (i.e. uncrossbred) music' (letter to Beier, 26 February 1972), he was drawing on images of peril and survival common to the worlds of mass culture theory, contemporary music and anti-communism. The understanding – at the heart of modernism – that music in the twentieth century had established a certain inescapable trajectory, that it must 'go forward or die', dovetailed neatly into a surrounding politics of extremes which allowed only the simple choice: this way, or that.

For the world of contemporary music, the perceived threat was not, on the whole, Soviet music but rather the commercial world which introduced popular forms whilst also appearing to appropriate and dilute the Western classical tradition. Confronted by competition and a dwindling constituency, those involved in the production of art music had increasingly to justify the activity: this was quite new. In her study

---

20   Reich points specifically to the way US politicians drew on this myth to rally their citizens against the Communist threat: Both FDR and Dean Acheson, for example, warned of 'rotten apple' nations that spread their rot to others, Eisenhower and Kennedy continuing in the same vein (see the following note on the very similar use of disease metaphors in mass culture theory).

21   There was a need, apparently, to 'quarantine kitsch' (Harold Rosenberg) against 'the spreading ooze of mass culture' (Dwight Macdonald), to 'avoid contamination' (Jeffrey Kronenberger) from 'parasites on the body of art' (Irving Howe).

of IRCAM, Georgina Born observed that 'in the absence of validation through the market, legitimation is the primary concern in the avant-garde and subsidised spheres' (Born, 1995, p. 27). She might have added that it was the very rise of the cultural mass market in the twentieth century which introduced a crisis of legitimacy into a high cultural field previously characterised by assurance and certainty. The crisis was, and is, about cultural power which, as Andrew Ross has pointed out:

> ... does not inhere in the contents of categories of taste. On the contrary, it is exercised through the capacity to draw the line between and around categories of taste; it is the power to define where each relational category begins and ends, and the power to determine what it contains at any one time (Ross, 1989, p. 61).

Art music in the mid-twentieth century faced a situation of eroded and declining private patronage, with patchy and embryonic public support. It had to urgently establish, and constantly renew, its legitimacy as the precondition of subsidy. All this took place at a time when intellectuals could no longer exercise cultural power – 'the capacity to draw the line between and around categories of taste' – unchallenged. In this sense, the world confronting Nabokov and his contemporaries was a worrying one. With a growing audience for 'classical music', the monopoly of musical authority previously enjoyed by composers and academics was increasingly under siege: by the market itself (which is to say by the benchmark of record and ticket sales); by the promotional and marketing activities of the music industry; and by what Nabokov's friend and collaborator Virgil Thomson called the 'music appreciation racket'. Such rival centres of middlebrow cultural authority offered their own definitions of which music was 'great music', and what exactly qualified it as such but they had also, from the perspective of Nabokov and his CCF colleagues, been powerfully augmented by the Soviet cultural offensive.

Expositions of the 'middlebrow' naturally considered the institutions of the culture industry which both powered the phenomenon and gave rise to these rival centres of authority. They also examined the new audience in terms of its aesthetics and its reception of both old and new music. This new mass audience, as Adorno argued and as Nabokov observed in the case of the American generals and Soviet officers, received music in the wrong way – emotionally and sentimentally – far from the disinterested contemplation of form which constitutes the modernist ideal. They also tended to be attached to a canon which admitted little, if any, of the twentieth century.

This new audience might demand a new type of composer, operating according to new principles. Nabokov could see that Shostakovich – assisted by the 'maestros and managers' of the culture industry – held the American concertgoing public in thrall. And the nature of Shostakovich's public seemed significant: surveying the crowd gathered to see him speak at the Waldorf-Astoria in 1949, William Barrett of *Partisan Review*

> ... speculated that the Communists remained popular with those segments of the American middle class most susceptible to contrived publicity and manufactured opinion ... the audience looked principally composed of professionals, college students and delegates from Hollywood and Broadway – in sum, the producers and consumers of mass culture. (Pells, 1985, p. 123)

Shostakovich's public appeared to be precisely the 'pernicious pests' of the sentimental, easily-influenced middle class who endangered both democracy and art. As we have seen, this alliance of Soviet culture and mass culture evidently worried Nabokov, who was all too aware of the difficulties faced by the many composers he considered far worthier of prestige and attention. In his own life there had been a period (after arriving in the USA) best described as a fragmentary and disagreeable patchwork of tutoring, college teaching, lecturing and musical arrangement work, interspersed with appeals to 'lady patrons' and rich friends (Nabokov, 1975, pp. 196–9). It was a highly insecure life – even a Diaghilev commission in one's resumé offered no immunity. Against this background, questions of the legitimacy of contemporary music and the location of musical authority were not merely issues of abstract-sounding 'cultural power' but of absolute economic necessity: the very survival of the composer (and therefore of 'music *tout court*') was at stake. Nabokov's American experience, then, contributed to the siege mentality which is found magnified in the wider world of contemporary music. One part of that experience demands our special attention.

Shutting the gates

Around the time that he became part of Bohlen's 'Russian Circle', Nabokov found himself teaching at St John's College in Annapolis, Maryland. This was a most unusual institution, around which educational debate had raged since the arrival of Scott Buchanan as dean in 1937. Buchanan had instituted a radical curriculum with almost no choice of content: undergraduates were simply expected to study the 'One Hundred Great Books' of the Western intellectual tradition.[22] This was radical, but not unprecedented. At the end of the First World War, John Erskine had been offering a 'great books' course called General Honors at Columbia University in New York. In 1926 Buchanan, then a teaching fellow at Columbia, and one of Erskine's students, Mortimer Adler, began offering seminars modelled on General Honors at the People's Institute, an early free university with no requirements or examinations. The idea became more visible and controversial after Adler's move to the University of Chicago, where he and President Robert Hutchins replaced the entire undergraduate curriculum with 'great books' courses in the period 1936–42. Chicago's Liberal Arts Committee revised and added to Erskine's original list of 75 books, and it was the Chicago list which was taken up by Buchanan for his 'New Program' at St John's.[23]

Buchanan's central idea – the idea which formed the cornerstone of the St John's revolution – was that 'knowledge was one but that men did not perceive that unity' (Buchanan, 1978, p. 44). As such, the College was intensely opposed to specialisation, to all that appeared to render knowledge fragmentary and piecemeal. There was an

---

22   In his account of teaching at St John's, the sceptical Nabokov habitually uses both quotation marks and capitals, thus – the 'One Hundred Great Books'. See Nabokov (1975), pp. 203–8.
23   This remained largely unchanged in the mid-1970s: see Riesman and Grant (1978).

egalitarian, socially progressive side to all this, carried over from the People's Institute with its largely working-class, often unemployed, students, and embodied in a faith that the test of a work's 'greatness' was its capacity to speak, unaided, to wide audiences (Rubin, 1992, p. 164).[24] Following his mentor, Erskine, Buchanan believed that the 'great books' should *not* be placed in historical context, and that students should *not* be fed the tutor's interpretations and that they should merely confront the raw, undiluted texts (see Haase, 1997). Perhaps unsurprisingly, the confines of these methods – not to mention the restrictions imposed by the list *per se* – could be demanding and problematical for tutors. According to Riesman and Grant, when Buchanan took over at St John's some, at least, of the existing faculty felt that it must result in superficiality (Riesman and Grant, 1978, p. 46),[25] a view which seems to have been shared by Nabokov. Looking back, he was to write:

> Reflecting now upon the St John's pedagogical flea circus and its whirlwind 'One Hundred Great Books' reading acrobatics, I cannot but think of the last scene of Alban Berg's *Wozzeck*: A child, a waif, jumps back and forth on a wooden horse and singsongs: 'Hop-hop ... hop-hop.' Hop-hop from *Faust* to Freud. Hop-hop from Dostoevsky's Karamazovs to the Communist Manifesto, and hop-hop lightly and swiftly through the cumbersome expanses of our 2,500-year-old 'cultural heritage' to – where? For what purpose? (Nabokov, 1975, pp. 204–5).

He also considered the list itself somewhat arbitrary, and mused that the convenient total of 100 books might be designed to 'elicit the same psychological response or conditional [*sic*] reflex that haberdashers aim at when they advertise the sale of three ties for ten dollars'. Furthermore, Nabokov and his teaching colleague Elliott Carter faced special difficulties in trying to work music into the New Program. They drew up a companion list of great works of music, stretching from a Gregorian mass to a single twentieth-century work – the *Rite of Spring* (this virtual exclusion of the contemporary reflected Buchanan's philosophy and the emphasis of the Great Books list[26]). These were to be timetabled chronologically through the four academic years of the Liberal Arts course. In each case an 'aesthetically objective lecture' would be followed by discussion in the usual St John's manner. To this the two composers added compulsory classes in notation, which they deemed essential before any serious discussion of music could take place. It was this which was to lead to a rift with Buchanan: for Nabokov and Carter, 'musically illiterate, or at best half-literate'

---

24   Rubin goes on to argue that the 'great books' idea was politically contradictory – on the one hand it seemed concerned to re-distribute knowledge, whilst on the other it could be said to have reinforced, through the conservatism of its list, existing centres of authority (pp. 176–8).

25   Fifty years later, however, they note that 'tutors do not regard themselves as generalists so much as elementalists ... [dealing with] the fundamental problems that have plagued mankind' (Riesman and Grant, 1978, p. 46).

26   Riesman and Grant found that, in the 1970s, the same situation pertained. As if to underline the College's distance from the modern, by then *Rite of Spring* had been replaced by *Symphony of Psalms*, a work which perhaps allows modern music to be presented more easily in terms of 'continuity' rather than 'rupture'. See Riesman and Grant, (1978, Appendix 3, p. 388).

students could be taught nothing useful about music; Buchanan, by contrast, believed that great music – like a great book – could *reveal itself* to an inquiring mind. As Nabokov tells the story, all was going well until:

> ... one day Dean Scott Buchanan sat in on one of my lectures on musical notation, and afterwards called me to his office. There was a battle of wits, during which I tried to explain to him that you couldn't teach anything about music before teaching its language. We agreed on an experiment in which together we would expose some students to a Beethoven quartet without the preliminary explanations, 'goading' them to learn – Buchanan's favorite method. The experiment quickly revealed the error of Buchanan's method. It turned into a comic fiasco, and Buchanan never forgave what he called my foolish, gratuitous joke. In April 1942 I knew that my days at St. John's were numbered. (Nabokov, 1975, p. 207)

This brief stay in the 'Great Books Nursery'[27] may have been significant. Consider the central features of the New Progam: the hostility towards specialisation; the idea that great art can always, potentially, reach a broad audience; and the stress on students' unmediated 'discovery' of the works. We know from Nabokov's own account that he and Carter had set out to provide something better than the 'slipshod "Music Appreciation" courses that flourished in colleges all over America'; we also know that he became frustrated, sceptical, that he left after a confrontation with Buchanan over what he saw as the necessity of remedial notation classes. It is fair to speculate that, for Nabokov, the St John's approach could lead only to generalities, programmatic readings and shallow emotionalism – very 'music appreciation' and very middlebrow. Certainly the great works philosophy provided no contact with contemporary music. The Paris festival of 1952 was effectively an attempt to set out a new canon, starting just where the St John's curriculum – and the mass audience – left off.

In *The Making of Middlebrow Culture*, Joan Shelley Rubin notes the resistance which the 'great books' idea generated within academia, since:

> ... while ... in the case of American literature, the promulgators of the canon in the early twentieth century worked to 'underwrite their own new cultural authority by selecting texts so difficult as to require "expert assistance"', the original 'great books' ideology was predicated on precisely the opposite idea. No doubt sensing that threat to their power, many of Erskine's colleagues objected to his plan when it came before them for debate late in 1916. (Rubin, 1992, p. 167, quoting Richard Brodhead)

For Rubin, then, one response to the middlebrow challenge was a new stress on difficulty and complexity – as a defensive strategy. In this view, intellectuals were merely protecting their interests, by ensuring that the supply of their 'product' would remain restricted. Modernism, then, is to be seen not as an autonomous development, but as a reaction, at least in part, to the spread of literacy and education. In the same way John Carey, surveying English literature in the same period, has argued that:

---

27   The term appears in a letter from Nabokov to Mike Bessie of the publishing house Secker and Warburg. In his synopsis of a proposed autobiography, Chapter 5 was to deal with his 'second pedagogical exile – life in the great books Nursery; an ironic essay' (letter to Bessie, 3 November 1958, p. 3).

... intellectuals could not, of course, actually prevent the masses from attaining literacy. But they could prevent them from reading literature by making it too difficult for them to understand – and this is what they did. The early twentieth century saw a determined effort, on the part of the European intelligentsia, to exclude the masses from culture ... the ingredients were basically similar, and they revolutionised the visual arts as well as literature. Realism of the sort that it was assumed the masses appreciated was abandoned. So was logical coherence. Irrationality and obscurity were cultivated. 'Poets in our civilisation, as it exists at present, must be difficult,' decreed T.S. Eliot. (Carey, 1992, pp. 16–17)

As in literature, so in music, where the dominant postwar trends eventually required the systematic denial of tonality, rhythmic pulse and, at the extreme, audibly repeating patterns of any sort. The 'morbid fear of the expressive image' which Serge Guilbaut identified in the avant-garde painting of the period seems, if anything, even more appropriate here (Guilbaut, 1992, p. 246).[28] Across the spectrum, from Nabokov to Boulez, modernist composers tended to claim that this music (however they variously defined it) had displaced all previous styles and methods; its complexity, its privileging of the cerebral and its distanced contemplation of pure form provided the new benchmarks for serious creation whilst also, crucially, forming a barrier to entry. We have seen that the blurring of boundaries, the loss of distinction, was a particular charge levelled at mass culture in general and at middlebrow culture in particular. Modernism redrew the lines, in an attempt to build a firebreak between a world of serious music and the middlebrow culture which – demanding only cheap emotion and superficial effect – had appropriated part of the Western canon. As Christopher Small puts it:

> ... anyone today who possesses the price of a concert ticket or of a gramophone record can gain admission to the 'World of the Great Composers', as the record-club advertisements so picturesquely put it. Exclusiveness has to be gained by other means, and it is appropriate that ... intellectuals should define themselves by references to musical performances that are too 'difficult' and complex for the ordinary music lover ... (Small, 1987, p. 364)

Critics of the Congress for Cultural Freedom have argued that self-interest was a vital component of intellectuals' involvement in it: politically, they could demonstrate that their experience and polemical skills made them vital Cold War assets; in the world of the arts, they sought, through mass culture theory, to raise the prestige of their own 'difficult' high cultural preserves (and, as we have seen, they argued that to attack both Stalinism and middlebrow culture was logical). Of these 'anti-communist liberals' gathered around the CCF, Daniel Bell has said: 'from them and their experiences we have inherited the key terms which dominate discourse today: irony, paradox, ambiguity and complexity' (quoted in Brookeman, 1984, p. 8).

---

28   Guilbaut's comment, aimed especially at Pollock, de Kooning, Rothko and Still, may seem paradoxical given their description as abstract *expressionists*. His point, however, is that these artists were concerned to avoid content and meaning. In this they were powerfully supported by Greenberg, who argued that 'new American painting ought to be modern, urbane, casual, and detached, in order to achieve control and composure ... [previously] it had never been able to restrain itself from articulating some sort of message, describing, speaking, telling a story' (Guilbaut, p. 245).

Whether or not they deserve the influence with which this credits them, we are reminded that this highly engaged Cold War group was also involved in securing modernism. Perhaps, then, the contingency of the Cold War *was* used – not narrowly, as Hugh Wilford suggests, to promote a few isolated personal projects – but within a contest which was both broader and altogether longer-term. Described by Rubin, Carey and Small, this process was one in which intellectuals sought to reinforce their authority and, by insisting on modernist complexity as the starting point for any serious work, to restrict access to the field of high culture. Nicolas Nabokov – with his fight against provincialism, his fears about the new era heralded by Shostakovich, his opposition to musical 'cross-breeding' and 'pollution', his contempt for all that was 'easy' or 'sentimental' – was engaged on the musical front of this struggle as well as in the Cold War. His project was consistent with the defensive strategy of a contemporary art music world facing a loss of prestige and legitimacy, under threat from rival values and rival musics: as such, it stands jointly implicated in the creation of the remote self-serving and exclusive enclave that the contemporary music world was made to be.

Appendix

L'Oeuvre du XXe Siècle
(Masterpieces of the XXth Century)

Paris, 30 April–1 May 1952

List of Works Performed

Note: Titles are given in the form, and with the spellings, which were employed in the festival brochure. See footnotes for clarifications.

Georges Auric
   Coup de Feu

Samuel Barber
   Sonata for Piano
   Overture: 'The School for Scandal'

Elsa Barraine
   Suite for Violin and Piano

Henri Barraud
   Le Testament Villon

Bela Bartok
   Deux Portraits
   Divertimento for chamber orchestra
   Second Piano Concerto
   Suite de Dances

Yves Baudrier
   Melodies

Alban Berg
   Wozzeck

Boris Blacher
   Variations on a Theme of Paganini

Pierre Boulez
Music for Two Pianos[1]

Benjamin Britten
Billy Budd

Ferrucio Busoni
Turandot

Andre Caplet
Septet for cords, vocal and instrumental

Alfred Casella
Paganiniana

Aaron Copland
The Pied Piper

Luigi Dallapiccola
Canti de Prigionia

Claude Debussy
Trois Images
La Mer
Prelude a l'Apres-Midi d'un Faune
'Syrinx' for solo flute

Sem Dresden
A Capella Chorale[2]

Henri Dutilleux
Choral and variations for piano

Manuel de Falla
Concerto for harpsichord and six instruments
Suite from 'The Three Cornered Hat'

Jean Francaix
Double Variations for cello and strings

Gabriel Faure
Second Quintet for Piano and Strings

Paul Hindemith
Four temperaments
Nobilissima Visione
Metamorphoses

---

1   The piece was *Structures*, Book 1, which received its first performance by Boulez and Messiaen on 7 May.

2   Dresden's work was one of five pieces of 'secular music for a capella choir' performed by the Nederlands Kamerkoor on 29 May. According to *Grove*, the composer had completed 12 such pieces up to that date, the most recent being the *Beatus Vir* of 1951.

Arthur Honegger
Symphony No. 2
Symphony No. 5

Charles Ives
Concord Sonata

Leos Janacek
Concertino for piano and instruments

André Jolivet
String Quartet

Zoltan Kodaly
A Capella Chorale[3]
Psalmus Hungaricus

Charles Koechlin
Piece for solo flute

Constant Lambert
Concerto for piano and nine instruments

Arthur Lourié
Little Gidding, four intonations for tenor and instruments

Gustav Mahler
Das Lied von der Erde

Francesco Malipiero
La Terra

Roland Manuel
Suite in Spanish Style for Harpsichord, Oboe, Bassoon and Trumpet

Frank Martin
Concerto for Violin and Orchestra

Bohuslav Martinu
Sonate di Camera, for Violin and Orchestra

Olivier Messiaen
'Les Visions de l'Amen' for two pianos

Darius Milhaud
Les Choephores
Finale 'Les Euménides'
Protee, Suite No. 2

---

3   This piece is something of a mystery, as it cannot be located in the festival's programme. Kodaly wrote a vast number of pieces for vocal groups of every kind, so the exact work – if, indeed, one was performed – cannot be identified.

Roman Palester
  Trois Sonnets à Orphée

Walter Piston
  Toccata

Francis Poulenc
  Stabat Mater

Serge Prokofiev
  Scythian Suite
  The Prodigal Son

Willem Pijper
  Symphony No. 3

Serge Rachmaninoff
  Second Piano Concerto

Maurice Ravel
  Concerto for Piano
  Rhapsodie Espagnol
  La Valse
  Valses Nobles et Sentimentales
  Daphnis et Chloé, Suite No. 2

Vittorio Rieti
  Don Perlimplin

Albert Roussel
  Suite in F
  Bacchus et Ariadne

Erik Satie
  Socrate

Henri Sauguet
  Cordelia

Arnold Schoenberg
  Erwartung
  Second Quartet for Strings and voice

William Schuman
  Symphony No. 3

Alexander Scriabin
  Sonata No. 10 for piano

Dmitri Shostakovich
  Concert Suite from 'Lady Macbeth of Mtsensk'

Richard Strauss
Til Eulenspiegel
Don Juan

Igor Stravinsky
The Firebird
Orpheus
The Rite of Spring
Concerto in D
Scènes de ballet
Oedipus Rex
Symphony in C
Capriccio for Piano
Symphony in three movements

Virgil Thomson
Four Saints in Three Acts

Michael Tippett
A Cappella Chorale

Edgard Varèse
'Ionisation' for percussion orchestra

Heitor Villa-Lobos
'Choros' for three horns and trombone

Johann Wagenaar
A Capella Chorale

William Walton
'Façade' for narrator and instruments

Anton Webern
A Capella Chorale[4]
Five Pieces for String Quartet

Ralph Vaughan Williams
Fantasy on a Theme of Thomas Tallis
Five variants of 'Dives and Lazarus'

---

4   A piece by Webern was due to be included in the concert of 29 May (see note 2). *Grove*, however, does not list any completed unaccompanied pieces for choir. Possibilities would be Op. 2 of 1908 – *Entflieht auf leichten Kähnen* – with harmonium accompaniment, or perhaps the *Two Songs* (from Goethe) of 1926, Op. 19, using a small chamber group of clarinet, bass clarinet, cello, guitar and violin. Some items that evening were accompanied, so this is a possibility. Other pieces listed in *Grove* are either sketches, or for choir and orchestra.

Bibliography

Writings by Nicolas Nabokov

Published

(1942a), 'Music under Dictatorship', *Atlantic Monthly*, **187**, January.
(1942b), 'Sergei Prokofiev', *Atlantic Monthly*, **187**, July.
(1943), 'The Case of Dmitri Shostakovich', *Harper's Magazine*, **186** (1114), March.
(1948a), 'The Music Purge', *Politics*, Spring.
(1948b), 'The Atonal Trail: A Communication', *Partisan Review*, May.
(1949a), 'Russian Music after the Purge', *Partisan Review*, **16** (8).
(1951a), 'Music under the Generals', *Atlantic Monthly*, **196**, January.
(1951b), 'Festivals and the Twelve-Tone Row', *Saturday Review of Literature*, 13 January.
(1951c), 'Changing Styles in Soviet Music', *The Listener*, 11 October.
(1951d), *Old Friends and New Music*, London: Hamish Hamilton.
(1952a), 'Introduction a L'Oeuvre du XXe Siècle', *L'Oeuvre du XXe Siècle: 1*, Paris: Congress for Cultural Freedom.
(1952b), 'Élégie Funèbre sur quatre notes', *Preuves*, May.
(1953), 'No Cantatas for Stalin?', *Encounter*, **1** (1).
(1971), 'Introduction: Twentieth Century makers of Music', Virgil Thomson, *American Music since 1910*, London: Weidenfeld and Nicholson.
(1975), *Bagázh: Memoirs of a Russian Cosmopolitan*, New York: Atheneum.

CCF publications: unacknowledged, probably by Nabokov

In all these cases the projects concerned were devised and executed by Nabokov: it therefore seems likely that these manuscripts, though unattributed, were written by him.

Music in the XXth Century, brochure for festival in Rome, held between 4 and 15 April 1954, IACF.
Masterpieces of the XXth Century, festival brochure, Paris: Congress for Cultural Freedom 1952, IACF.
'An International Institute for Comparative Music Studies', undated, unattributed typescript, marked 'Executive Office *East West Music Encounter*' (Tokyo, 1961), IACF.

Unpublished

(nd 1), 'Draft Proposal for the CCF', undated typescript, IACF.
(nd 2), 'La Musique en Russie Sovietique et dans les Pays Limotrophes', undated typescript, NN.
(nd 3), 'Free or Controlled Music', undated typescript, NN.
(nd 4), 'The Changing Styles of Soviet Music', undated typescript, IACF.
(nd 5), 'Allocution de M. Nicolas Nabokov', undated typescript, IACF.
(nd 6), 'Masterpieces of our Century (Tentative Title): A Retrospective Festival of the Main Artistic Achievements of the First Half of This Century', undated typescript, IACF.
(1949b), 'Music and Peace', typescript undated but marked 'for release Sunday March 27', NN.
(1951e), 'Masterpieces of the 20th Century: International Exposition of the Arts of the Western World: Progress Report by the Executive Secretary of the Congress for Cultural Freedom', dated 17 December, IACF.
(1952c), 'Speech at Anglo-American Press Club', unpublished manuscript, dated February, IACF.

Correspondence

Letters from Nicolas Nabokov

Bessie, Mike, 3 November 1958, SW.
Beier, Ulli, 26 February 1972, NN.
Boulez, Pierre, 14 September 1954, IACF (trans. Marie-Pierre Corrin and Ian Wellens).
Burnham, James, 6 June 1951, IACF.
Cabot, H.E., 27 June 1951, IACF.
Craft, Robert, 13 February 1958, IACF.
Craft, Robert, 24 March 1958, IACF.
Dorati, Antal, 18 November 1957, IACF.
Executive Secretary of National Music Council (not named), 25 February 1952, IACF.
Fleischmann, Julius, 22 May 1953, IACF.
Hook, Sidney, 17 December 1954, IACF.
Hunt, John, 13 November 1961, IACF.
Josselson, Michael, 24 August 1975, NN.
Kennedy, Jacqueline, 23 February 1961, NN.
Lasker, Albert (Mrs), 12 June 1964, IACF.
Schlesinger, Arthur, 19 July 1951, NN.
Stein, Sol, 1 February 1955, IACF.
Stokowski, Leopold, 25 January 1952, IACF.
Kluger, Pearl, 20 December 1951, IACF.
Panufnik, Andrzej, 3 November 1954, IACF.
Panufnik, Andrzej, 19 January 1955, IACF.
Parsons, Geoffry, 28 December 1951, IACF.
Rosznyay, Zoltan, 13 August 1957, IACF.
Schlesinger, Arthur, 5 August 1959, IACF.
Stone, Shepard, 13 February 1952, IACF.
Stokowski, Leopold, 25 January, 1952, IACF.
Thomson, Virgil, 18 October 1951, IACF.

Letters to Nicolas Nabokov

Berlin, Isaiah, 21 December 1976, NN.
Boulez, Pierre, undated, IACF (trans. Marie-Pierre Corrin and Ian Wellens).
Farfield Foundation, unsigned, 30 September 1954, IACF.
Flanner, Janet, 7 August 1952, NN.
Hook, Sidney, 12 June 1952, IACF.
Hook, Sidney, 31 March 1955, IACF.
Kallin, Anna, 7 August 1951, NN.
Kristol, Irving, 30 October 1952, IACF.
Menuhin, Yehudi, 29 April 1957, IACF.
Schlesinger, Arthur, 18 June 1951, NN.
Fleischmann, Julius, 13 December 1951, NN.

Other

Donnelly, Albert to Fleischmann, Julius, 15 November 1951, IACF.
Dorati, Antal to Fuerstenberg, Georg, 8 November 1957, IACF.
Josselson, Michael to Spender, Stephen, 23 April 1967, MJ.
Kennan, George to Stone, Shepard, 9 November 1967, MJ.
Menuhin, Yehudi to unknown respondent, 9 November 1967, MJ.
Stein, Sol to Josselson, Michael, 1 September 1954, IACF.
Stein, Sol to Josselson, Michael, 20 January 1955, IACF.

Books and articles

Adorno, T.W. (1994), 'On Popular Music', in John Storey (ed.), *Cultural Theory and Popular Culture*, Hemel Hempstead: Harvester.
Arendt, Hannah (1964), 'Society and Culture', in Norman Jacobs (ed.), *Culture for the Millions? Mass Media in Modern Society*, Boston: Beacon Press.
Becker, Howard S. (1982), *Art Worlds*, Berkeley and Los Angeles: University of California Press.
Bell, Daniel (1979), *The Cultural Contradictions of Capitalism*, London: Heinemann.
Bender, Thomas (1987), *New York Intellect: A History of Intellectual Life in New York City from 1750 to the Beginnings of Our Own Time*, New York: Alfred A. Knopf.
Bloom, Alexander (1987), *Prodigal Sons: The New York Intellectuals and their World*, London: Oxford University Press.
Blum, Joseph (1988), 'Review of Arnold Perris: *Music as Propaganda: Art to Control, Art to Persuade*', *Ethnomusicology*, Winter.
Bogdanor, Vernon (1998), 'Party Pieces', in *BBC Proms 98*, London: BBC.
Bohlen, Charles E. (1973), *Witness to History: 1929–1969*, London: Weidenfeld and Nicholson.
Born, Georgina (1995), *Rationalising Culture: IRCAM, Boulez and the Institutionalisation of the Musical Avant-Garde*, Berkeley: University of California Press.
Botstein, Leon (1995), 'After 50 Years: Thoughts on Music and the End of World War II', *Musical Quarterly*, **79** (2), Summer.
Braden, Thomas W. (1967), 'I'm Glad the CIA is "Immoral" ', *Saturday Evening Post*, 20 May.
Brindle, Reginald Smith (1987), *The New Music: The Avant-Garde Since 1945*, Oxford: Oxford University Press.

Brody, Martin (1993), 'Music for the Masses: Milton Babbit's Cold War Music Theory', *Musical Quarterly*, **77** (2), Summer.

Brookeman, Christopher (1984), *American Culture and Society Since the 1930s*, London: Macmillan.

Brooks, William (1993), 'The Americas 1945–1970', in Robert P. Morgan (ed.), *Modern Times: From World War I to the Present*, London: Macmillan.

Carey, John (1992), *The Intellectuals and the Masses: Pride and Prejudice among the Literary Intelligentsia 1880–1939*, London: Faber and Faber.

Chomsky, Noam, and Herman, Edward S. (1979), *The Washington Connection and Third World Fascism*, Nottingham: Spokesman.

Clements, Andrew (1993), 'Western Europe 1945–1970', in Robert P. Morgan (ed.), *Modern Times: From World War I to the Present*, London: Macmillan.

Cockcroft, Eva (1992), 'Abstract Expressionism, Weapon of the Cold War', in Francis Frascina and Jonathan Harris (eds), *Art in Modern Culture: An Anthology of Critical Texts*, London: Phaidon Press.

Coleman, Peter (1987), 'Sidney Hook and Cultural Freedom', *The National Interest*, Fall.

Coleman, Peter (1989), *The Liberal Conspiracy: The Congress for Cultural Freedom and the Struggle for the Mind of Postwar Europe*, New York: The Free Press.

Coppock, Jane (1978), 'A Conversation with Arthur Berger', *Perspectives of New Music*, **17**.

Cox, Annette (1977), *Art-as-Politics: The Abstract Expressionist Avant-Garde and Society*, Ann Arbor, Mich.: UMI Research Press.

Craft, Robert (1972), *Stravinsky: The Chronicle of a Friendship 1948–1971*, London: Gollancz.

Craft, Robert (ed.) (1984), *Stravinsky: Selected Correspondence Volume II*, London: Faber and Faber.

Downes, Olin (1944), 'Politics versus Symphonies', *New York Times*, 30 April.

Eimert, Herbert (1959), 'The Composer's Freedom of Choice', *Die Reihe 3: Musical Craftsmanship*, Bryn Mawr, Penn: Theodore Pressner.

Fanning, David (1993), 'The Symphony in the Soviet Union', in Robert Layton (ed.), *A Companion to the Symphony*, London: Simon and Schuster.

Fay, Laurel E. (1980), 'Shostakovich versus Volkov: Whose Testimony?', *Russian Review*, October.

Fiedler, Leslie (1955), 'The Middle Against Both Ends', *Encounter*, **V** (2), August.

Flanner, Janet (1952a), 'Festival of Free-World Arts', *Freedom & Union*, September.

Flanner, Janet (writing as 'Genet') (1952b), 'Letter from Paris', *The New Yorker*, 31 May.

Gay, Peter (1978), *Freud, Jews and Other Germans*, Oxford: Oxford University Press.

Giannaris, George (1972), *Mikis Theodorakis: Music and Social Change*, New York: Praeger.

Glanville-Hicks, Peggy and Carr, Bruce (1980), 'Nicolas Nabokov' in Stanley Sadie (ed.), *The New Grove Dictionary of Music and Musicians*, London: Macmillan.

Glock, William (1985), *Notes in Advance*, Oxford: Oxford University Press.

Greenberg, Clement (1985), 'Avant-garde and Kitsch' in Francis Frascina (ed.), *Pollock and After: The Critical Debate*, London: Harper and Row.

Guilbaut, Serge (1992), 'The New Adventures of the Avant-Garde in America: Greenberg, Pollock, or from Trotskyism to the New Liberalism of the "Vital Center"', in Francis Frascina and Jonathan Harris (eds), *Art in Modern Culture: An Anthology of Critical Texts*, London: Phaidon Press.

Haase, Leif Wellington (1997), 'Democracy and Excellence: Rhodes Scholar Scott Buchanan's Search for a Great Books College', *The American Oxonian*, **LXXXIV** (1), Winter.

Haskell, Harry (1988), *The Early Music Revival: A History*, London: Thames and Hudson.

Hofstader, Richard (1962), *Anti-Intellectualism in American Life*, New York: Vintage Books.

Holst, Gail (1980), *Theodorakis: Myth and Politics in Modern Greek Music*, Amsterdam: Adolf M. Hakkert.

Hook, Sidney (1987), *Out of Step: An Unquiet Life in the Twentieth Century*, New York: Harper.

Horowitz, Joseph (1987), *Understanding Toscanini: How He Became an American Culture-God and Helped Create a New Audience for Old Music*, New York: Alfred A. Knopf.

Howe, Irving (1949), 'The Culture Conference', *Partisan Review*, **XVI** (5), May.

Isaacson, Walter and Thomas, Evan (1986), *The Wise Men: Six Friends and the World They Made*, London: Faber and Faber.

Khrennikov, Tikhon (1984), 'Formalism and its Roots', *Soviet Art*, 28 February.

Kozloff, Max (1985), 'American Painting during the Cold War', in Francis Frascina (ed.), *Pollock and After: The Critical Debate*, London: Harper and Row.

Kuisel, Richard F. (1993), *Seducing the French: The Dilemma of Americanisation*, Berkeley: University of California Press.

Lasch, Christopher (1965), *The New Radicalism in America 1889–1963: The Intellectual as a Social Type*, New York: Vintage.

Lasch, Christopher (1968), 'The Cultural Cold War: A Short History of the Congress for Cultural Freedom', in Barton J. Bernstein (ed.), *Towards a New Past: Dissenting Essays in American History*, New York: Pantheon.

Leavis, F.R (1994), 'Mass Civilisation and Minority Culture', in John Storey (ed.), *Cultural Theory and Popular Culture*, Hemel Hempstead: Harvester.

Lebrecht, Norman (1985), 'Boulez and the Well-Tempered 4X', *Sunday Times Magazine*, 17 February.

Lipman, Samuel (1989), 'The Encounter Group', *The Washington Post*, 17 September.

List, Kurt (1944), 'The Music of Soviet Russia', *Politics*, May.

Luethy, Herbert (1952), 'Selling Paris on Western Culture', *Commentary*, 14 July.

McCarthy, Kathleen (1987), 'From Cold War to Cultural Development: The International Cultural Activities of the Ford Foundation, 1950–1980', *Daedalus*, **116**.

McClary, Susan (1989), 'Terminal Prestige: The Case of Avant-Garde Music Composition', *Cultural Critique*, Spring.

Macdonald, Dwight (1994), 'A Theory of Mass Culture', in John Storey (ed.), *Cultural Theory and Popular Culture*, Hemel Hempstead: Harvester.

Muggeridge, John (1990), 'Belles-Lettresgate', *The American Spectator*, June.

Norris, Christopher (1989), 'Introduction', in Christopher Norris (ed.), *Music and the Politics of Culture*, London: Lawrence and Wishart.

Panufnik, Andrzej (1987), *Composing Myself*, London: Methuen.

Pells, Richard H. (1985), *The Liberal Mind in a Conservative Age: American Intellectuals in the 1940s and 1950s*, New York: Harper and Row.

Pells, Richard H. (1997), *Not Like Us: How Europeans have Loved, Hated and Transformed American Culture since World War II*, New York: Basic Books.

Perris, Arnold (1985), *Music as Propaganda: Art to Persuade, Art to Control*, Westport, CT: Greenwood Press.

Phillips, William (1990), 'Comment: The Liberal Conspiracy', *Partisan Review*, **57** (4).

Radway, Janice (1990), 'The Scandal of the Middlebrow', *South Atlantic Quarterly*, **89** (4).

Reich, Robert B. (1987), *Tales of a New America*, New York: Times Books.

Riesman, David and Grant, Gerald (1978), *The Perpetual Dream: Reform and Experiment in the American College*, Chicago: University of Chicago Press.

Roche, John P. (1989), 'On the Intellectual Barricades', *The New Leader*, 13 November.

Ross, Andrew (1989), *No Respect: Intellectuals and Popular Culture*, New York: Routledge.

Rubin, Joan Shelley (1992), *The Making of Middlebrow Culture*, Chapel Hill: University of North Carolina Press.

Salzman, Eric (1964), '*Modern Music* in Retrospect', *Perspectives of New Music*, Spring/Summer.

Schlesinger, Arthur (1949), *The Vital Center: Our Purposes and Perils on the Tightrope of American Liberalism*, Cambridge: Riverside Press.

Schwarz, Elliott and Godfrey, Daniel (1993), *Music since 1945: Issues, Materials and Literature*, New York: Schirmer.

Shils, Edward (1964), 'Mass Society and its Culture' in Norman Jacobs (ed.), *Culture for the Millions? Mass Media in Modern Society*, Boston: Beacon Press.

Shils, Edward (1990), 'Remembering the Congress for Cultural Freedom', *Encounter*, **XXV** (2), September.

Sinfield, Alan (1987), 'The Migrations of Modernism: Remaking English Studies in the Cold War', *New Formations*, **2**, Summer.

Small, Christopher (1977), *Music: Society: Education*, London: John Calder.

Small, Christopher (1987), *Music of the Common Tongue*, London: John Calder.

Smith, Geoff, and Smith, Nicola Walker (1994), *American Originals*, London: Faber and Faber.

Stonor Saunders, Frances (1999), *Who Paid the Piper? The CIA and the Cultural Cold War*, London: Granta.

Volkov, Solomon (1979), *Testimony: The Memoirs of Shostakovich as Related to Solomon Volkov*, London: Hamish Hamilton.

Wald, Alan M. (1987), *The New York Intellectuals: the Rise and Decline of the Anti-Stalinist Left from the 1930s to the 1980s*, Chapel Hill and London: University of North Carolina Press 1987.

Wall, Irwin M. (1991), *The United States and the Making of Postwar France 1945–54*, Cambridge: Cambridge University Press.

Werth, Alexander (1949), *Musical Uproar in Moscow*, London: Turnstile Press.

Wicker, Tom *et al.* (1966), 'CIA Spies from 100 Miles Up; Satellites Probe Secrets of Soviet; Electronic Prying Grows', *New York Times*, 27 April.

Wilford, Hugh (1994), ' "Winning Hearts and Minds": American Cultural Strategies in the Cold War', *Borderlines*, **1**.

Wilford, Hugh (1995), *The New York Intellectuals: From Vanguard to Institution*, Manchester: Manchester University Press.

Unpublished manuscripts

Daniélou, Alain (nd), 'Problems of the Preservation of Traditions', typescript, IACF.

Executive Committee of the American Committee for Cultural Freedom (1955), 'Draft Statement for the Congress of Cultural Freedom', unpublished typescript, 6 January, TL.

Lee, Ruth (1992), 'The Composers Collective of New York City and the Attempt to Articulate the Nature of Proletarian Music in the Writings of Charles Seeger, Marc Blitzstein and Elie Siegmeister in the 1930s', unpublished PhD thesis, University of Keele.

Schuyler, George (nd), 'The Negro Question Without Propaganda', typescript, IACF.

Index